Ignite Your Passion for Jesus

Your Guide to Experience Personal Revival

Tom Phillips
WITH EMILY ADAMS

BroadStreet
PUBLISHING

BroadStreet Publishing® Group, LLC
Savage, Minnesota, USA
BroadStreetPublishing.com

Ignite Your Passion for Jesus: Your Guide to Experience Personal Revival

Stock or custom editions of BroadStreet Publishing titles may be purchased in bulk for educational, business, ministry, fundraising, or sales promotional use. For information, please email info@broadstreetpublishing.com.

Cover and interior by Garborg Design at GarborgDesign.com

Printed in the United States of America
19 20 21 22 23 5 4 3 2 1

*To my wife Ouida
and our children, Cara, Matt, and Molly.*
TOM PHILLIPS

*To Anne Marie Armistead,
who first believed I could write
and set me free to do so in unconditional faith.*
EMILY ADAMS

Contents

Foreword

By Dr. David Ferguson

Legacy is often defined as "what you leave behind when you leave." In his earthly ministry, Jesus lived each day with legacy in mind. Even from his baptism, Christ was preparing the disciples for his eventual departure. Jesus certainly ended his time on earth with clear evidence of purpose!

My friend, Tom Phillips, is living out part of his legacy as a global champion of spiritual awakening. This significant resource not only reflects Tom's legacy, but it will also bring clarity to your legacy as a passionate follower of Jesus.

Since we develop and deepen our legacies with intentionality and purpose, this interactive, experiential resource provides a clear framework for a life lived on purpose. You will realize more of your purpose through exercises that guide you in how to love the Lord and live His Word, love people, and live His mission.

Across the pages of the Gospels, we find people who encountered Jesus and went away different, changed, and transformed. Lives were changed because they had been with Jesus. Far too often, our contemporary resources, classes, and small groups leave us unchanged. To make matters worse, we realize we are unchanged, and the people in our lives *notice* we are unchanged. Not so with this resource! Thanks to Tom's stewardship of passion and leadership for a Jesus Now Awakening, the power of the Gospel is transforming pastors, churches, and communities across the faith spectrum. With Tom's commitment to spiritual awakening, your commitment to fresh encounters with Jesus, His Word, and His people, you can realize the transformation that was possible in the first century!

Tom's book, *Ignite Your Passion for Jesus*, is unique. It is unlike any of the resources you've likely read before because the exercises in each chapter were written with the specific goal of engaging you in a Spirit-empowered faith. These exercises are created to move beyond seeking to simply know or study God's truth and move toward actually experiencing it. Why is this important? It's only an experiential, Spirit-empowered faith that can live out a Jesus Now Awakening.

Our team (from the Great Commandment Network) has developed the experiential exercises included within *Ignite Your Passion for Jesus*. The Great Commandment Network is an international collaborative network of strategic, kingdom leaders from the faith community, marketplace, education, and caregiving fields who prioritize the powerful simplicity of the words of Jesus to love God, love others, and see others become His followers (Matthew 22:37–40;

28:19–20). You will find the exercises we added within brackets throughout this resource. When you see the brackets, pause to prayerfully complete each prompt. These exercises are designed to encourage a Spirit-empowered faith—moments when you move beyond knowing God's Word to actually experiencing it.

This book is part of the *Jesus Now Awakening* resource series, which has been designed to engage followers of Jesus as they impart both the Gospel and their lives while living out a relevant, daily faith (1 Thessalonians 2:7–8). Just as the Word of God became flesh and "moved into the neighborhood" through the prompting and power of His Spirit, so we can live out a Jesus Now Awakening in our world (John 1:14 MSG).

We have drawn a framework for spiritual growth from a cluster analysis of several Greek and Hebrew words, which declare that Christ's followers are to be equipped for works of ministry or service. Therefore, within *Ignite Your Passion for Jesus*, you'll find specific exercises that we designed and organized around four themes. A Spirit-empowered disciple:

- Loves the *Lord* (Acts 13:2 NASB) – Exercises designed to strengthen this area of spiritual growth are marked L1–L10.

- Lives His *Word* (Acts 6:4 NASB) – Exercises for building up this aspect of spiritual growth are marked W1–W10.

- Loves *People* (Galatians 5:13 NASB) – Exercises intended to equip this area of growth are marked P1–P10.

- Lives His *Mission* (2 Corinthians 5:18 NASB) – Exercises provided to strengthen this area of growth are marked M1–M10.

Imagine this: You're on a journey in *Ignite Your Passion for Jesus*. It's as if you're going for a walk. As you read through this resource, we invite you to walk:

- In the light of God's Son—John 8:12

- In the light of God's Word—Psalm 119:105

- In the light of God's people—Matthew 5:14

The bracketed boxes and exercises in them incorporate these three sources of God's light. They'll encourage your awakening journey as a Spirit-empowered disciple of Jesus. God's Word reminds us that it's vitally important to walk in the light: "Walk while you have the Light" (John 12:35).

The Great Commandment Network has developed the experiential exercises, the Spirit-empowered discipleship framework, and the Spirit-empowered outcomes that we included in the appendices of this resource. We have listed each of the forty outcomes in Appendix 2. With all these contributions, the Great Commandment's deepest desire is to serve our friend, Dr. Tom Phillips, and the Jesus Now Awakening.

Be sure to use *Ignite Your Passion for Jesus as* a personal devotional, small group study, or in one-on-one discipleship. Tom has combined the power of story with practical exercises and passionate encounters with Jesus to help rekindle your First Love!

Read it and reap great reward.

Dr. David Ferguson
GreatCommandment.net

Foreword to the first edition

By Bill Bright

On July 5, 1994, I felt God lead me to begin a forty-day fast for two purposes. The first was to pray on behalf of a great spiritual revival and awakening in America and the world. The second was to fast and pray for the fulfillment of the Great Commission throughout the world. Though I have been committed to these two purposes since my conversion to Christ in 1945, I have recently sensed a special urgency.

As believers in Christ, we are at war with the enemy of our souls, and I think it is a matter of life and death to hundreds of millions that we be faithful to our Lord and fight the battle for the souls of men like never before in history. Unprecedented opportunities to help fulfill the Great Commission are now open to us.

The world in which we live is rapidly changing into a place where suicide, drug addiction, and murder are the norm, and being part of a normal nuclear family is unusual. Americans are selfish and cynical, and the church—the body of Christ—often seems asleep. *Ignite Your Passion for Jesus* is a call for the church to wake up to revival, one heart at a time.

We cannot ask God for too much as it relates to the fulfillment of the Great Commission if our hearts and motives are pure, and we do everything according to His Word and His will and for His glory.

Still, there are human hindrances that can stand in the way of fulfilling these goals, including pride, lack of faith, mediocrity, and carnality. There is no place for such attitudes. In the front lines of battle, soldiers know that their very lives depend on unity and cooperation as they support their fellow soldiers.

In this book, Tom Phillips encourages the church to stop waiting for God to pour out revival and to aggressively become a vehicle through which God can do that very thing. Revival begins in our hearts as we say, "Spirit of God, breathe on me. I'll be obedient. I'll walk in faith. I'll fast. I'll pray. I'll share Your Word with all You put in my path." As we take these steps, we will become vessels God can use to help bring revival to believers and an awakening to seekers after truth—an awakening to those around us, to our country, and to the world.

Ultimately, if we are going to see the world reached for Christ, you and I must die to self (Galatians 2:20), a biblical truth Tom emphasizes in this book.

I appreciate the heart Tom has carried for revival for so many years. He shares his heart in this guidebook, and if you listen carefully, you'll learn and grow. It's time to change the world through personal revival. I stand on tiptoe with anticipation to see what God is going to do in and through His church and in and through you and me.

Bill Bright
Founder and President Emeritus, Campus Crusade for Christ (now CRU)

INTRODUCTION

The Time Is Now

Everywhere you turn, the news looks bad. Reports of violence fill the national and international news. Countries are at war. Millions of children suffer abuse while others are aborted daily. Senseless crimes and terrorist acts have stunned many. Consider these recent headlines: More than one thousand people die in the destructive path of Cyclone Idai;[1] Two teens who survived Florida school shooting commit suicide;[2] Sri Lanka mourns nearly three hundred who died in Easter Sunday terror attacks.[3] Throughout the world, darkness erupts in every setting.

Some people choose not to read newspapers or magazines or listen to the nightly news. They wave it off, proclaiming, "It's all bad. What's the point?" Perhaps it's a matter of perspective. You can see those events from your view as a human or from Jesus's view. I read the news with extreme interest as I desire to see world events from Christ's perspective. My prayer has been from 1 Chronicles 12:32, to be like the people in the tribe of Issachar who "had understanding of the times, to know what Israel ought to do." I've prayed and asked Jesus to help me be a person who understands the times, to see through His eyes what He is doing, and then to know how to respond during a particular "*chairos*" moment in time.

A *chairos* moment is a special moment in time that is predetermined in history. The Greek word appears only a few times in the Bible; it's not the normal Greek word for time, *chronos*, from which we derive "chronology" or "time." One of the places Scripture uses *chairos* is in the word "times" in Acts 17:26–28, which states:

> And He has made from one blood every nation of
> men to dwell on all the face of the earth, and has deter-
> mined their preappointed times and the boundaries of
> their dwellings, so that they should seek the Lord, in

the hope that they might grope for Him and find Him,
though He is not far from each one of us; for in Him we
live and move and have our being, as also some of your
own poets have said, "For we are also His offspring."
(NKJV)

The Lord of the universe used this concept of *chairos* to indicate a special moment, and today in history our world stands in such a time—a time when our world looks incredibly dark. We wonder, "Where is the Good News?" God reveals a bit of His purpose in this passage in Acts—that we should seek the Lord, grope for *Him*, and find *Him*. Those words mean that we have an invitation and responsibility as Christians to grow in our intimacy with Christ.

Why? Because, as the Scriptures note, it is in Him that we live, move, and have our being. Our life and breath are based on our relationship with God— intimacy with the Creator through Jesus Christ. It is only through this intimacy with Jesus that we can move out and effect change in our world. Revival begins with "Christ in you, the hope of glory" (Colossians 1:27).

A *chairos* moment may have begun, or is about to begin, in your own life. Henry Blackaby, coauthor of *Experiencing God,* wrote that people should determine where God is working and jump in the middle of it.[4] Dark events are taking place on earth, but perhaps Jesus is working in the midst of them. If you and I turn our attention to focus on Jesus, we will see how He is working personally in our hearts and calling us to open the door for revival in our communities, our country, and the world. He is beginning a worldwide awakening to revival one person at a time. Jesus is leading you and me into refreshing, experiential, and personal revival.

As you choose to take advantage of this *chairos* moment and seek personal revival, be kind to yourself and understand that sustaining a lifestyle of revival is by faith and trust in Jesus. The journey toward igniting your passion for Jesus will ultimately require you to give Him everything, all of yourself, in exchange for all of Him. The pilgrimage throughout the meditations in this book must impact your life and transfer into daily surrender to Christ. Otherwise this would be only an intellectual exercise. "You will seek me and find me, when you seek me with all your heart" (Jeremiah 29:13).

Before we begin, here are some steps to consider:

The experiential devotionals in the "Walking in the Light" section at the end of each day will help you chew on and respond to what you read. Give yourself permission to move at your own pace. Probe for honest answers to issues. A key ingredient of reflection is looking deeply. Remove any masks or self-doubt and look deeply into yourself. Seek the guidance of the Holy Spirit. Remember Jesus's promise: "He, the Spirit of truth, . . . will guide you into all truth; for He will not speak on His own authority, but whatever He hears He will speak; and He will tell you things to come" (John 16:13 NKJV).

Each day you will find quotations, definitions, and, in some cases, songs to help you think and worship. Take time to read and listen to these treasures. Eat them. Stop and sing the songs. Look them up online and listen to them. Offer them back to Jesus. Post them in your world if they're particularly inspiring. Worship is key to rekindling our fire.

You will also find Bible passages within every day. Meditating on and memorizing these verses will throw wide the gates of your heart and invite the Holy Spirit to move in every moment of your life. You will begin to see Him work out His Word in specific situations in your everyday life so that you come to know it experientially. Hiding God's Word in our hearts and minds is vital to rekindling spiritual fire.

Jesus is calling the world to revival *now*, one heart at a time. In *Ignite Your Passion for Jesus,* you can find anew your personal and loving Lord and Savior. Revival begins with knowing and proclaiming, "God, I know that you love me." A word of warning, though. If your primary focus is on yourself or only things confined to this earthly world, this book will frustrate you. When Emily Adams first started working and writing with me on revival a few years ago, the Lord gently began to bring her into ongoing personal revival. Here is what she wrote about the process:

A Beginner's Experience of Personal Revival

Then Jesus said to his disciples, "If you truly want to follow me, you should at once completely reject and disown your own life. And you must be willing to share my cross and experience it as your own, as you continually surrender to my ways. For if you choose self-sacrifice and lose your lives for my glory, you will continually discover true life. But if you choose to keep your lives for yourselves, you will forfeit what you try to keep." (Matthew 16:24–25 TPT)

Get ready to die. Personal revival isn't a lifestyle, it's a deathstyle—constant dying to self. You will probably feel like a camel passing through the eye of a needle. Prepare to be crucified into Jesus. "The way is narrow" may begin to have entirely new meaning for you. You should probably read Matthew 22:1–14, Luke 14:7–35, Philippians 3, and 1 Peter 4 before deciding if you really want to do this.

If you are going to receive all that God has for you, you have to want it as much as your next breath. You have to be willing to sacrifice organization, time, normalcy, ability, eating, drinking, sleeping, family, friends, career, security, money, fame, ambition, arrogance, strength, weakness, pride, entitlement, self-promotion, fear of man, inadequacy, perfectionism, independence, lust, idolatry, and above all, YOURSELF. To be empty enough to receive all Jesus wants to give you, you have to be willing to give up all else besides Him.

You will have to carry around a towel to mop up the blood of Jesus's grace as it pours off the people around you. You will also have to let others mop up the blood of Jesus's grace as it pours off of YOU. This process will be harder if you demand pristineness of yourself. Don't be afraid of messiness. The grace you're going to need to give birth to sustained personal revival is comparable to the grace you received for salvation.

As you become truly aware of God's goodness, you will want to allow yourself to die in Jesus. The only way to come through the fires of revival is in the presence of Jesus. Believe that He is good. Believe that He loves you. If you believe those two things, He will take you through the fire. He doesn't let those who aren't ready have ears to hear or hearts to understand this message. Ignorance is the bliss of His mercy. Be sure you want to wake up, for once you do, there is no going back. Do not "stir up or awaken love until it pleases" (Song of Songs 2:7). You have to want more of Him so much that you are unwilling to go on unless He gives it to you.

You might feel like you are losing your sanity. Jesus

will shake loose every structure in your life that is not from His Kingdom. You will lose the kingdom of this world. But you will gain the Kingdom of God. When you lose it all, you will gain permission to be the glove that God's hand uses to bring about "the blind receive their sight and the lame walk, lepers are cleansed and the deaf hear, and the dead are raised up, and the poor have good news preached to them" (Matthew 11:5).

The battle is not between life and death—Jesus defeated death on the cross. The battle is between hope and despair. If you can have faith to DIE in the hope of God's love, you will inherit Jesus's new creation life on earth as it is in heaven.

CHAPTER 1

A LIFEstyle OF Revival

When people think of revival, they often think of it as a tent meeting during the summer, somewhere in the Bible belt. Shouting itinerant preachers predict doom for unrepentant sinners as they pound out their message on a wooden podium. "Bringing in the Sheaves" or "Amazing Grace" ring through the tent as the preacher gives the altar call. "Come now and give your life to Jesus," the preacher says. "Recommit your life to Christ."

"Quit sinning. Quit drinking. Quit having sex outside marriage. You can't quit by yourself, but God can deliver you," the messenger explains. "Return to Him. Let God help you." Then he adds, "Don't let God pass you by!"

It sounds cliché, but many have come to salvation through these meetings. Commitments were real. God was present. But what happened when the meeting was over, when the preacher left, when the people resumed their daily lives?

For some, their relationship with God culminated at the end of the Sunday night meeting. For others, it was just a beginning. God met them in that tent, and nothing was ever the same. What made the difference? For the first group, "The Revival" was an event to be planned, to be experienced, to come to an end. For the others, "revival" became a way of life. It wasn't a one-night or one-week experience but rather how they began, ended, and lived each day. A constant spiritual renewal of their relationship with Christ.

And that is true revival—an ongoing renewal within. We cannot limit revival to a specific planned event. But revival does change lives, communities, and even the world.

Day 1

The Foundation— A Personal Relationship

In Mississippi, as an eight-year-old in my church's biannual evangelistic event called a "revival," I committed my life to Jesus Christ. It wasn't a hell-fire-and-brimstone time. The pastor simply asked us, "Do you want to love God completely all your life?" He didn't storm his audience with sin but talked about the love of Jesus. At the conclusion of his sermon, I responded to his invitation.

As I began to move forward, my neighbors in the pew tried to grab me. Luckily, I was so tiny—my nickname was Mouse—that they missed. They thought I was far too young to make such an important decision. Later the pastor agreed to talk with my parents, to pray about the validity of the decision. In the end, they all agreed, "Tom does know what he is doing."

Almost twenty years later, one of my cousins said to me, "You really met Jesus Christ that night when you were eight years old, didn't you?"

"Yes, I did," I said. "How could you tell?"

"Well, most of us in the South joined a church when we were young. And that's all we did. But you were different. Before that day, you were one of the meanest kids I had ever known, and you changed!"

> *"I am praying for an old-fashioned, heaven-sent, Holy Ghost Revival that will sweep our nation from coast to coast." – Billy Graham, 1949 and 2012*

I have many faults. If you want the details, talk with Ouida, my wife! The Christian life has been a continual growth experience for me, a pilgrimage. But by meeting Christ personally, my heart and life changed. I am still on that pilgrimage.

The only way to understand the rest of this book is first to know Jesus Christ as Lord and Savior. The basis of our study in these pages is rooted in a relationship with Christ and His presence in our lives. The Creator of the universe loves you and wants you to know Him intimately, presently, and forever.

God has always loved you and will forever, whether you are His child or not. But He created us with the free will to choose whether to receive that relationship. The first man and woman chose to disobey God and go their own willful way. Many still choose to disobey God, and it results in a broken relationship. God's heart breaks for these people.

Throughout history, an unholy people have tried to reach a holy God through various routes: religion, good works, ethics, morality, and philosophy—all without success. Our Father God has provided a way for us to have a restored relationship through Jesus Christ, and He is the only way. Because Jesus died on the cross for your sins, He took your punishment and made a way for the restoration of your relationship with God.

God never forces us to respond. Each of us must accept that Jesus Christ paid for our sins through His death on the cross. As you give your life to Him, then you will have a right relationship with God.

If you have not given your life to Christ, is there any good reason why you shouldn't invite Him into your life right now? If you have already given your life to Christ, how is He calling you to greater depths? To connect with a Christian counselor and receive free discipleship materials as you make your commitment to receive Jesus as your Lord and Savior, go to www.PeaceWithGod.net.

STEPS TO PEACE WITH GOD

1. God's Plan—Peace and Life

God loves you and wants you to experience His peace and life.

The BIBLE says: "For God so loved the world that He gave His only begotten Son, that whoever believes in Him should not perish but have everlasting life" (John 3:16).

2. Our Problem—Separation

Being at peace with God is not automatic, because by nature you are separated from God.

The BIBLE says: "For all have sinned and fall short of the glory of God" (Romans 3:23).

3. God's Remedy—The Cross

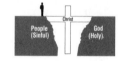

God's love bridges the gap of separation between God and you. When Jesus Christ died on the cross and rose from the grave, He paid the penalty for your sins.

The BIBLE says: "He personally carried the load of our sins in his own body when he died on the cross" (1 Peter 2:2-4 TLB).

4. Our Response—Receive Christ

You cross the bridge into God's family when you receive Christ by personal invitation.

The BIBLE says: "But as many as received Him, to them He gave the right to become children of God, even to those who believe in His name" (John 1:12).

To receive Christ you need to do four things:

    1. ADMIT your spiritual need. "I am a sinner."

    2. REPENT and be willing to turn from your sin.

    3. BELIEVE that Jesus Christ died for you on the cross.

    4. RECEIVE, through prayer, Jesus Christ into your heart and life.

    CHRIST says, "Behold, I stand at the door and knock. If anyone hears My voice and opens the door, I will come in" (Revelation 3:20).

    The BIBLE says, "Whoever calls upon the name of the Lord will be saved" (Romans 10:13).

What to Pray:

Dear Lord Jesus, I know that I am a sinner and need Your forgiveness. I believe that You died for my sins. I want to turn from my sins. I now invite You to come into my heart and life. I want to trust and follow You as Lord and Savior. In Jesus's name, Amen.

Go to www.PeaceWithGod.net

Revival Truths

- Revival is a lifetime process, not only a one-time event.
- A personal relationship with Jesus Christ is the beginning of revival.
- Scripture assures us of God's forgiveness.

Everyone who calls on the name of the Lord will be saved.

ROMANS 10:13

Walking
in the Light
of God's
Word

His Abundant Gifts

As His divine power has given to us all things that pertain to life and godliness, through the knowledge of Him who called us by glory and virtue, by which have been given to us exceedingly great and precious promises, that through these you may be partakers of the divine nature, having escaped the corruption that is in the world through lust.

2 PETER 1:3–4 NKJV

Consider your relationship with Christ. Reflect upon how God has given you everything you need for life and godliness, enabled you to participate in the divine nature, and made you a joint heir of Christ.

When you became a follower of Christ and accepted His gift of salvation:

- You were adopted (placed as an adult heir) into the family of God (Romans 8:15, 23; Ephesians 1:5).
- God forgave all your sins (Ephesians 1:7; 4:32; Colossians 1:14; 2:13; 3:13). They have been removed "as far as the east is from the west" (Psalm 103:12).
- You have been brought near and made a citizen of God's Kingdom (Ephesians 2:13, 19; Philippians 3:20; Colossians 1:13).

- You are no longer a slave to sin. You are free by His Spirit to yield to God, obeying Him out of a desire to love Him (Romans 6:17–18).

- Christ has purified you and made you eager to do what is good (Titus 2:14).

- Jesus prays for you and the concerns of your heart (Romans 8:34; Hebrews 7:25).

What does it do to your heart that not only did God love you so much that He did all the above for you, but that He also delighted in it? That He is eager and passionate in His love for you to give you a life of continuing revival. Express your heart to God.

Dear God, as I consider these truths revealed to me by You in Scripture—all that you have done for me when You saved me, how You have blessed me through your Holy Spirit with so many different blessings because of Your infinite love for me, my heart is stirred with _____ . Please continue to reveal who I am in Your eyes so I can live intimately in Your transforming love.

L4. A Spirit-empowered disciple rejoices regularly in their identity as "His beloved."

Day 2

Delighting in Discipline

After meeting Jesus personally, I began the discipline of reading the Bible and praying nearly every day. Even as a young boy, God showed me the need to be disciplined and purposeful in life. I had a clear set of personal guidelines. Each night before I went to bed, I read a chapter of Scripture. If I forgot, then the next morning I would read two. If something prevented my reading and I missed again, the next night I read three. With this primitive schedule, the chapters could stack up quickly. Fortunately, I was lazy enough to not want to get too far behind. It wasn't the purest motive, but it kept me on schedule. Through the discipline of Bible reading, I was learning more about God. In the process, I was changing, for something supernatural occurs in the heart when it absorbs the truth of God's Word.

In addition to reading Scripture, I began talking daily with God through prayer. That beginning of my relationship with God was the sweetest part of my childhood. I couldn't understand why anyone would not want to know God. If God made us and had a plan for our lives, then a person would be foolish not to know Him. Perhaps this view was a tangible example of coming to God as a child—living obediently through childlike faith. I learned that reading Scripture and praying were the way to grow in my relationship with Christ, so I innocently obeyed.

When I was in high school, our church had "cold turkey" visitation on Thursday evenings where we knocked on doors in our neighborhood to talk with others about Christ. That may sound like bold intrusion today, but in the South in those days, it was not. Back then, you usually didn't call ahead; you just stopped by. If it was at mealtime, you had a meal. If the neighbor was out on the tractor, you got on and rode along. The farmer kept working while he talked with you.

What an adventure! As a young boy, I went from a rewarding personal relationship to moving outside myself to share Christ with others. It was a logical progression of spiritual growth. God's love had changed me, and I wanted others to have the same opportunity. At times, the listeners openly received my message. At other times, they did not. What a shock to learn that not everyone had the contentment and security of a relationship with Jesus. What an even bigger shock to realize that many people rejected Christ.

Yet, it was these adventures of sharing my faith, along with prayer and Scripture study, that caused me to grow.

It is not just prayer and sharing that help us to grow in our faith. God gives us many exercises to "flex" our spiritual muscles. Richard J. Foster, in his excellent book *Celebration of Discipline*, listed several disciplines for spiritual growth. He discussed corporate disciplines like worship that reflect our part in the body of Christ, our need to connect others. These outward disciplines, such as service, relate to the way we live. Foster also discussed inward disciplines, which include meditation, prayer, fasting, and study. While discipline often conjures thoughts of punishment, or at best a negative influence, Foster stated that "God has given us the Disciplines of the spiritual life as a means of receiving His grace. The Disciplines allow us to place ourselves before God so that He can transform us."[5]

> *"No one experiences the secret of freedom, except by discipline." – Dietrich Bonhoeffer[6]*

In one of his sermons, Jim Tomberline, also discussed spiritual disciplines. He referred to them as "habits of the heart." In 1 Timothy 4:7–8, we read, "Rather train yourself for godliness; for while bodily training is of some value, godliness is of value in every way, as it holds promise for the present life and also for the life to come." What are the spiritual exercises that keep a person spiritually fit? Here are eight key areas that Pastor Tomberline noted:

1. Renew your strength through worship (Isaiah 40:31).

2. Deepen your peace of mind through prayer (Philippians 4:6–7).

3. Strengthen your commitment through fellowship (Hebrews 10:24–25).

4. Expand your perspective through biblical exposure (John 8:31–32).

5. Increase your joy through witnessing (1 Peter 3:15).

6. Practice your love through giving (2 Corinthians 8:7–8).

7. Develop your talents through serving (1 Peter 4:10).

8. Restore your soul through retreating (Matthew 11:28–29).[7]

Growing in our relationship with Christ requires discipline. The word *training* in 1 Timothy 4:7–8 comes from the Greek word *gumnazo,* from which we get *gymnasium.* It is continual discipline in training that produces growth. In athletics, one often hears, "No pain, no gain." It's a comfort to know that any pain we might encounter is merely a growing pain. With Jesus, who has gone before us, we are to "lay aside every weight, and sin which clings so closely, and let us run with endurance the race that is set before us" (Hebrews 12:1).

Amazingly, we can receive discipline from Jesus by resting in Him instead of striving in ourselves, and true delight and love for God can motivate our discipline. Relationship is the key to consistent discipline: "Delight yourself in the Lord, and he will give you the desires of your heart" (Psalm 37:4).

Revival Truths

- It is through spiritual discipline that we exercise our spiritual muscles for growth.

- Discipline is not punishment but a way to put us before God so He can bring us into freedom in Jesus.

- Delight in Jesus is the key to resting in discipline.

Let us also lay aside every weight, and sin which clings so closely, and let us run with endurance the race that is set before us.

HEBREWS 12:1

Walking
in the Light
of God's
People

What Would Jesus Do?

Jesus said, "Follow Me."

JOHN 1:43

Two simple but profound words can guide my daily walk as Light in a dark world: "Follow me." Whatever may come my way today, Jesus has gone before me. He has led, and I'm to follow as I live in the "disciplines" of intimacy with Him.

"WWJD" is my key to following Him as I practice the "habits of the heart."

- What would Jesus *do* becomes a guiding principle when uncertainty abounds.

- What would Jesus *choose* guides me away from a broad road of destruction onto the narrow road of life abundant.

- What would Jesus *say* guides my speech from unwholesome words and into words that edify.

- What would Jesus *think* guides my thoughts away from this world into His Word, which renews my mind.

- I find clarity and adequacy for daily living in the powerful simplicity of two words from the Gospel: "Follow Me."

Pause to celebrate with a partner or small group:

"Recently I sensed an important "following" of Jesus as I faced and found strength to _____ ."

L9. A Spirit-empowered disciple yields to the Spirit's fullness as life in the Spirit brings supernatural intimacy with the Lord, manifestation of divine gifts, and witness of the fruit of the Spirit.

Day 3

A God-Directed Life

When I entered college, it was time to decide on a career. Medicine was a natural for me. I enjoyed people, I could think fast in an emergency, and I loved to witness while helping others. Medicine would be a great platform for sharing my faith because a doctor is often helping people in crisis as they consider serious life issues. But I felt a spiritual force pulling me toward the ministry, a pull I worked hard to ignore.

Around this time, my girlfriend, Ouida (who eventually became my wife), and I had been dating for two years. We came to a point in our relationship that we either needed to get married or break up. So we broke up—for two weeks!

During that time, I asked out another girl. We went to dinner and then returned to her apartment. While in the living room, I saw other couples, partially dressed, go in and out of a bedroom. I could see what was going on and walked out of the apartment, probably hurting the girl's feelings. I didn't belong in the midst of such obvious temptation. I knew God watched over me all the time, but I was also young with budding hormones. The Bible says, "Flee youthful passions" (2 Timothy 2:22)—so I did.

My date stood at the window watching me walk down the outside stairs of her apartment building. When I reached the bottom step, these wise words spoke to my mind: "What's more important? Helping someone live seventy years with quality of life or helping someone live eternally?" God was speaking to me, and in an instant His profound, simple truth overwhelmed me. My legs lost all energy, and I fell to my knees. It was a *chairos* moment with God. I looked up to realize this girl was still watching me from her window above, while my weakened knees were glued to the concrete walkway. I couldn't get up.

I prayed, "God, you've got to let me get up. This is one of the most embarrassing experiences of my life." Finally, I was able to get up and walk away, and probably to her relief, I never saw that girl again.

You'd think that after hearing God loud and clear I would have submitted to His call, but I still held on to my dream of becoming a doctor. Later that same summer, the Lord spoke to me again. "Tom, you're going to be a preacher." Immediately I protested. These were not the words I wanted to hear, even though I had been asking His direction for my life. Intellectually I wanted God's direction to be the same as my desire.

> *"If we really knew just how much He loves us, we would always be willing to receive anything from His hand."*
> – *Brother Lawrence*

One day during the early part of the summer, I read Billy Graham's syndicated column, "My Answer," in the *Daily Corinthian*, the local newspaper of Corinth, Mississippi. Dr. Graham wrote that he prayed about everything. He even prayed when he parked his car because if he prayed about where to park, then he could help people as God guided him.

So I too began praying about where to park. Every time I prayed about parking, I sensed God's direction, and each time I left my car, someone with a need would be there. After helping them, I often had an opportunity to talk about Christ. It was amazing, and the many opportunities began to convict my heart because I thought, *Wow, God cares about all the details in people's lives, including mine. Even parking is important to Him. Well, if where to park is important, then everything is important—especially my calling in life.*

Perhaps as you read this, you feel discouraged, as though you may have missed God's call for your life. Remember that there is nothing wasted in the kingdom of God. Though my journey of faith started at a young age, Jesus will begin with you right now where you are, regardless of your stage in life. Don't feel discouraged if you are further along in life but just now beginning to follow His plan for you. God will redeem lost years for His children.

As we grow in our relationship, we grow in our obedience, and His plan and purpose for our lives come forward. Perhaps God is not calling you into "professional" ministry, but He is calling you to minister as He directs you in your daily life. When Jesus Christ walked the earth, He carefully followed God's direction in His life. One of His keys to following God's will each day was to focus on God's desires and not His own.

It may be completely new to you to realize that God cares about the intimate details of your everyday life. Even if thinking about God's direction isn't new, it may be a good reminder for you. God's direction in your life isn't always specific. The Lord wants you to trust Him step by step for His direction.

Revival Truths

- Everything in your life is important to God.

- God will guide you in making decisions if you ask Him.

Jesus said to them, "Truly, truly, I say to you, the Son can do nothing of his own accord, but only what he sees the Father doing. For whatever the Father does, that the Son does likewise.

JOHN 5:19

Walking
in the Light
of God's
Word

Reveal, Empower, Provide

Lazarus became very sick to the point of death. So his sisters sent a message to Jesus, "Lord, our brother Lazarus, the one you love, is very sick. Please come!"

JOHN 11:2–3 TPT

Jesus heard the word of His Father and courageously yielded to it. He lived life directed by His Father. In John 11, we observe an example of the Father revealing His word and the Son exhibiting courage to yield to His Father's will despite a request from His friends.

Living a God-directed life:

- Informs judgment: "He remained where he was for two more days" (John 11:6 TPT).

- Empowers courage: "Finally, on the third day, he said to his disciples, 'Come. It's time to go to Bethany'" (v. 7 TPT).

- Clarifies vision: "This sickness will not end in death for Lazarus, but will bring glory and praise to God. This will reveal the greatness of the Son of God by what takes place" (v. 4 TPT).

Pause and practice, allowing God's Spirit to direct your life.

- Ask God to reveal through His Word the areas in your life in which your opinions might be coloring your judgment: *Lord, help my beliefs, behaviors, and relational encounters to align with Your Word.*

- Ask the Lord to empower your decision making: *Heavenly Father, may I have the boldness to address issues in my own life and to offer courageous confessions when appropriate. Help me to stand for what is right and not "cave in" to others' pressure. Also, Father, grant the awareness and the grace to hold others accountable for their growth.*

- Ask God to provide clarity and confirmation through His Word regarding His will in your current situation: *Lord, give me a clear purpose in life and the ability to support and encourage others in following a clear purpose.*

L2. A Spirit-empowered disciple listens to and hears God for direction and discernment.

SPIRIT-
EMPOWERED
Faith

27

Day 4

Decision Time

As Billy Graham pointed out, God cares about our prayers for parking—and a lot more. After realizing God cares not just about parking but also about what I did with my life, I finally asked, "God, what do you want me to do?"

During the final night of another evangelistic campaign in my hometown, the voice that responded to my question was so booming I thought everyone in the church heard it—yet no one seemed to notice a thing. God was again speaking to my mind. I clung to the back of the pew with white knuckles, weeping because I realized God had called me to preach. It wasn't what I wanted. At the age of nineteen, my only goal was to be a wealthy physician. I didn't want to put up with church boards or elders or people who think they are the majority stockholders in the pastor's life. Raised in the church, I had seen preachers tormented by carnal congregation members. I didn't want that for me or my future family.

My mind filled with stereotypes about pastors. I didn't want to eat a lot of chicken. I didn't want to get fat. I didn't want to spend days counting nickel-and-dime offerings. I didn't want to be a preacher, but I knew God had called me; I knew His voice. I wanted to trust Him, but I wept thinking of giving up *my* dreams to follow God's call.

From listening to God, I knew I should respond publicly and make a commitment, but I just didn't want to. I was proud and fearful. I didn't go forward. After the service that night, I was desperate to find Leroy Tubbs, our pastor. I felt like I would burst open. I finally spotted him outside the church. I grabbed him, jerked him into a side room off the narthex, and fell on his shoulder broken and bawling.

At first, he didn't understand my tears, but when I finally could tell him, he rejoiced. Pastor Tubbs knew that Jesus had been working in my heart for about two years, but neither of us could understand the purpose. At that moment, he knew. He encouraged me to transfer to a Bible college instead of returning to the University of Mississippi. After my decision to change careers, my concerned parents brought me back home to attend a local junior college. They thought I was mentally cracking up. As a pre-med student at Ole Miss, I was a success, making excellent grades, and they couldn't comprehend the apparently sudden switch in career choices.

Confusion reigned. I headed toward the pastorate, for I wanted to be obedient to Jesus's call on my life. Meanwhile, my family and friends thought I was nuts and told me so. But I knew that the Lord would guide my decisions. He had prompted me and was leading me. It was a *chairos* moment—a "Wow!"—when God intervened in my life and I responded.

> *Worship Experience*
> **Listen to "New Wine," by Hillsong Worship:**
> **"In the crushing,**
> **in the pressing,**
> **You are making new wine."**

God speaks in many ways but mostly through His Word. Another way God speaks is through people in our lives. Through a "multitude of counselors there is safety," the Bible says in Proverbs 11:14 (NKJV). At times God also speaks in the still, small voice or through circumstances of life—positively and negatively. When God speaks, we must trust Him.

Revival Truths

- Following Christ and His goals for our life is a matter of obedience.

- God speaks through the Scriptures, to our minds during prayer, and through other people.

Trust in the Lord with all your heart, and do not lean on your own understanding. In all your ways acknowledge him, and he will make straight your paths.

PROVERBS 3:5–6

Walking
in the Light
of God's
Word

Opportunities for Nourishment

As newborn babes, desire the pure milk of the word,
that you may grow thereby.

1 PETER 2:2 NKJV

One of the Millennium Development Goals of the United Nations is to reduce malnutrition, a condition that occurs when the body doesn't get enough nutrients. Christ followers are nourished into personal revival as we receive and yield to God's Word. To receive the nourishment of God's Word, we must take full advantage of every opportunity to encounter God in Scripture and experience its nourishing benefits and blessings.

- As we *hear* the Word of God taught, preached, and shared, our faith will be strengthened: "faith comes from hearing the message" (Romans 10:17 NIV).

- As we *read* the Word, we will receive blessings: "Blessed is the one who reads aloud the words of this prophecy" (Revelation 1:3 NIV).

- As we *study* the Word, God will approve us as "a workman who . . . correctly handles the word of truth" (2 Timothy 2:15 NIV).

- As we *memorize* it, we will be less vulnerable to sin: "I have hidden Your word in my heart that I might not sin against You" (Psalm 119:11 NIV).

- As we *meditate* upon God's Word, we will increasingly yield to it: "This Book of the Law shall not depart from your mouth, but you shall meditate on it day and night, so that you may be careful to do according to all that is written in it. For then you will make your way prosperous, and then you will have good success" (Joshua 1:8 ESV). Our meditation on the Word will also produce spiritual prosperity, health, and fruitfulness (Psalm 1:1–3).

Consider these five opportunities for nourishment from God's Word. How many have you taken advantage of this week? Sadly, too many of God's children remain "babes" in their faith as they come to hear God's Word preached or taught by others, but rarely take advantage of other avenues of nourishment.

Pause now and take a moment to express your gratitude to God for providing so many different ways for us to be strengthened by His Word. Decide which one these opportunities you will take advantage of today. Will you memorize the suggested Scripture passage for this week? Will you spend time meditating on particular passages or stories of Christ? Will you spend time studying this week's sermon text for yourself, allowing God's Spirit to impress you with insights?

Lord, I sense your prompting to more deeply nourish my life in Your Word through additional priority on _____.

W1. A Spirit-empowered disciple is frequently led by the Spirit into deeper love for the One who wrote the Word.

Day 5

Revival 101

Throughout this week, we have focused on our personal relationship with Christ. We've considered our initial commitment, the importance of spiritual disciplines, and the need to hear God and obey His call in our lives. These are the foundations for personal revival and spiritual renewal. Let's begin to look at revival as a concept that moves beyond our personal lives to impact the lives of others.

Lewis Drummond, a gifted evangelist and professor, became my mentor during seminary. Dr. Drummond loved to tell people how to know God, and I took every course I possibly could from him. One of those courses was entitled Revival 101. I went into the class with a preconceived notion of its content. To me, revival was an evangelistic campaign, and I thought this course would teach me the how-tos. I signed up believing I knew what to expect, but I found something totally unexpected.

Dr. Drummond described great periods of history when the Holy Spirit moved on a people in a powerful fashion. He began in the Bible where God intervened in the affairs of men and women, then in history with nations transformed through His intervention, or *chairos* moments. Dr. Drummond challenged us regarding how such movements came through prayer, brokenness, and humility. Once an individual is spiritually broken, then God can intervene in a mighty manner.

I learned that revival is a continual process of brokenness and restoration, not just a one-night event or even a series of meetings. As I listened to his explanation, my heart jumped. I suddenly knew that I was born for revival and to be part of a spiritual awakening—an awakening that I believe is now in the toddling stages of touching America and the world!

This call to revival is not exclusive or only for me. I believe the Holy Spirit is right now in the process of establishing the call to revival over the lives of many, if not all, of His children. When the Lord gripped Emily Adams's heart for revival at twenty-one years old while she was sitting in the breakroom of the Billy Graham Library in Charlotte, NC, she said to me, "You have shown me that for which I could live the rest of my life—Jesus REVIVED in us!"

> *"Revival is about God. His children meeting with God, the nation being confronted with Him." – Colin Urquhart*

There are many glimmers of hope regarding this spiritual awakening, but here are a couple of examples. On October 4, 1997, an estimated one million men from all races and denominational backgrounds gathered in Washington, DC, for prayer and reconciliation in an event organized by Promise Keepers, a group focused on bringing revival to the hearts of men. Reports said the event, "Stand in the Gap: A Sacred Assembly of Men," was the largest religious gathering in American history. Spiritual and racial reconciliation has been enhanced immeasurably in recent years, and we have seen much greater trust and desire to work together locally and nationally from spiritual brothers and sisters of all ethnic groups and denominational backgrounds. Promise Keepers announced in May 2019 that it is planning a new season of men's ministry using digital media resources and connecting men through a national event in the summer of 2020. They are expecting eighty thousand men to attend the event in person and another five million to join the gathering digitally, courtesy of simulcast.[8]

Or consider the commitment of young people gathered at the flagpoles of their schools to pray for their teachers, principals, parents, city leaders, and each other—unprecedented in the youth movements of history. Since its small beginnings in 1990, the Lord has exploded See You at the Pole™ through elementary, middle, high school, and college students from public, private, and homeschools in more than sixty-four nations. It took only a few years for the movement of student-led prayer to move beyond America. Across the globe, from Canada to Korea, in places as unlikely as Japan and Turkey, more than one million students gather each year to participate in See You at the Pole™, responding to God's call and accepting His invitation to pray.[9]

In 2016, Franklin Graham spoke at every United States state capital in all fifty states, calling the nation to return to prayer and Jesus. The Billy Graham Evangelistic Association organized this as a "cry out and up" to our Heavenly Father in trying times. Averaging about five thousand people per stop, an estimated 236,950 joined the Decision America Tour.[10] At these events, Franklin called Americans just like you and me to put God first in their lives and go to their knees in prayer, laying a foundation for increased faith in our nation. Franklin Graham and the continuing Decision America Tours have been instrumental in establishing a prayer movement for the Kingdom of God. They have become a basis for what God will continue to do as Jesus moves America back to His love, biblical values, and principles of life.

These signs of rekindled spiritual renewal are appearing across our world and nation. Each sign gives us hope and encouragement for our daily walk with Jesus Christ. As each person walks in obedience, God weaves those individual acts of obedience together into a greater move of His Spirit.

The purpose of revival is to renew Jesus in the believer and to then bring the lost to Jesus. Being a goal-minded person, I determined a mission statement for my life. "I exist to help others know God personally through Jesus Christ through the spiritual awakening of the church and the resulting action which brings salvation to all possible and justice for all possible globally."

This seemed to be an impossible mission statement to fulfill. Alan Redpath, a great British preacher, told me in 1983 that when God wants to do an impossible thing, He takes an impossible man (or woman) and crushes him. God uses the broken vessel He reconstructs. Be encouraged.

Jesus's ways are a part of my daily life as I die to Tom and open myself by faith to Him. As I experience personal revival and grow in my intimacy with

Christ, it increases my desire to be obedient to His Word and to share Him with others. And as others experience personal revival, they will live holier lives and share Christ too. Again, be encouraged.

We desire to see the reality of 2 Chronicles 7:14. We pray for a spiritual awakening in the United States. We want God to heal our land. In a world full of self-help and New Age teaching, our hope for revival must be found in Christ alone. For God to heal the land, He must heal one person at a time, beginning with you and me. If revival is to spread, it must begin with individuals.

More than any other time in recent history, Americans are aware of their growing spiritual needs. Printed material on spirituality has been in great demand during recent years. Why? It's an indicator of the searching heart.

Revival Truths

- World revival begins with personal revival, through *chairos* moments with God.

- Personal revival begins with daily and consistent intimacy with God through prayer and Bible study.

- Personal revival requires daily obedience to His call.

> You are the light of the world. A city set on a hill cannot be hidden.

MATTHEW 5:14

Walking in the Light of God's Son

Test and Reveal

> Search me, O God, and know my heart! Try me and know my thoughts! And see if there be any grievous way in me, and lead me in the way everlasting!

PSALM 139:23–24

Each of us was born with a human nature that goes our own way. We are born separated by our sin from a holy God. Each of us has fallen short of His perfection and that means we are disconnected from God. We become separated from the very One who most loves us and can help us.

Could you take the next few moments and ask God to reveal any areas in which you fall short of His perfection? Pray the Psalmist's prayer: Ask God to search your heart and reveal the things that ought to worry you about your life. Could it be: anger, pride, selfishness, lying, arrogance, self-centeredness, being rude, disrespectful, unkind, gossip, lust, unforgiveness, bitterness, sexual sin, insensitivity to others, judging others, betrayal, critical to others, withholding love, disobedience, coveting, filthy language, ungrateful attitude, envy, jealousy, unacceptance, deception, short temper, addiction, or theft? Confess these things to Him as He reveals them.

- *God, one area in which I fall short of your standard is . . .*

- *God, I ask for your forgiveness. I know Jesus gave up His life for this sin in me. I ask you to forgive me and revive my heart.*

A part of why Jesus chose to go to the cross was because of what you and I have just named. He chose to take our sins upon Himself. God is certainly a God who is rich in mercy and He is a holy God. God is so holy that He cannot relate to sin in any form (Ephesians 2:4; Habakkuk 1:13). So rather than lose relationship with us, God restored the possibility of relationship by sacrificing His Son.

How does your heart respond knowing that Jesus gave His life in order to lift these burdens and sins from you?

Jesus, I feel _____ (amazed/grateful/astounded) as I think about how You gave Your life for my _____ (name one of the struggles you have just identified.) I'm especially grateful because . . .
I am astounded by your love for me, Jesus. I choose to receive your forgiveness and ask for your continued transformation.

L10. A Spirit-empowered disciple practices the presence of the Lord, yielding to the Spirit's work of Christlikeness.

SPIRIT-
EMPOWERED
Faith

Looking Forward

Revival begins in the hearts of individuals. As we personally experience revival, growing out of a relationship with Christ, we then share this hope with others. It's a process that bears the fruit of God in our lives—not an event. Next week we will learn about the methods God uses to bring us to a point of personal revival.

CHAPTER 2

Beginning with BROKENNESS

The journey to rekindle the fire of your passion for Christ often begins at an unlikely spot. It begins with a word not usually spoken from the pulpit today, yet the early church fathers fully recognized it as the route for spiritual wholeness: *brokenness.*

Our world displays plenty of examples opposing brokenness—examples of pride. Pride is the slogan of the day on Wall Street. "You deserve it. You can make it yourself. You are capable and independent and sufficient." The big You—without need of Jesus. Pride puffs you up instead of allowing you to realize your own inadequacies, your humanness, your dependence on Him. Ironically that realization is what sets you free.

During this week, let's examine the concept of spiritual brokenness. What does it mean? How do you discover it? What impact can it have to rekindle your love relationship with Jesus Christ?

Day 1

Pitiful Pride

Jesus can't use a prideful person. The Bible says, "Pride goes before destruction, and a haughty spirit before a fall" (Proverbs 16:18). Paraphrasing St. Augustine, pride in who you truly are in Christ is not a sin, but pride in who you think you are, inordinate pride, is a sin. It's perfectly normal to be glad that you are a child of God or a joint heir with Christ, but we're talking here about pride in yourself apart from God. True humility is agreement with how God sees you.

In my own journey with pride and brokenness, I have gone through several stages, and I expect more stages will come. The first stage I experienced was an awareness of pride in my life. As with most issues, God worked through circumstances and other people to bring this to light.

During high school, I competed in the high hurdles track-and-field event. During the regionals, I had one last chance to go to the state championship, and I felt confident I would qualify. The runners lined up, the gun sounded, but there was a false start—someone left the starting blocks too soon. We returned to our positions. The second time the gun sounded, I saw another false start. There was a difference this time, however. I saw it, but the official did not. He didn't signal it false. Confident I was right, however, I had halted in the blocks until I saw the entire field race ahead of me. I finally took off, chasing the pack.

As I started clearing those hurdles, I *knew* the guys around me started early. I was sure the official would call us back to the starting line. Yet the race continued, and no false start was called. I had to push hard to catch them. To qualify for state, you had to finish either first or second in the heat. I came in third. Afterward my coach asked, "Why did you stop?"

"Coach, it was a false start."

He said, "Yeah, but you aren't the one who calls it false, are you?"

I was devastated. I knew I was good enough to compete at the state level, but my pride kept me from achieving my goal. Right wasn't right that time.

> "Revival is that strange and sovereign mark of God in which He visits His own people—restoring, reanimating, and releasing them into the fullness of His blessing."
> – Stephen Olford

Looking back, I am grateful now to see God's hand in these situations. I had an enormous amount of pride, and I argued a lot, convinced I was always right. I don't remember ever losing a debate or argument throughout high school or college or even during points in my marriage, but I believe I lost friends and at times alienated my wife. God hates pride and will eventually allow us to be humbled. There are always consequences to pride in our lives. God needed to deal with my pride. He continues to deal with my pride. It requires daily confession and repentance. My desire is that I would be humble before God, but sometimes I still struggle. I want to be worthy of use by God, but His vessel needs periodic purifying.

Revival Truths

- Whether or not you are aware of it, pride can hinder your relationship with the eternal God.

- The Lord wants you to consider pride in your life, then remove it. He wants you to be proud only of Him and His work in and through your life.

One's pride will bring him low, but he who is lowly in spirit will obtain honor.

PROVERBS 29:23

Walking in the Light of God's People

How Might You Yield?

And Jesus, crying out with a loud voice, said, "Father, into Your hands I commit My spirit." Having said this, He breathed His last.

LUKE 23:46 (NASB)

In His last words from the cross, Christ expresses both His identity and His legacy to us: In humility, He yielded! This is the key that unlocks the mystery of Jesus and the Father being One—whatever the Son did, it was only what He had seen the Father doing. In the same way, the key that will empower our living expression of God's glory will be our humble commitment to yield to whatever the Father reveals.

Consider some of these Bible passages that testify of how Jesus yielded. Ask the Holy Spirit to prompt your heart with any areas where you could further demonstrate your own love for the Father by yielding to Him.

- Jesus yielded as He left heaven's riches and became a servant (Philippians 2:5–8). How might you yield to the Father and become more of a servant today?

- Jesus yielded His actions to the Father. He did not seek to please Himself, but desired only to please the Father (John 5:19, 30). How might you yield your actions to the Father today? How might you please Him with your life today?

- Jesus yielded to the leadership of the Holy Spirit (Matthew 4:1). How might you yield to the leadership of the Holy Spirit today? How might you become more attentive to His direction and guidance?

- Jesus yielded to the Holy Spirit when He was tempted as we are so that He might help us when we are tempted (Hebrews 2:18; Luke 4:1–13). How might you yield to the Holy Spirit in overcoming sin?

- Jesus yielded to human authority (John 19:1–22). How might you yield to the Father and the human authorities that God has placed in your life today?

Now consider John 20:21: "Jesus said to them again, 'Peace be with you; as the Father has sent Me, I also send you'" (NASB). Consider the areas and issues in your life in which the Holy Spirit is longing to work. What do you sense will be the fresh work of humility that the Lord is longing to see in you?

- To be more convinced of God's love for me
- To better please Him in all things
- To be more attentive to the Spirit's direction
- To better overcome evil, reoccurring sin
- To be more yielding to others' input and wisdom

Consider praying with one or two others:

Lord Jesus, I wish to have an attitude of humility and look for opportunities to serve those in my life. Help me with my stubbornness because I tend to want things to go my way. Usually, I want to do my own thing and not follow the counsel of others. Specifically, I yield to Your Spirit so that I might be _____

_____.

L5. A Spirit-empowered disciple lives with a passionate longing for purity and desire to please Him in all things.

Day 2

Rusty Pipes

In San Diego, I met with an ex-professional football player, an NFL Hall of Fame member then in his early eighties. He was a truly great man and a dear friend. In spite of this physical and spiritual giant's age, God was still working on his pride. He was experiencing some personal difficulties, and he asked me, "Why is this happening in my life?"

"Is it possible God is working on your pride?" I asked. Instantly he responded, "I don't have any pride."

"Oh really? Maybe that's the problem. When you think you don't have any pride, then that's when you may struggle with this very issue."

The giant of a man looked at me with a shocked expression. He said nothing—one of the few times I had known him to be at a loss for words.

Consider the promise of 2 Timothy 2:21: "Therefore, if anyone cleanses himself from what is dishonorable, he will be a vessel for honorable use, set apart as holy, useful to the master of the house, ready for every good work."

Do you want to be prepared for every good work? Do you want Jesus to use you as a holy vessel? If so, then you must get anything extraneous and unnecessary out of the way, often beginning with pride. The Bible tells us that personal character flaws are difficult to see, and pride is often the foundational flaw to keep us from seeing other issues. For that reason, God may use other people and circumstances to reveal our pride. The Bible says that "iron sharpens iron" (Proverbs 27:17). We can sharpen one another's lives.

> *"Here is the outstanding feature of revival: Suddenly, without warning, God is present, and the people are brought face to face with God's holiness and their sin. It seems that God is dealing with them alone so that whatever the spiritual state of the person, saved or unsaved, a mighty work of transformation occurs. The unsaved are brought to salvation and the saved are brought to further holiness." – Dale Schlafer*

I once saw a building containing a huge steam plant for a large complex. Projecting out of this building were several massive pipes. At key points the pipes bent at right angles. An engineer explained to me the strange looking pipes: "That's the steam plant, and the steam comes out in force. If we don't constrict the flow by making it go through several turns, it will blow the pressure valves when it hits the radiators in other buildings." The engineers reduced the power of the steam by hindering its flow.

Unlike the steam pipe, where too much power poses a danger, God wants us to have the unrestricted power of the Holy Spirit. Picture God's heart connected to your heart by a pipe. Is there rust in your pipe that keeps the power of the Holy Spirit from flowing freely into your thoughts and everyday actions? The rust may not block the pipe entirely, yet any time the flow of the Holy Spirit has to go around constrictions, it cuts down the power of the flow. Or do you have a lot of bending in your pipes, where you try to go around things God has for you? Our pipes should be straight, open to the flow of God's Holy Spirit.

We try to "clean" our spiritual pipes by self-revelation, self-actualization, and self-renewal. These self-centered activities will prove useless and frustrating. Conviction, confession, and turning to Him for cleansing are the keys to an unhindered flow of the Holy Spirit. Only Jesus can remove the rust and straighten the pipes.

We need personal brokenness and humility, and then God can heal our land. God heals the land as He flows through unconstricted vessels, and you are one of those precious vessels. People mistakenly believe that worldwide revival happens when God opens the windows of heaven and pours the Holy Spirit from a big bucket. That's not the way it works. The Holy Spirit flows through God's people, His vessels—one at a time.

So if God is working in your heart, asking you to release your pride and submit to Him, then you, as an individual, are a key part of corporate revival. We are the means through which God reaches this world.

It's difficult to stand outside yourself and see character flaws. You need others to help you see areas for growth. It is through brokenness that we are able to grow, and as you continually grow in Christ, the power of the Holy Spirit can flow through your life.

Consider your vessel. Is there rust in your pipes? Are they constricted? What rust needs to be removed? Pray now for God to clear the rust and straighten the bends.

Revival Truths

- God uses brokenness to build strength into our lives.

- God desires to clean any blockage in "our pipes" so we can be free and clear for Him to flow through.

- We need to be prepared for God to work through us.

If anyone cleanses himself from what is dishonorable, he will be a vessel for honorable use, set apart as holy, useful to the master of the house, ready for every good work.

2 TIMOTHY 2:21

Walking in the Light of God's Word

Can You Hear Him Now?

I saw the Lord sitting on a throne, high and lifted up, and the train of His robe filled the temple.

ISAIAH 6:1

The prophet Isaiah's dramatic encounter with the Lord brought with it the need to put away the sin of "unclean lips." He confessed his sin: "'Woe to me!' I cried. 'I am ruined! For I am a man of unclean lips, and I live among a people of unclean lips, and my eyes have seen the King, the Lord Almighty'" (Isaiah 6:5 NIV). Then God cleansed him by sending an angel with a live coal. The angel touched Isaiah's mouth and said, "See, this has touched your lips; your guilt is taken away and your sin atoned for" (vv. 6–7 NIV). Isaiah then heard the voice of God saying, "Whom shall I send? And who will go for us?" The man of God then yielded to the Lord and said, "Here am I. Send me" (vv. 8–9 NIV).

The story of this Old Testament prophet reminds us that cleansing must precede clarity concerning God's voice and discernment about His will. Christ followers long to hear the Lord so that they, like Isaiah, will want to put away anything that might hinder hearing from Him.

Consider a fresh experience of Hebrews 12:1: "Therefore, since we have so great a cloud of witnesses surrounding us, let us also lay aside every encumbrance and the sin which so easily entangles us, and let us run with endurance the race that is set before us" (NASB).

Do you need to lay aside and seek cleansing for:

- Particular areas of sin through confessing to God and receiving His forgiveness? Write about them.

- Unresolved emotions, like guilt, anger and bitterness, condemnation and fear? Write about them.

- Childish things, such as finger-pointing or blame? Preoccupation with self? Idle chatter or gossip? Write about them.

Pause now and consider your own ability to hear from the Lord:

Ask His Spirit to reveal anything that might need to be cleansed. Sit quietly before the Lord and allow Him to speak to your heart. Be open to the gentle voice that urges you to purify yourself so that you might have deepened intimacy with the Creator.

Dear Lord Jesus, help me to put away sins that are derailing me. I no longer wish to carry the burden of these unresolved emotions. I'm sorrowed by my childish behaviors and want to renounce these. I wish to hear Your voice and no longer listen to the distracting noise of transgression.

L10. A Spirit-empowered disciple practices the presence of the Lord, yielding to the Spirit's work of Christlikeness.

Day 3

Becoming Accountable

Several years ago, one of my friends, Joe Leininger, moved from Chicago to Colorado Springs. For ten years, he had traded in the Eurodollar pit of the Chicago Mercantile Exchange, and he captured his unusual business experiences in a book, *Lessons from the Pit*.[11] Two weeks after he arrived, Joe and I met for lunch at a local deli. He said, "I have a request. Would you disciple me?" My answer surprised Joe. "No, I don't do that." He looked at me oddly, certain I had discipled other men. After all, for over twenty years, I worked with Billy Graham and my spiritual mentor, Charlie Riggs, a discipler of men.

He said, "I thought you did that."

"No. You have to be consistently available to disciple someone, and I travel too much. But I will be in a Barnabas/John Mark relationship with you. I'm older, so I'll be Barnabas and you be John Mark—brothers in Christ with a commitment to each other. The only commitment I will make is one you have to make to me too: I'll challenge you to grow as I see things in your life, but only if you'll help me grow. Like iron sharpening iron, the relationship has to be a two-way street. I need to learn too. I'm teachable and want to grow."

Joe accepted this condition, and we began to meet. After laying ground rules to discuss our growth in Christ, I dug into the conversation. "All right. The first thing I want to discuss is brokenness."

He said, "I don't want to talk about brokenness."

"Why not?"

"Because I don't like brokenness," Joe said, leaning on the table with sincerity. "It's like you're weak or something." His response wasn't surprising considering he had been a University of Illinois athlete and then spent years in the competitive locker-room-like environment of the Chicago trading pit. In either of those situations, one would be unwise to show weakness.

I responded, "No, it's not weakness at all. It is strength. There is strength in weakness. Paul says that the less you have the more you depend on Him. The Bible also says that when you are weak, He can be strong in you" (2 Corinthians 12:10).

Joe was adamant, saying again, "I don't want to talk about that."

"Okay, we're not going to meet together then," I said, "because that's what God is doing in my life right now. He's continually breaking the old me, and I need it. Not that I like the pain of being broken, but I believe in the end result. If you are going to meet with me, then we'll talk about brokenness."

Reluctantly he said, "Okay, if that's what it takes."

Again I affirmed, "That's the only way I can do it because it's where I am. I can't change from where I am in my growing relationship with Christ."

A few months later, Joe wrote in a letter, "You taught me a great deal about what it means to be a man of God. I no longer associate the idea of brokenheartedness with a killjoy Christian paranoia. Now I see it as the sort of humility that is needed for God to truly use a person to accomplish his purposes."

> **"Revival is a going of God among His people."**
> – Duncan Campbell

If you are serious about working on your pride and other character issues, you need accountability with someone else. My accountability relationships have fostered significant growth in my Christian life, and I'm convinced we can continue growing in our love relationship with Christ through accountability with another person.

Do you have an accountability partner to help you with character issues such as pride? If not, find one, possibly with the help of your local church leader. Establish a few ground rules for your session together such as:

- The purpose of our meeting is to talk about areas of growth.

- Our conversation will be confidential.

- Our partnership is equally balanced—each person has an opportunity for growth.

- We'll commit to pray for each other.

- We'll commit to a regular schedule of meeting together.

As you evaluate a person as an accountability partner also consider: (1) Is this someone I enjoy meeting with on a regular basis? (2) Is this someone I can trust with my confidences? (3) Is this someone I can see meeting with over a long period of time? (4) Will this person's schedule or heart allow for a commitment to this relationship?

When you come together, one way to promote deep conversation is with a series of questions. Each party should agree to these questions and their use ahead of time. John Maxwell, in his ministry, has used such questions. Questions might include: (1) Are you reading your Bible and praying every day? (2) Consider what's running through your thoughts. Are they pure? (3) Are you misusing or violating any trust that someone else has given you? (4) Are you living every day in total obedience to God? Maxwell mentions that partial obedience equals disobedience.

Then ask a fifth and final question: Have you lied about any of the previous questions? You may think the fifth question is unnecessary, but it's another call into accountability. Without penalty, it gives the person an opportunity to revisit any of the previous four questions.

Revival Truths

- Pride and other character issues are hard to see in ourselves.

- For character development, we need to have an accountability relationship.

Iron sharpens iron, and one man sharpens another.

PROVERBS 27:17

Walking
in the Light
of God's
Word

Get Close

Be holy, for I am holy.

1 PETER 1:16

This passage in 1 Peter might seem a little unrealistic. Is God really asking us to reach a goal that will never be attainable? Is God seriously demanding our perfection for personal revival? Why would God want our holiness? Why is He telling us to be like Him?

Our God isn't holding out an impractical standard. Peter is letting us know that because God is holy, He wants us to live out our lives always striving for holiness and maturity because the more we are like Him, the closer we are to Him. God's motive behind His hope for our personal revival is that He deeply longs for a closer and closer relationship with us.

How does it make you feel as you consider God's motive for your spiritual maturity? The reason He wants you to mature and grow spiritually is because God deeply desires a closer relationship with you.

When I consider God's motive for my spiritual growth, I feel
_____ because _____ .

What might it look like to be a maturing follower of Jesus?

- Children frequently go to great lengths to justify their poor choices, but as maturing followers of Jesus, we are called to be accountable to God and to take responsibility for our actions (Romans 14:12).

- Children tend to talk a great deal and often have trouble listening carefully, but as maturing disciples of Jesus we are called to speak less and listen more both to God and other people (James 1:19).

- Children are often intensely selfish and focused on their own desires, but as maturing disciples of Jesus, we are called to abandon self-preoccupation and to direct our energy toward loving and serving God and others (Philippians 2:3–4).

- Children generally have a very limited, simplistic understanding of most subjects, but as maturing disciples of Jesus, we are called to pursue knowledge and understanding of God's Word and to live with wisdom and discernment that comes from time spent with Him (Psalm 111:10).

Now, tell Him about your willingness to grow:

Father, my heart wants to be mature in all that I do and say. Help me to see any of my childish ways and help me to trade them for more mature choices because I want to be closer to You. Specifically, I sense a renewed importance for me to:

- *Be more accountable and responsible.*
- *Listen more to God and others and talk less.*
- *Be less self-preoccupied and more willing to serve others.*

- *Be more of a student of God's Word and His ways.*

W-6 A Spirit-empowered disciple encounters Jesus in the Word for deepened transformation in Christlikeness.

Day 4

A Normal Relationship with God

As you seek the heart of Jesus in your pilgrimage, you will more readily accomplish God's purpose in your life. Some people think that brokenness is abnormal, but from the Bible, we learn that it's really the foundation on which God can build.

Our normal relationship with God hinges on the ability to communicate with Him on a consistent basis. The Bible says that we can "pray without ceasing" (1 Thessalonians 5:17). God has told us that we "ought always to pray" (Luke 18:1). This means that our hearts should be in utter communion with Him. Of course, it's so easy for us to move away from God and follow the ways of the world that seem to bring us possessions and power but often do not bring us joy. Even our thoughts are vitally involved in this process.

When I was dating Ouida, I met her Methodist minister, Jack Williams, a remarkable man. Reverend Williams led his church with tremendous spiritual depth and was one of the godliest men I'd ever met. As a high school student, when I went to church with her, I was always impressed by his emphasis on consistent prayer and our thought life. Every Sunday he opened the altar of his suburban Methodist church and people flooded to the front for communion with the Lord—individually and corporately. It was a sweet time. The power of the Holy Spirit was deeply present.

Each Sunday Brother Jack had a habit of handing out little mimeographed pieces of paper at the door after Sunday service with quotations on them, which always meant much to me as I meditated on each one. One touched my heart deeply, and I remember it to this day. It said, "What's in the conscious mind sinks down into the unconscious to influence our moods and our health. If we indulge negative, resentful, impure, or unkind thinking, we become tense and have a depressed spirit as individuals. But, if we fill our lives with what is positive, worthy, and beautiful, we gradually grow poised, power-filled lives."

That quotation applies to Philippians 4:8–9: "Finally, brothers, whatever is true, whatever is honorable, whatever is just, whatever is pure, whatever is lovely, whatever is commendable, if there is any excellence, if there is anything worthy of praise, think about these things. What you have learned and received and heard and seen in me—practice these things, and the God of peace will be with you."

Our thoughts are vitally connected to our actions in the normal Christian faith. They produce a flow in the relationship with God. In context, this simply means "being occupied with God and seeing ourselves in relationship with Him. It means that we see ourselves as creatures but we see Him as Creator."[12]

What some people see as brokenness is alignment with His will and purpose for our lives. God wants to work His perfect will through us as He says in Philippians 2:13, "For it is God who works in you, both to will and to work for his good pleasure." That is our normal Christian life—allowing God to flow through us unhindered.

> *"Revival is nothing more than a return to normal Christianity." – Tom Phillips*

When I was a college senior, I needed a one-hour, upper-level art course to graduate. With only one summer left to complete a double major in biology and English, my opportunities to secure an art course were limited, and to my chagrin, the only one that I could take was pottery. I couldn't believe that was a course they gave credit for in a university. But to my utter amazement, I loved the course and did well in it.

One day, at the wheel, as my feet moved rapidly on the stone below that turned the table above, I placed a ball of clay. Most pottery pieces begin with a thumb hole in the middle of the clay, and then with deft finger movements, the potter pulls the clay into a tube and widens into the desired shape. That day I pulled the tallest and best tube I'd ever made. I was overjoyed. But to my horror, I inadvertently stuck a hole in the side with my finger.

I looked at the clay on my finger and with relief realized that I could affix the lump back into the hole and smooth it out. Delighted, I began to push my feet against the wheel and bring the upper table to full momentum. I began to work the clay only to watch the reattached lump finally shoot off and fall to the floor. Oh, well, so much for repairing a broken vessel. I had to crush it and start over.

It is similar with our relationship to God. Though He does not make mistakes in fashioning us, He desires a perfect vessel. With each blemish, our loving Father uses brokenness to make us more like Him. It is not enough to be repaired; it requires a new start. It's normal life on the Potter's wheel. Initially, we may resist the process of brokenness, but it's a normal act of faith in our pilgrimage with Jesus. Today make a fresh commitment to view your life as God sees you—in true humility, flaws and all.

Revival Truths

- Constructive brokenness is a normal part of our life with Christ.

- Without brokenness, sin hardens our hearts to God's work in us.

All these things my hand has made, and so all these things came to be, declares the Lord. But this is the one to whom I will look: he who is humble and contrite in spirit and trembles at my word.

ISAIAH 66:2

Walking
in the Light
of God's
People

Transformed Priorities

Simon Peter answered and said, "You are the Christ, the Son of the living God." Jesus answered and said to him, "Blessed are you, Simon Bar-Jonah, for flesh and blood has not revealed this to you, but My Father who is in heaven. And I also say to you that you are Peter, and on this rock I will build My church, and the gates of Hades shall not prevail against it.

MATTHEW 16:16–18 NKJV

We live in a day in which material possessions, status, leisure, enter-tainment, and many other things seem to take priority while our important relationships are suffering.

Notice in the text above that when Christ affirmed Peter, He highlighted the Father's "revealing," and He affirmed Peter for hearing the Father's revelation. Peter, after all his bold pronouncements, was being humbled and broken. It was as if Jesus was saying to Peter, in his brokenness, "You got it! And the reason you got it is because the Father revealed it to you." Jesus acknowledged both the Father's revealing and Peter's brokenness to hear. This foundational process of God revealing and His followers yielding—hearing and responding in brokenness—is the "rock" upon which Christ is even now building His church.

This foundational truth must shape our walk with Him: As we faithfully follow Him, our life priorities will change from what we are seeking to accomplish, acquire, or achieve to a divinely prompted longing to hear Him and yield to Him. The longing for the Holy Spirit within us to nourish and prompt us reorders our priorities. Just as certainly as we need food to nourish our bodies in order to mature physically, so also our spiritual nourishment must become a priority if we are to mature as faithful disciples and express His presence.

Consider your own priorities now. Are you more concerned about what you will accomplish, acquire, or achieve? Or is your heart longing to hear from the Lord and ready to yield to Him? Recommit yourself to hearing from God and yielding your heart to His plans and desires.

Pause now with one or two others to pray together, asking God to reorder your priorities as the Holy Spirit longs to reveal His ways to you and empower your yielding.

Dear God, there are many voices calling for my attention today, and often I'm not listening for Yours. I acknowledge that You do not have a speaking problem; rather, I have an attunement issue. I want to recommit my heart to hearing Your voice as You redirect me to focus on the important people and Kingdom issues in my life.

L2. A Spirit-empowered disciple listens to and hears God for direction and discernment.

Day 5

The Key to National Healing: Brokenness

To be fully filled with Jesus, we must first be fully emptied of ourselves. Only one thing prevents Jesus from filling our cup—sin. And the dirtiness in the cup of America looms large as we're absorbed with ourselves: our self-image, self-indulgence, self-pity, self-complacency, and self-seeking. The source of these "self-exhortations" is unbelief, an inverted form of pride. They hinder our intimacy with Christ.[13] Such is our nation. In the article "Prodigal Nation," published by *Washington Watch,* Peter Marshall wrote that the United States has become a prodigal. We have:

- Rejected the "right way to do things" . . . in every . . . area of American life.

- Trashed the reputations of our nation's founders.

- Ended the practice of reforming our society in light of God's Word.

- Rejected education with a biblical worldview.

- Rejected the notion of our founding fathers that "religion is the basis and foundation of government" (James Madison).

- Rejected the fact that our constitution only works when the people whom it governs are moral and religious.

- Rejected Benjamin Franklin's comment that "only virtuous people are capable of freedom."

- Rejected the fact Americans of faith must be involved in current and moral civil government.[14]

This leaves us needing God's discipline. The decadence of our society, the corruption of our religious leaders, and the ever-present example of abortion, division, and hatred make us a prodigal nation.

We know God is concerned for our nation. In many ways the Lord holds the church of Jesus Christ responsible for the nation. Yes, the church is made up of people just like you and me. Therefore, as we look at the concerns relative to our nation, we as individuals must address the hope that is in Christ for the entire nation. Revival in the church is the way God will bring a renewal to our country. The foundation for that is brokenness and prayer. We all must pray, believing He has a plan for our nation and that the power of the Holy Spirit has defeated the enemy.

> *"Revival is God bending down to the dying embers of a fire that is just about to go out, and breathing into it until it bursts again into flame." – Christmas Evans*

Matthew Henry once said, "When God intends great mercy for His people, He first of all sets them a-praying."[15] We *are* seeing a praying nation. Through so many prayer efforts, like The Call, the International Houses of Prayer, the World Prayer Center, the National Prayer Committee, the National Day of Prayer, Generals of Intercession, Intercessors for America, and so many others, there is an amazing movement of prayer building in individual's lives, small prayer groups, and selfless national organizations. A.T. Pierson said that "There has never been a spiritual awakening in any country or locality that did not begin in united prayer."[16] Prayer has always preceded any great national or regional move of the Spirit of God, concerted, united, persistent, persevering prayer. When God intends to move in His children's lives, He first calls His people to prayer.

Prayer and brokenness are united in the principles of 2 Chronicles 7:14. As we are humble, convicted, and obedient, God can heal our land. What can we do to open the door for God to heal our land? We can:

- Die to self.

- Ask God to cleanse and purify our hearts.

- Ask God to search our hearts for bitterness or hate. Ask for forgiveness and make amends.

- Lift Christ's love above our differences so He is what others see in us. We can do this without changing our convictions.

- Be open to confession and repentance for historic acts relative to the way one people group has treated another, both in this nation and in the world.

- Condemn violence toward other people because of racial, ethnic, or any other differences.

- Realize that, though some sins are less "socially acceptable," we're all sinners in God's eyes.

- Love others who express differences in their lives, even if those differences are sinful. The saint must truly love the sinner regardless of the sin.

Brokenness in our nation will come when believers humble themselves before God. With that humility, God can pour His spirit into our lives, and through our lives into the lives of others. National brokenness is necessary for God to heal our land.

Revival Truths

- We can see the pillars of our nation crumbling, yet they crumble with God's purpose to revive a nation with a broken, humble spirit to the Lord.

- National brokenness begins with personal brokenness.

He said to me, "My grace is sufficient for you, for my power is made perfect in weakness." Therefore, I will boast all the more gladly of my weaknesses, so that the power of Christ may rest upon me.

2 CORINTHIANS 12:9

Walking in the Light of God's People

Hungry to Yield

He said to them, "I have food to eat of which you do not know."

JOHN 4:32 NKJV

The "food" which nourished Jesus wasn't something that could've been served for dinner or ordered for breakfast. It wasn't a five-course meal or even a taste of Galilee's finest produce. Christ was strengthened, sustained, and nourished by yielding to whatever His Father revealed. Just as we also get hungry for the nourishment of physical food, we must become hungry to yield to God. The things of this world simply are inadequate for personal or national revival.

Perhaps this is what the beatitude speaks of: "Blessed are those who hunger and thirst for righteousness, for they will be filled" (Matthew 5:6 NIV). Could righteousness that produces satisfaction of hunger be the tangible expression of Christ followers yielding to what they have heard from God? As a personal revival is multiplied among His people, we will see national revival.

We have the opportunity to receive the same nourishment that strengthened and sustained our Lord. As God reveals Himself to us in our personal brokenness, He brings the opportunity to yield. We, too, can receive nourishment from the joy of knowing that we have heard and yielded to the Father.

Just imagine, when the Father revealed Christ to you for salvation, in brokenness before Him, you yielded to Him. You responded with trusting faith. You came to see your hopeless state and yielded to Christ as your only hope. You came to see Christ as life eternal and yielded to His abundant life. You and I, like Peter, were challenged to yield to the reality of what the Father was revealing to us: Christ was who He claimed to be, and we desperately needed Him. Such is the hope of our world.

Pause now with one or two others and share a few words of gratitude with God. Thank Him for the marvelous revelation of Christ as your Savior. Thank Him for revealing Jesus and drawing you to Himself. Finally, express the joy that comes as you consider how you have already received His revelation, yielded to His Spirit, and are now an expression of His presence!

Heavenly Father, I'm grateful for salvation through Christ. And I appreciate the peace, joy, and satisfaction from the nourishment of Your presence. May I impart life and hope to others in our desperate world as I yield to You. I ask you to continue to nurture me in my walk with You as You reveal Yourself and Your ways.

L10. A Spirit-empowered disciple practices the presence of the Lord, yielding to the Spirit's work of Christlikeness.

Looking Forward

Brokenness is the antithesis of all that modern culture promotes. Pride is the foundation for many sinful behaviors. We think we're too good or too smart to let one little sin enslave us. Or we think we're more pure and holy than others who commit less "socially acceptable" sins. It's pride. In God's upside-down kingdom, it's the weak who are strong and the broken who are whole. Once we are open to brokenness, God can convict us and call us to freedom and joy through *repentance*.

CHAPTER 3

JOY IN True Repentance

Spiritual revivals throughout history have another common thread—repentance. Many people are praying for God to touch the United States. Though the corporate need is certainly present, it will only begin as individuals turn from sin and turn to Christ.

When a military officer does an about-face, he turns from one direction and heads resolutely in the opposite. That's a picture of repentance. If, as a Christian, you have turned from God in any area of your life, ask God to convict you of your sin and to help you see it as He does. Then as you confess this sin, agree with Him that it's wrong. Next, turn away from repeating the sin as you turn toward God.

Repentance leads us not just to change our actions but also to change the way we think. The Greek word for repent, *metanoeō*, literally means to think better. It is only when the grace of Jesus begins to renew our minds that we are able to consistently think better and see our actions turn lastingly away from sin and toward Jesus.

We often don't realize what it means to be a "normal" follower of Christ. Words like *confession* or *repentance* are whispered or never spoken. But confession and repentance are normal Christian experiences in our daily walk with Christ. They are redemptive actions that God established to overcome evil. True repentance leads to great joy as we experience the love and forgiveness of Jesus.

Day 1

Revival Requires Repentance

Today's world has an urgency and desperation unlike any other period of history. The darkness in the world seems cavernous, but points of light are breaking through. Repentance opens the door for God's light to shine in darkness. These laser points from Jesus shine in spite of the darkness. In revival, you and I are the light of the world, the light that dispels the darkness.

Some time ago, in the fall of 2016, I had a dream. I usually do not remember dreams, but I did this one. I have never been able to forget it—it has become monumental in my life. I was at a football field in a small town. There were absolutely no lights on; there was no moon or stars, no reflections or ambient light. It was an unusual completely dark night. I was standing in the stands about halfway up, on the home-team side fifty-yard line looking at a black football field. It was so dark that the grass showed up as black.

Then it was as if I left the field and then came back. When I got back, there were about ten lights spread throughout the entire surface of the football field—spread over all 100 yards long and fifty yards wide. But these ten little lights were like the tiny white lights on a Christmas tree. Wherever there was a little light, darkness was dispelled, and I could see a little green illumination—the life of the grass.

I went away and came back again. Standing in the same place again on the home-team side, I could now see about a hundred of those little lights, the tiny ones, several mid-sized ones, and a couple of large ones. And of course, everywhere I saw a little light, I saw a little life in the green grass.

I went away and came back a third time—instantaneously—as if jumping from one frame to another. From the stands, I could see that the little lights had increased again. Some of the bulbs had been replaced by much larger bulbs. There were sections of the field beginning to show life with extensive patches of green.

I went away again and came back. The lights were now completely across the field— larger bulbs, smaller bulbs, medium sized bulbs of all types, but concentric circles of light were beginning to overlap. The multiplied pinpricks and pinpoints of light completely lit the field, a fully green field covered in life.

I went away again and came back a fifth time to the same location. I could see exactly the same view as before but with one addition. The top of the field was now transparent, and I could see as if with x-ray vision through the life of the grass to the fiber-optic cables below that connected everything from the grassroots up—a tapestry of connections. It was as if Jesus spoke to me and said, "Those connecting cables have been there all along. I put them there to bring light out of the darkness." The entire dream only lasted about a minute.

Grassroots revival is what we are seeing in America and internationally today—lights springing forth by the millions. Light always dispels darkness, both physically and spiritually. Jesus is doing His work among His people, bringing forth light, life, and joy through repentance. We must remember that darkness never defeats light; repentance opens the door for God's light to shine in darkness. Will you be the light the Lord is forming you into in this Jesus Now Awakening?

Most people stop at confession and don't enter the next step, repentance. Sin is putting the "I" before God. Conviction says, "Yes, God, I put myself before you." Confession says, "I will get the *I* out of the way in these specific areas." Most people think of confession as a horrendous guilt trip. Confession isn't negative; it's God's design to allow us to come to Him for cleansing. "God's kindness is meant to lead [us] to repentance" (Romans 2:4).

Confess your sins or failures to God. He already knows, and He loves you. Confession comes from two words that mean to simply agree with God. Say something like, "God, I agree with you that I was unduly angry in that situation." Or "God, I agree that pride clouded my judgment in that situation." Confession, or agreeing that you have sinned, must always precede repentance, which is turning from that sin, turning to Jesus.

Finally, there is repentance: turning from sin to Jesus Christ. It is not a crushing blow from God but a surrendering into His loving arms, thereby experiencing incredible joy. Imagine your life like that of a wise pilot. If he or she continues heading toward the mountain, a crash will occur; continue heading into sin, and you may crash into the mountain of spiritual separation from God, ruining your life. Instead, a wise pilot—like a believer—turns away from the mountain (sin and death) and heads for the airport (Jesus Christ). That is repentance.

> *"What happens when four people face the consequences of ignoring life's warning signs? Watch the power of repentance and restoration when God breaks through."*
> – *Flying Blind, TV special, Billy Graham Evangelistic Association,*
> *billygraham.tv*

I can tell when I am "in the flesh." If Ouida and I disagree on something, I will win if I'm not careful—right from my flesh. I know it's not God's Spirit in me, so I have to back off. I've made a commitment to my wife that I would not go for the jugular in an argument—that's the old Tom. I have repented of that sin and desire to turn from it.

I talked over this particular struggle with Joe Leininger, my accountability partner, and he said, "Tom, you've probably won so much in your life that now Ouida needs to win nine to one just to catch up for the past." Of course, Joe is right.

Even when we see our faults, a voice inside says, "Don't apologize." Or it says, "Deal with it later." Unfortunately, those comments leave us in denial and "later" never comes. If you want to deepen your relationship with Jesus Christ, then immediately apologize to Him for rebelling—despite the embarrassment. Then confess and repent—first to God and then to any person you have hurt by your sin.

When our daughter Molly was about twelve years old, I began to understand and be sensitive to the many flaws in my life. They were habitual flaws like impulsiveness or intensity or lack of patience—qualities that can put great burdens on other people living or working with me. And those flaws can lead to sin. I also struggled with my speech. I periodically hurt Molly and other members of our family through my sharp tongue.

Look, I determined, *I'm just going to begin confessing my sin immediately, apologize, and deal with this habitual problem. I am not going to let it ride and ignore it.* My flaws surfaced so often that I feared my apologies would become meaningless to my children and my wife, though I was sure Jesus would understand, accept, and appreciate my repentance. I sat with my family and declared the five areas that I felt Jesus wanted to change in my life. I told them, "I will ask for your forgiveness immediately, and I am sincere about it—even though I may do it many times."

Months later, my wife told me that Molly declared, "I'm just sick of this."

"What are you sick about?" Ouida inquired.

Molly is a child similar to her dad and impulsively said, "I'm sick of Dad saying that he's sorry all of the time."

My wife told me that Molly thought for a minute and then declared, "But, I'm so glad he does." My daughter knew the difference between a dad who infrequently declared his sorrow, who didn't repent, compared to my numerous apologies and continuing commitment to change. Will you commit to continually allow Jesus to lead you in repentance so you can be the light He has called you to be in this grassroots revival?

Revival Truths

- Repentance opens the door for God's light to shine in darkness.

- Repentance is moving beyond confessing sin to turning away from sin and toward Jesus.

- Revival, either personal or corporate, cannot occur without repentance.

If you return, I will restore you, and you shall stand before me. If you utter what is precious, and not what is worthless, you shall be as my mouth. They shall turn to you, but you shall not turn to them.

JEREMIAH 15:19

Walking in the Light of God's Son

Through Frequent Experiences of Scripture

"Whatever Jesus tells you, make sure that you do it!"

JOHN 2:5

What an awesome key to life abundant and a life pleasing the Lord! This was the simple secret of Jesus's love for the Father. Nowhere in Scripture does it speak of the Father obeying the Son, but uniquely, the Son loves the Father by doing whatever the Father asks.

Jesus would describe His own love of His Father with these words: "I am doing exactly what the Father destined for me to accomplish, so that the world will discover how much I love my Father" (John 14:31 TPT).

The Son loves the Father by yielding to the Father's every word, and so it's to be with His followers. Sometimes His speaking is through His Word or a fellow disciple, sometimes He speaks in prayer, and at other times it's the gentle impression of the Holy Spirit upon our spirit.

Implicit to this life in the Spirit is:

- First saying "yes" by faith even before we've heard Him speak.

- Next, "hearing" the Lord as we faithfully yield to young Samuel's prayer: "Speak, Lord, your servant is listening" (1 Samuel 3:8–9).

- Finally, full and immediate obedience to what we hear.

The first miracle at the wedding feast of Cana illustrates the powerful simplicity of "doing what He says." Our daily accountability to do the same will empower a fulfilling and impactful life.

Consider this discipline as you reflect on the close of each day:

"Lord, today I heard you say _____

__and your Spirit empowered me to _____

_____.*"*

W8. A Spirit-empowered disciple lives "naturally supernatural" in all of life as His Spirit makes the written Word (logos) the living Word (Rhema).

SPIRIT-
EMPOWERED
Faith

Day 2

Control and Conviction

Confession and repentance are not possible without conviction. It requires boldness to pray for conviction and a heart softened to hear God's voice directly through prayer, Scripture, or other people. Many people avoid situations where they might feel convicted. It's not a comfortable feeling.

Conviction also requires that we give up control, which is something our American culture teaches us never to do. We must release control from thinking that we know ourselves best. We must release control from thinking that we are always right. We must give up control from thinking that we can always act and respond exactly as we choose. We must release control from believing that we are a finished product rather than a work in process. As long as we hold tightly to the reins of control, conviction will not come.

Jesus brings conviction from many avenues. It is better to seek conviction than hide from it. By actively seeking those areas where Jesus wants to change you, you will be more able to cooperate with the Holy Spirit as He works, which is always a better way. First Corinthians 11:31 says, "But if we would examine ourselves, we would not be judged by God in this way" (NLT).

You can seek conviction through prayer. Ask Jesus to reveal to you areas of your life, your character, your personality, or your emotions that He would like to change. Wait on Him; He will answer. Another way is to look in the mirror of Jesus Christ and study Him. Study a Gospel like Mark and ask the Holy Spirit to clearly reveal Jesus to you. Then ask Him to show you yourself in light of Himself.

Jesus loves you and knows you desire to grow in your relationship with Him. Stop now and ask Jesus to show you areas for growth so you can be more like Jesus. What does He show you?

We also receive conviction through others who know us well. In 1983, as the coordinator of counseling and follow-up preparing for six Billy Graham crusades in England, I met regularly with my counterpart in England, Eddie Gibbs from the Bible Society.

Because we worked closely for six months, Dr. Gibbs and I spent a great deal of time together. We saw each other in a variety of situations and with many different people. We took many walks, prayed about the crusades, and became close brothers in Christ. Eddie and I have different personalities with diverse temperaments and different social skills. I am straightforward like other Americans, and Eddie is more reserved and polished. In truth, both of us were just a couple of God's kids from humble roots, seeking to walk with Christ daily in the midst of a rigorous schedule. Eddie's father was an auto mechanic, mine a carpenter.

By the end of the Crusade, we had grown to appreciate each other immensely. We committed to writing a candid letter that would detail the other's strengths and weaknesses. Each of us took time to think and pray before we wrote the letter. Then we exchanged letters, read them, and talked about them. This was a valuable exercise for both of us, and we each learned and grew immensely from the other's feedback. No matter who we are—professor, leader, auto mechanic, carpenter, homemaker—we can learn from others.

> **"Revival is God revealing Himself to men in awesome holiness and irresistible power."** – *Arthur Wallis*

The Holy Spirit can also help by giving conviction through individuals. The Spirit can give us a heart to receive honest feedback from others if we are willing to relinquish that control. God may have given you tremendous strengths, but He wants you to continue to grow. So we ask the Holy Spirit to control our weaknesses and manage our strengths.

Charlie Riggs, my spiritual mentor, always challenged me to find Bible verses that would be my "plumb bobs," which spoke to me to help balance my life. A plumb bob is the weight hooked beneath the tripod below a surveyor's telescope. Without this weight hanging under the center of the telescope, the surveyor cannot level the telescope. Plumb bobs often take the form of learning and heeding the truths of Scripture. I memorized and meditated on them. For example, each day I review Ephesians 6 where Paul details our spiritual armor. By faith I prepare to face the day, putting on each piece of spiritual armor.

Over the years, this chapter has become a part of my life.

Also, plumb-bob verses give you God's Word for your various weaknesses. It might be temptation, bitterness, envy or pride, or the unwise use of the tongue or the eyes. Find the appropriate passages and use them to walk each day in the conviction and power of the Holy Spirit.

Revival Truths

- Jesus calls us to release our control and seek His conviction.
- Jesus works through many avenues to bring conviction.
- It is better to seek conviction than have it hit you over the head.
- Scriptural plumb bobs are tools for stability that mark the truth.

Seek the Lord, all you humble of the land, who do his just commands; seek righteousness; seek humility; perhaps you may be hidden on the day of the anger of the Lord.

ZEPHANIAH 2:3

Walking
in the Light
of God's
People

At All Costs

Even a child is known by his deeds, whether what he does is pure and right.

PROVERBS 20:11 NKJV

If you've ever been in love, you know what it means to go out of your way to please another person. If you love someone, you're careful not to do anything that would jeopardize the relationship; at all costs, you avoid things that would hurt them.

We must ground out convictions concerning what is right and wrong in this same framework. Because of our deep love for Jesus, we want to be careful not to do anything that would jeopardize the relationship. Because of our deep love for Jesus, we'll want to avoid doing things that would hurt him.

Take the next few moments and remember how Jesus has loved you. How has he provided for you? How has he cared for you? How has he been attentive to you, forgiven you, supported you, or accepted you?

- *Jesus, I am so grateful that you loved me by . . .*

- *I am particularly glad about the time when you . . .*

Now, take time to express your love to Him, specifically regarding your commitment to live out your convictions. What are the convictions that you want to live out because you want to please him?

- *God, I am committed to living out my conviction to . . .*

What are your convictions of things you want to avoid because at all costs you don't want to hurt your relationship with Jesus?

- *God, I am committed to living out my conviction to avoid*
  _____ because I know that to do these things
  would hurt you.

Consider praying with one or two others

Jesus, I know that my ways are not always the right ways. I want to live out my convictions because You do always know what's best for me. You love me, and I'm grateful. Help me to remember that doing what is right pleases You, and I want to do that because I love You. Help me to remember that doing what is wrong hurts You. And at all costs, I don't want to hurt the One who has given His life for me.

W3. A Spirit-empowered disciple yields to the Scripture's protective cautions and transforming power to bring about life change.

Day 3

The Roadblock of Sin

Many years ago, when I was in seminary, I rode in a car with a friend, discussing sin. Larry Hart, who eventually became a professor at a seminary, was driving, and I began to describe a habitual sin that affected my life. Periodically the sin would overwhelm me, I told Larry. I would repent and ask God to forgive me, but it returned again and again. This debilitating process caused me great concern, I explained.

"Tom, your problem is focusing on the sin rather than the Savior," Larry said as he continued to drive. "When you ask God to forgive you of that sin, you don't forgive yourself. He has already forgiven you, so why do you keep thinking about it? Don't focus on the sin. Focus on the Savior."

He went on to say: "Tom, the Bible says that satan is a deceiver, liar, and mocker. You are letting satan deceive you, lie to you, and mock you. The devil is tricking you. Don't let him do that." That simple truth from God's Word was like a revelation. It brought a profound release unlike anything I had ever experienced and great joy flooded my heart, which exists to this day. Victory in Jesus over small or large matters is real.

I was already a Christian, but this moment changed my life. Before this point in time, I tried taking back control after repentance. The reality was, I was not in control. But Jesus was and is. I allowed satan to use guilt and shame to keep that sin fresh in my mind. And as that sin sat in my mind, it often led to action. I needed to treat that sin as God did, casting it away and considering it no more.

I had been trying to drive forward while only looking in the rearview mirror. The place to focus in repentance is not on the sin from which we are turning but on the glory of Jesus toward which we are turning. Turning from sin is important. Turning toward Jesus is more important. It is much easier to say yes to Jesus than it is to say no to sin. As we choose to continuously say yes to Jesus, our no to sin will become an automatic result.

We must fix our eyes on Jesus, the author and perfecter of our faith (Hebrews 12:2). The process can be painful and awkward, but it does give us freedom. We need to trust God for the forgiveness He promises.

Some time ago, a female colleague described to me the deep repentance that she and her mother had seen among women in a large city in northern California. Almost eighteen thousand women listened to a speaker describe how to deal with past abortions. The shame of abortion often overrides the burden of the sin. Many women have kept silent about their sin because they feel so much condemnation from themselves and others, especially the church. Yet Jesus was using the speaker, who has herself had five abortions, as the instrument to deliver others.[17]

She asked the women to respond by symbolically holding up their aborted children as an offering to the Lord. According to my colleague, an audible wailing rose from deep within their souls and spirits; it was unnatural and unnerving. Her mother turned to her and said, "I have sometimes wondered what hell sounded like. After hearing this, I never want to hear the sound of hell again."

What a burden when we've had to carry the shame of sin alone, whether from an abortion, a theft, or cruel words we later regret. We may feel the guilt of sin that we have given to Jesus for forgiveness but have not been able to air openly. Even men may now be feeling the challenge to repent for their part in abortions.

The Lord tells us that the truth does set us free. "And you will know the truth, and the truth will set you free" (John 8:32). Also, "If the Son sets you free, you will be free indeed" (v. 36). For those women in northern California, giving

Christ the sin in their lives removed the shame as well as the pain of taking an innocent life. There were torturous moans in the audience, yet victory was also present for all.

Often people try to hide their guilt and shame with drugs, alcohol, isolation, overeating, or hostility. But Jesus promises release to all through His redeeming work: "The Spirit of the Lord . . . has anointed Me to preach the Gospel to the poor; He has sent Me to heal the brokenhearted, to proclaim liberty to the captives, and recovery of sight to the blind, to set at liberty those who are oppressed; to proclaim the acceptable year of the Lord" (Luke 4:18–19 NKJV).

Worship Experience
Listen to "Out of Hiding" (Father's Song),
by Steffany Gretzinger:
"You're safe here with Me . . .
No need to cover, What I already see."

Revival Truths

- Even confessed sin can be a roadblock if we don't receive God's forgiveness.

- Satan will try to remind us of past sins. He is a liar.

- We must fix our eyes on Jesus.

- Healing comes from accepting Jesus's death as complete atonement for our sin.

I tell you, there will be more joy in heaven over one sinner who repents than over ninety-nine righteous persons who need no repentance.

LUKE 15:7

Walking
in the Light
of God's
Son

When Obedience Is Not Enough

Looking unto Jesus, the author and finisher of our faith, who for the joy that was set before Him endured the cross, despising the shame, and has sat down at the right hand of the throne of God.

HEBREWS 12:2 NKJV

Jesus scorned the shame of Calvary because of His joy in pleasing the Father. In a similar way, true repentance is grounded in a "deep dread" of displeasing Jesus. Christ's obedience to humble Himself to the point of death on a cross was rooted in this joy of pleasing His Father.

Would it have been genuine obedience if Christ had lived a perfect outer life, endured the cross, but felt irritated in having to do so? Outward obedience without this joy-filled longing to please may not be real obedience. Is it possible that our obedience is only pleasurable to God when this joy of pleasing Him is our motivation?

Unfortunately, too often we can be "going through the motions" as Christians—outwardly complying with external standards of right and wrong, or saying the right things, all the while motivated by only duty or obligation. The Christian life is meant to be more than mere dutiful obedience; it must include a relational passion to please a person—and His name is Jesus!

How about you? How will you know if you have been "going through the motions?" Are you:

- "Doing" Christianity rather than "being" Christlike? Christ's disciples don't *do* Christianity but rather express His presence by *being* Christlike.

- Becoming prideful or self-exalting as you try to live out right behaviors?

- Becoming selfish and almost trying to *take* God's blessings?

- Becoming self-condemning as you fail to live out your beliefs, and now questioning if you are even worth God's forgiveness and other blessings?

Pause now and consider your own walk with Christ. Has it been a growing, thriving relationship or mostly dutiful compliance? Consider how much more the Savior wants for you. He wants your life to be filled with His joy—the joy that comes from loving Him so much that you can't bear the thought of hurting Him.

Meditate quietly on the Great High Priest praying for you—and you listen and hear these words: These things I have spoken to you so that My joy may be in you, and that your joy may be made full (John 15:11).

God, I want to have this kind of relationship with You and a kind of obedience that is empowered by my deep love for You.

L3. A Spirit-empowered disciple experiences God as He really is through deepened intimacy with Him.

Day 4

To Be Like Christ

Have you ever noticed that you start acting like the group of people with whom you are hanging around? Parents of teenagers are well aware of the dangers—and sometimes the benefits—of this truth. Parents want their kids to spend time with other children who hold moral and ethical values that the parents agree with because parents know that groups of kids will act in similar ways. Otherwise it wouldn't concern parents if their sweet and innocent teenage girl became friends with another girl who smoked and drank and was promiscuous. It's not a given fact, but the chances are there would be some negative influence. Even adults can be prone to picking up habits, whether positive or negative, since we often develop characteristics like the people with whom we spend the most time.

Our desire should be to act like Jesus. The more time we spend with Him, the more we will be like Him. We have discussed the importance of prayer and Scripture reading, and also of practicing His presence. As we repent and turn our hearts toward Christ and away from sin, it's important to walk with Him daily.

> **"We shall not become like Christ until we give Him more time."** – Frank Laubach

An outstanding example of someone who walks each day with Christ, with the goal of being more like Him, is Mike MacIntosh. I first met Mike in 1976 while teaching a Christian life and witness class for the Billy Graham Crusades. We were preparing for the San Diego Crusade, and I led a class at a church filled with youth called Calvary Chapel (now called Horizon Christian Fellowship).

Pastor Mike MacIntosh was almost thirty, and he taught simply out of the Bible as he told the young listeners to follow God's Word. He gave an invitation, and scores came to the front to make decisions for Christ. To each new believer, the counselors gave a New Testament and told the new believer to go, read it, and do it. What a follow-up program, and the young followers of Christ did just that!

Afterward I met Pastor Mike, the best Bible teacher under whom I had ever sat. He was so practical and easy to understand, and the Holy Spirit flowed through this man with such strength that he radiated Jesus.

Before coming to Christ, Mike had been a salesman and heavy drug user. A tremendous extrovert, Mike could charm almost anyone. But he owed a lot of money to the drug pushers. One day they caught Mike, put a bag over his head, and shot a pistol by his ear. He was so stoned from his drug use that for many months, Mike actually thought he was dead. Eventually, through the outreach of Calvary Chapel (Costa Mesa) to the southern California youth, Mike met Christ as his Lord and Savior.

In his early days of walking with Christ, Mike became the founding president of Maranatha Music, initially selling music records and tapes from the trunk of his car. Then at God's direction, he and another believer went to

San Diego and started a Bible study in an apartment. Eventually this study grew into one of the fastest growing churches in America, now named Horizon Christian Fellowship. This simple gathering was the start of a worldwide congregation that now includes more than a hundred churches and parachurch movements.[18]

In the beginning, Mike didn't have a college degree. Since those humble beginnings, Mike has received his undergraduate degree, two masters, and a doctorate, and he's become a certified jet pilot and an author. Yet more important than his accomplishments, Mike is someone who humbly reflects Jesus day in and day out.

Mike MacIntosh is a good example of Jesus's power in the life of someone who, at one time in the eyes of others, had little hope. Yet through the power of the Holy Spirit, Mike has reflected Jesus Christ to thousands because he lives in the power and joy of God's Spirit. Jesus took Mike in his obedience and love for the Bible and did something incredible, and it's still happening today.[19] Mike was willing to repent, to totally change his life.

How is it that Mike, who came from such a horrible place in life, can be such a clear reflection of Christ? Because Mike spends time with Christ, and he imitates what Christ does. It's not a complicated system of dos and don'ts. He also continues a lifestyle of ongoing repentance to be more like Christ.

Each day you and I need to make a fresh commitment to grow more like Jesus. This growth flows from our love relationship with Him.

Revival Truths

- Through repentance in your life, you can grow more like Jesus each day.

- We are more like those with whom we spend time.

- Only by spending time daily with Christ, by knowing and obeying Him, can we be more like Him.

May the God of endurance and encouragement grant you to live in such harmony with one another, in accord with Christ Jesus, that together you may with one voice glorify the God and Father of our Lord Jesus Christ.

ROMANS 15:5–6

What's God Saying?

As each one has received a gift, minister it to one another,
as good stewards of the manifold grace of God.

1 PETER 4:10 NKJV

When God created you, it wasn't some cookie-cutter approach or assembly line procedure. God is a craftsman. And as the Master Craftsman, He carefully shaped each intricate detail of your being. He was like a painter who carefully adds the perfect mix of color with just the right stroke of the brush in order to create an original, beautiful masterpiece. The things that make you unique were intentional. God knew what He was doing. The Master Craftsman created His original masterpiece—in you!

You are God's creation, so you can count on Him knowing everything about you. Because He formed you and added every special touch, He knows you deeply and intimately. He is fully aware of all your thoughts, fears, hopes, dreams, insecurities, joys, sorrows, talents, needs, and quirks. God made you, He knows you, and every day, He steps back to admire His work.

God has lovingly created you as a unique individual because He hopes the two of you can share a great relationship.

- God has also created you as a one-of-a-kind individual so that He might entrust certain missions and callings to you.

- He created you with certain gifts and talents so that you will be able to live out your life purposes to serve Him and to bring Him glory.

- God handcrafted you with the intention that you would experience His love for you and in turn, love Him in grateful response (Matthew 10:8). But we're not supposed to stop there.

God deeply desires that you extend His love to others in the ways that are uniquely your own. God called Jeremiah to be a prophet to the nations. God called Moses to lead of the children of Israel. What do you hear God saying about your life? Ask God to reveal or confirm your life's calling and mission.

Father, You made me. You created me with a special purpose in mind. You created me so that I might enjoy You and You might enjoy me. You created me to share your love with others. Open up my heart to hear Your voice calling out to me. Help me to be confident in who You've created me to be and the special calling you have for me.

> ### L9. A Spirit-empowered disciple yields to the Spirit's fullness as life in the Spirit brings supernatural intimacy with the Lord, manifestation of divine gifts, and witness of the fruit of the Spirit.

Day 5

Forgiveness

When I began my ministerial career, a Southern Baptist minister approached me and said that he knew a church of about two hundred members south of town that was looking for a pastor. In my naïveté I inquired, and eventually I became the pastor of the church. I don't know who was more naïve—them or me.

I preached vehemently every Sunday like the boy-preacher I was. On one particular communion Sunday, I admonished that the congregation shouldn't come to the altar for communion unless they had first obeyed Matthew 5:23–24 that said, "So if you are offering your gift at the altar and there remember that your brother has something against you, leave your gift there before the altar and go. First be reconciled to your brother, and then come and offer your gift." Fortunately, Jesus used that sermon to also convict me. I realized that I too had a situation in my own life that needed attention.

"Mrs. Davis" was a godly but dominating older woman who had basically run the church. She meant well, but she often spoke the truth so abrasively that it was painful to others. In a conversation with the chairman of the deacons, I mentioned my opinion about Mrs. Davis's behavior. Of course, this comment made its way to her. I realized that I was wrong and needed to make amends. I didn't want to. Mrs. Davis could be so tough; she didn't display much grace that I could see. But how could I ask others to be right before the Lord if I didn't also? I had sinned and needed to make it right with Mrs. Davis and with God.

I made my way to Mrs. Davis's house. The gate to her fence was locked, and for a moment I thought that was my escape. But conviction rose in me again, so I jumped her chain-link fence. Sheepishly approaching the back door, the entrance for friends, I rang the bell.

"Mrs. Davis, I'd like to speak with you, if you don't mind." She opened the door. I sat down, baring my soul and the conviction God had placed on my heart about my attitude and behavior. I said that I needed to make this right before the next communion service. I asked for forgiveness.

You can imagine my shock as the tears began to roll down Mrs. Davis's face. She approached me, put her arms around me, and wept. She thanked me for my sensitivity and released the bitterness from her heart she held toward me. I was amazed.

Though not every situation ends in such a positive way, Jesus does call us to ask for forgiveness and make amends. Perhaps the person you speak to won't offer the forgiveness you seek. That's okay. It's between that person and God. What matters is not the person's response to you but your response in obedience to Jesus. Unforgiveness can lead to bitterness, rage, and anger. It grieves God to see His children fighting against each other.

> *"Once we understand the depth of our sin and the distance it placed between us and God, and once we get a glimpse of the sacrifice He made to restore fellowship with us, we should not hesitate to forgive."* – Charles Stanley

Lack of confession and unforgiveness of personal sin affects the closeness of our walk with Jesus on a personal level but also has the potential to affect our families, workplaces, churches, and even our nation. In 2017 at the 66th Annual National Observance of the National Day of Prayer in Washington, DC,

Reverend Pat Chen led those gathered in the capitol building in repentance for our personal sins as a nation, including: ingratitude, neglect of Bible reading, unbelief, prayerlessness, pride, envy, critical spirits, slander, lying, hypocrisy, tempers, and arrogance. Men and women around the room knelt on the floor and bowed their heads in the seats of their chairs as they repented and prayed. This is exactly the type of corporate, national confession and repentance that ignites revival within the forgiveness of Jesus.

Revival Truths

- God calls us to confess our sins to others and to ask for forgiveness.

- We are called to make any amends necessary for damage repair.

- The other person's response is not up to us; our obedience to Jesus is what counts.

- Unforgiveness and lack of confession does not just affect our personal relationship with Jesus but also our families, churches, workplaces, and our nation.

- The forgiveness of Jesus sparks revival.

Jesus said to him, "I do not say to you [to forgive] seven times, but seventy-seven times.

MATTHEW 18:22

Walking
in the Light
of God's
Son

Worth Talking About

But I have trusted in Your mercy; My heart shall rejoice in Your salvation.

PSALM 13:5 NKJV

One of the greatest truths we can share with those we encounter is our gratitude for how a God of mercy and forgiveness loves us unconditionally. Think about one of the times when you have messed up. Think about those times when you have failed, fallen short, or times when you have sinned against God. Remember those times. Think about the guilt or regret you felt. Remember the pain of consequences and the heaviness of your heart.

- *I remember the times when I have failed and fallen short. Times like*
  . . .

Now, take the next few moments and experience the unconditional love of Christ once again.

Imagine that you have gone for a walk. You're trying to clear your head and heart of the guilt, regret, hurt, and anger you're feeling. You've messed up, and it hurts. Just as you round the corner and see your house, you notice that Jesus is waiting for your return. When He sees you in the distance, He is moved with compassion. He doesn't even wait for you to arrive. He runs to you! He leaps quickly and anxiously off the front porch because He can't wait to see you. He hugs you and whispers in your ear (Luke 15:20).

Jesus doesn't give a lecture or criticism. He doesn't fuss at you or remind you of how you've messed up. Jesus knows the consequences of your sin. He's fully aware of how things have gone wrong, but his voice is filled with care. Christ's eyes are kind and His body language is gentle and relaxed as He talks with you. Jesus tells you that He loves you and that His mercy is fully available to you.

As you consider Christ and how He has mercy in spite of your failures, how does that move your heart? And how might you share your gratitude and celebration with people around you?

God, I celebrate how You have given me mercy in spite of my failures and sinful choices. Help me share this same startling, forgiving love with others.

P2. A Spirit-empowered disciple startles people with loving initiatives to give first.

Looking Forward

Repentance requires a determination to turn completely away from anything not of God and completely toward all of Jesus Christ. Though modern believers often see repentance as punishment, it is a normal and healthy part of our relationship with God and others. Without repentance, there can be no forgiveness, and without forgiveness, there can be no salvation. Without salvation, there can be no revival. True repentance leads to steadfast, daily joy as we commune with Jesus. In chapter 4, we will look at the role obedience plays in revival.

CHAPTER 4

THE FOUNDATION OF
Obedience

In the work of God worldwide, there are many unsung heroes. Mark Buntain is a great example. In 1954 Mark and Huldah Buntain went for a six-month missionary trip to Calcutta, India. They rented a small apartment for their short stay. Thirty-four years later, the Buntains were living in the same apartment. During the short-term trip, they heard God's call to stay in India. They obeyed.

Starting from an upstairs hall, they built a ministry compound, Calcutta Mission of Mercy, with a preaching facility that would seat 1,500 and a 167-bed teaching hospital that would welcome doctors, nurses, interns, and doctors in residence. Before Mark Buntain's death on June 4, 1989, they were feeding and teaching more than 10,000 children each day.[20] Today Huldah continues to run this work, which is just around the corner from the ministry of the late Mother Teresa, a close friend of the mission. Mark's obedience to God is a model of obedience to God's call and direction.

Once an American reporter was in the streets of Calcutta and saw a man sitting hunched on the concrete sidewalk, leaning against a wall. The reporter was a Christian, and the Lord impressed him to speak to the man about Jesus. He asked, "Do you know God?"

"Yes, I do. In fact, I've met him, and God will be here in the morning."

"Really?" the reporter said with a bemused look on his face.

"Yes; do you want to meet him? Well, meet me here at 6 a.m., and I'll show you God."

The next morning, the reporter came to the spot. He didn't expect the old man to be there, thinking it was probably a joke. But the same man was waiting and said, "Come with me." At first, they began walking down a fairly wide street in the city, but as they continued, the street began to narrow. Finally they were walking in the poor section of Calcutta with tiny walkways of dirt and running sewage between shack homes. As they wound through a maze of humanity, suddenly they turned into a small courtyard. Standing in the middle of the courtyard was Mark Buntain and his associates, who were passing out bread to the poor.

The old man pointed and said, "See, there's God." Through Mark's obedience to the Savior, he made a profound impression on the people of India about the love of Jesus Christ.[21]

God may not be calling you to India, but He does call you to obey in your daily life. Most people are almost as uncomfortable with the word *obedience* as they are with the word *repentance*. Yet obedience is foundational to rekindle your fire and to bring about revival. For the next five days let's explore the role of obedience in personal revival.

Day 1

The Call to Obey God's Word— Holiness

England's great revival in the mid 1700s started with an unlikely group of three young men who began a club to pursue spiritual disciplines in the midst of their theological education. In 1729, Charles Wesley and two other students began to meet weekly to discuss the subjects of a holy life. They started their meetings with prayer, studied the New Testament and Christian books, reviewed what they were going to do that day, and planned the next. Often they would meet again for supper. This desire to be holy grew until the group acquired the name the Holy Club.

The three men lived by stringent rules and had a method of:

- Daily self-examination
- Prayer
- Weekly communion
- Fasting on Wednesdays and Fridays—an imitation of the early church
- Meditating on different days on topics such as "The Love of God in

Simplicity," "The Love of Man," etc.

In addition, the three members of the Holy Club sought God's will in everything. They strove each day to develop a virtue such as humility or faith, and each day at nine, twelve and three o'clock they repeated the printed prayers of the Church of England. Soon others joined them, including Charles's older brother John, who years earlier had been a devout student while studying at Christ Church College in Oxford; there he earned his master's degree in 1727. John soon became the accepted leader of the group. Eventually, for their systematic approach, people in derision called them the Methodists.

They visited jails, teaching the prisoners to read and pray. They visited the sick. The Holy Club never exceeded twenty-five in number because such discipline deterred others. They assisted poor families and poor children, teaching them to read.[22] Out of these desires, God turned them into men who would realize that the disciplines were effectual only through a personal relationship with Jesus Christ. As John Wesley would later write in his journal, "I've come to convert the heathen, but, oh, who will convert me?" Then his heart was strangely touched at a meeting one evening where someone read aloud the preface to the book of Romans. He noted of that occasion, "I felt my heart strangely warmed."

The Church of England had become an institution. It did not promote the spiritual side of life described in the books John, Charles, George Whitfield, and the others began to read. But these men yearned for this personal relationship with Christ. And the Lord honored their seeking, as He promises He will. Through these committed young men of "methods," the church of Jesus Christ began to grow.

What an example of obedience. The sacrifices were overwhelming. History records that even when they preached in the open-air meetings, people hurled rocks, broken glass, punches, or even dead cats at them. Mobs who took offense by the simple proclamation of the Gospel often attacked them and their followers, once even shredding John Wesley's clothes. But Jesus was preeminent. He worked through key men who, within the Church of England, were nobodies. Yet, God raised them up to do His will in bringing revival.[23]

> *"In revival, holiness becomes a constant necessity rather than an occasional option."* – *Mark Stibbe*

As we look at our nation today, it's important to consider the disciplines of a holy life of obedience. These young men sought an intimate walk with Christ through obedience, and a nation was changed. They were obedient regardless of the consequences. Perhaps God is not asking you to change an entire nation. Perhaps He is calling you to change one aspect of your life. Are you willing to step out in faith and obey?

Revival Truths

- Jesus uses ordinary people, willing to obey and live holy lives, to make great changes.

- We are all called to a life of holy obedience.

- We must be willing to obey no matter what the cost.

I discipline my body and keep it under control, lest after preaching to others I myself should be disqualified.

1 CORINTHIANS 9:27

Walking in the Light of God's Son

Encounters with Jesus

But the Helper, the Holy Spirit, whom the Father will send in My name, He will teach you all things, and bring to your remembrance all things that I said to you.

JOHN 14:26 NKJV

Members of the so-called EPIC Generations of millennials and Gen Z are Experiential, Participatory, Image-driven, and Connected. Their emphasis on "experiencing" Christ is truly relevant as the Christian life is about relating to this One who lived, died, and rose again. Christianity and living a life of holiness will only occur as we come to truly relate to and encounter Jesus Christ. The Father's love-filled hope for our encounters with Jesus is that they will transform us into His very image. Faithful disciples diligently pursue fresh encounters with Jesus with yielded hearts, confident that such encounters will make them a little more like Him!

If events could sanctify the saints, Western-world Christians would surely be among the kingdom's most sanctified. If exposure to the Christian message and media could produce fully devoted followers of Christ, we would turn the world upside down for Christ, as did the first-century church. If camps, conferences, and concerts could instill the faith in the next generation, we would not be struggling to make disciples of our own children. In spite of all of these well-intentioned events, vast segments of God's people have come to think that a relationship with Christ is only about being able to claim, "I believe and I obey," while a life of holiness is only available to those who walk intimately with Him.

Pause now and ask the Lord to lead you into a deepened relationship with Jesus. Ask His Spirit to help you go beyond an important set of Christian beliefs for the moment. Ask Him to help you move beyond the all-important commands to obey. Ask the Lord to lead you into more of a transformed relationship with Him. Pray that you will come to know the Savior more intimately and be able to express His love and life more clearly.

Your prayer might sound like the following:

Father, I long to encounter Your son Jesus in deep, life-changing ways. I yield my life and heart to being transformed—whatever that may mean. I want Christ's promises to be real for me, and that the Counselor, the Holy Spirit within me, will teach me all things. Speak now, Lord. I long to hear You, yield to You, and be transformed into the likeness of Jesus.

L10. A Spirit-empowered disciple practices the presence of the Lord, yielding to the Spirit's work of Christlikeness.

SPIRIT-
EMPOWERED
Faith

Day 2

Obedience in the Small Things

Charlie Riggs, my spiritual mentor, used to say, "Small things are those from which large things flow." My mother believed that truth before I ever heard Charlie say it. As a sort of "forewoman" at a local factory, she observed many workers pulling discarded items from the garbage can. These items were genuine discards from the plant, such as old rolls of wire or small pincher pliers with a piece of the point broken off. These items were no longer usable at the factory but could possibly be useful at a worker's home. My mother determined these items didn't belong to her, and she would not take them.

As a little boy walking along the street one day, I found a dollar bill. In my day, that bill was a tremendous amount of money, and I wanted to pick it up. But Mother said, "Tom, leave it."

With a questioning tone, I echoed, "Leave it? Somebody lost this dollar, and they don't know where they lost it."

"Son, you don't know that they don't know where they lost this dollar. Whoever lost this money knows where they have been today, and they may retrace their steps to try and locate it. It may be very important to them. You must leave it. It's not yours."

As a child, that money was important, so I tried one more time. "But, Mom, it doesn't matter. It's lost. The next guy will pick it up."

"Tom, God sees you every moment of every day, and that money is not yours. The point is ownership, so don't pick it up." Through a practical (and painful!) example, my mother was teaching me that little things grow into big things. The big things in life are made of small choices. Big obedience comes from small steps of obedience. If you open the disobedience window, then you allow the cancerous growth of disobedience to begin in your life.

Worship Experience
Listen to "Into the Light," by Laura Woodley Osman:
"You said: . . . I choose you . . .
My blood has made you clean."

Once, as the director of the 1987 Denver Billy Graham crusade, I drove Dr. Graham to some appointments a few days before the crusade. The speed limit was fifty-five miles per hour, and I was driving between sixty-two and sixty-four mph. Dr. Graham turned to me and asked, "Tom, do you believe in obeying the speed limit?"

I stammered, "Well . . . yes," as I looked at my speedometer.

Dr. Graham continued. "I believe in obeying the law. The Bible says render unto Caesar the things that are Caesar's and unto God the things that are God's. I just don't speed. I don't think God can honor you when you are speeding."

Of course, before he had finished his explanation, my speed slowed to fifty-five mph, my face was flushed, and I was a little saint driving with my halo over the driver's seat. To this day, it impressed me how much Billy Graham cared about obeying the law. These little aspects of life are the building blocks of obedience.

Jesus told the parable of the talents in Matthew 25:14–30. In this story, the Lord is asking us to use what we have for the kingdom. If we have little, then we should use it faithfully, and God will give more. Jesus concludes His parable with the profound statement, "For to everyone who has will more be given, and he will have an abundance. But from the one who has not, even what he has will be taken away" (v. 29). It is the same with obedience. If we can be faithful in the small, painless areas of life, God can trust us with more.

Honesty is an area that has become particularly gray. We find many ways to avoid the whole truth. We keep secrets. We make promises and don't keep them. Acts 5:1–11 relates the example in the early Church of Ananias and Sapphira, his wife. They sold some land then supposedly gave the money to the church, but they lied about the actual sale price. The apostle Peter, speaking in the power of the Holy Spirit, pointed out their lies, and each died instantly. Their story was an example to the early Church and also to us. Each day we need to live honestly before the Lord. We also see from this example that when there is a choice between obeying God or obeying man, perhaps as in the case of Sapphira, it's best to obey God.

God calls us to be faithful with the small aspects of life, and that involves our consistent obedience to the Lord.

Revival Truths

- Obedience is a matter of faithfulness—with the small and large aspects of life.

- There is no area too small or too large to ignore God's call to obedience.

And being made perfect, [Jesus] became the source of eternal salvation to all who obey him.

HEBREWS 5:9

Walking in the Light of God's Word

Our Only Hope

So I say, walk by the Spirit, and you will not gratify the desires of the flesh.

GALATIANS 5:16 NIV

None of us is perfect. We each go our own way making wrong, sinful choices. The good news is that Jesus chose to go to the cross and give His life because of our sins. The Savior chose to take our sins upon Himself and receive our punishment. Here's the mysterious contrast: God is a God who is both rich in mercy and ultimately holy. He is so holy that He cannot relate to sin in any form. So rather than lose relationship with us, God restored the possibility of relationship by sacrificing his Son.

Because Christ gave His life on Calvary for you and me, we must face the truth that our sins have a direct connection to His death. He died because of my sins. He had to die because of yours. Our sinful choices are a part of what hurt Jesus at Calvary. It pains His heart to watch us make choices that are against His Word.

How do you feel as you consider the personal connection of your sin and Christ's death? Your sin and the pain it causes to God's heart?

- *I feel _____ as I reflect on the truth that my sins have a personal connection with Christ's death.*

- *I've come to realize that God's heart hurts when I make wrong choices. That truth makes me love God even more because . . .*

Our only hope of making right choices in line with his thoughts and his ways is to live our lives yielded to the direction and prompting of the Holy Spirit.

Our only hope is to declare our helplessness to live a life that is pleasing to God, apart from the Holy Spirit's guidance and power. Claim the promise that, in your humility, God will guide you with His Spirit (James 4:6).

Father God, I am helpless to make right choices without Your Spirit's help. Forgive me. There is no hope of my embracing Your ways instead of my ways unless Your Spirit empowers me. Guide me and help me. I need You every day.

L5. A Spirit-empowered disciple lives with a passionate longing for purity and desire to please Him in all things.

Day 3

Obedience in Your Relationships

To rekindle the spiritual fire in your life, you must be in right relationship with God, yourself, and others. If any one of these relationships is out of balance, it's difficult to rekindle your fire. We have to remove anything in the way that hinders the love between God and us.

As a child, "Sheila" had been molested by a woman claiming to be a friend of the family. The molestation continued for about two years until Sheila was twelve years old. Though they attended church, Sheila's own family neglected her, which opened the door for the abuse. It became difficult for this little girl to separate love from sex. Though she was molesting Sheila, her perpetrator was kind and nurturing—giving all that Sheila lacked in her own home.

When Sheila became a young adult, she entered into a sexual relationship with another woman. She knew it was not pleasing to God, but she felt it was what she deserved. It was love, after all, she told herself. Yet she was not at peace about her life and began to seek Jesus. In the process of seeking, she realized that to ever be free from the anguish that bound her, Sheila would have to walk away from the only caring relationship she knew. She had to obey Jesus in having relationships that honored Him and allow Him to work in her life. Sheila left the sinful relationship and found peace as she continued to seek Jesus's love.

Worship Experience
Listen to "Trading My Sorrows," by Darrell Evans: "For the sake of the Lord."

Perhaps you are in a relationship that is damaging to you. It may be a sexual relationship outside of marriage. Or it may be a friendship with someone who influences you away from Jesus. Any relationship that distracts your attention from Jesus is not pleasing to Him.

Most people have been wounded in some way. It is common to carry anger or unforgiveness against those who hurt us. But this is not God's plan. Pray now. Ask God to bring to mind any unforgiveness you carry against someone else. Scripture gives us pictures of healthy relationships. Just as we can be in an unhealthy relationship, God wants us to care for the relationships to which He has called us.

Today, make a new commitment to be in sync in your relationships with God, self, and others.

Revival Truths

- In obedience to the Lord, our relationships with God, self, and others need to be constantly growing and improving.

- We need to realize sinful relationships will hinder Jesus's work in our lives.

- Jesus calls us to forgive others and keep unhindered relationships with other members of the body.

- Jesus wants us to care for the relationships with which He has blessed us.

A new commandment I give to you, that you love one another: just as I have loved you, you also are to love one another. By this all people will know that you are My disciples, if you have love for one another.

JOHN 13:34–35

The Perfect Plan

Let all those who see You rejoice and be glad in You; And let those who love Your salvation say continually, "Let God be magnified!"

PSALM 70:4 NKJV

Broken relationships are at the root of many of the world's problems. A broken relationship with God and broken relationships with one another can be found underneath so many of the challenges we face.

The initial effect of the first sin—Adam and Eve's disobedience in the garden of Eden--was damaged relationships. Adam and Eve's sin caused brokenness in their relationship with God. But here's the good news: God went looking for Adam and Eve in the garden because He deeply longed for a relationship with them. And even as he encountered Adam and Eve's painful choices, God announced His plan for restoring relationships with Him and others.

God was sorrowed because of the loss of relationship with Adam and Eve. He couldn't bear the thought of being separated from the ones He loved, so God devised a plan to reconnect to His children . . . and to you and me. God's plan was to send His Son into our world to "dwell among us" (John 1:14). Jesus came to earth to cancel the brokenness of sin so you and I could know and experience God's love for us.

The Bible tells us that God is the same, yesterday, today, and forever (Hebrews 13:8). Just as He did with Adam and Eve, God looks for us because he wants a relationship with us. He longs to relate to you. He couldn't bear the thought of being disconnected from Adam and Eve, and He feels the same way about you and me. How does it make you feel to know that God's heart hurts when He thinks about being disconnected from you?

- *As I reflect on how God is saddened when He thinks about being disconnected from me, I feel . . .*

How does your heart respond as you consider God's plan for repairing His relationship with you? As you might need to receive Him as savior and Lord—do so! If you have already received His gift of relationship and have become a follower of Jesus, could you express your love by sharing Him with others? By forgiving others?

God, I want to magnify or show how great You are because . . .
Holy Spirit, prompt and empower my sharing of the Gospel and my very life with others around me (1 Thessalonians 2:7–8). Grant me a forgiving heart and gracious love towards others.

M8. A Spirit-empowered disciple attentively listens to others' stories, vulnerably shares their story, and is a sensitive witness of Jesus's story as life's ultimate hope.

Day 4

Obedience in Your Calling

In 1 Corinthians 12, the apostle Paul wrote about the interdependence of the body of Christ. In verse 18, Paul declared, "But as it is, God arranged the members in the body, each one of them, as he chose." Because of our uniqueness, God gives us each a different calling in life. Though we are all called to share the Gospel and minister to others, we do it differently.

God calls some to full-time Christian service as both a mission calling and as a vocation. This requires obedience. I wanted to be a doctor. I knew I was skilled to become a doctor. I saw an opportunity to serve Jesus as a doctor.

Jesus wanted me instead to be in a preaching ministry full time. I had to make a choice of obedience to follow where He led rather than where I thought was a good place to go.

God calls others to a "secular" vocation—to serve Jesus daily among the lost and hurting of the world. Such ministry also requires obedience. Susan, a young woman who loves the Lord, had an intense desire to go overseas as a missionary. For some time, Jesus called her to work in an office environment, to be Jesus to those around her each day. Before you get the wrong idea, Jesus does not immediately call us to the exact opposite of what we desire! I use Susan and myself simply as examples of being obedient wherever Jesus's call may lead.

If you are not full-time clergy, it's tempting to think that it's someone else's job to do the ministry. After all, the professionals get paid to do it. There is also a temptation for those in church, parachurch, and missions ministries to see themselves as holier or more special than those who serve elsewhere. In truth, we are all in ministry to others as we serve the Father. As we will discuss in chapter 7, often the difference between sacred and secular is the attitude with which we do the work, not the work itself. What matters is our obedience.

Jesus has called each of us to be ministers of the Gospel: We are His ambassadors wherever we work—"Therefore, we are ambassadors for Christ, God making his appeal through us" (2 Corinthians 5:20)—in the law office, on a construction crew, on an oil rig off the coast of Alaska, or working in a military installation. It's important to realize:

- God made us.
- God created us as His children through His Son.
- God has a plan for our lives.
- As we are disciplined, obedient, and pure, He will put that plan into practice in our lives.
- He made us as a piece of the mosaic. When we follow Him, He supernaturally puts us in His big picture of ministry, heart by heart, one by one, changing the world in the process.

Obedience in our vocation and calling means: (1) remembering that He sees us every moment, (2) wanting to please Him, (3) having a relationship with Him that makes pleasing Him naturally fulfilling, (4) being available through purity of heart in obedience to do what He has called us to do each day, and (5) being sensitive to His Spirit and asking Him to guide us to what He has in store for us that day.

> *"Revival, in its fullness, will see neighborhoods, schools,*
> *work places, and cultures changed and healed."*
>
> – *Mark DuPont*

When Ouida and I first came to Colorado Springs, we met Ann, a real-estate agent recommended to us. Ann was seeking spiritually and exploring New Age philosophies. Ouida and I instantly liked her. As we drove around viewing homes, Ann discovered that I had been working for Billy Graham. This was intriguing. Then Ann found out I was writing a book. I didn't know exactly how to tell her about the subject, revival, and I didn't want to use that word because I didn't know what connotations she might draw.

So I said, "It's a book about spiritual life."

"Well," she said, "spiritual life. I'm into spiritual life. What's it all about?"

I began to tell her about how Jesus could be a part of her life and bring tremendous fulfillment and joy. Then from that spiritual connection would come a balanced individual who can be successful, with Jesus's help. I got her a copy of the book when it was published, and our relationship continued to grow. Three and a half years later, my wife had the privilege of helping Ann come to a personal relationship with Christ.

Today, both Ann and her husband are faithful worshipers and growing in the Lord. Recently Ann told us, "You will never know how much it means to us that Ouida and you guided us to Jesus." I was being obedient by following Jesus's call to move to Colorado for a new ministry job. Ouida was following her call as my wife. Through this obedience, we were in the right place at the right time to minister to someone Jesus brought to us. Through obedience in our calling, we can change the lives of people who cross our path.

Revival Truths

- Our vocation or calling (no matter what) is to serve in obedience to the Lord.

- Our work is secular or sacred only in attitude, not in the work itself.

- Jesus can use us to change the lives of others if we are obedient.

Power belongs to God, and . . . to you, O Lord, belongs steadfast love. For you
will render to a man according to his work.

PSALM 62:11–12

Walking
in the Light
of God's
Son

Radical, Sensitive Love

He had compassion on her.

LUKE 7:13

The widow of Nain doesn't get a lot of attention, but hers is one of the purest, most telling pictures of the heart of Jesus and a life of yielded obedience.

The funeral procession began at her home and then wound its way through the dusty streets of Nain. Just as the widow and the mourners came to the city gate, another crowd of people was entering. This crowd was following Jesus. The two crowds converged. One group followed the coffin. The other followed the Christ.

And as the two crowds converged, Jesus saw the widow. Because he is God, Jesus would have looked deep into her heart and known that she was alone. She was a widow who had just lost her only son. That meant no husband to provide for her, no one to take care of her, no security, and no guarantee of safety.

Jesus would have also seen the woman's future. She had no one to grow old with, no one to cook for, and no one to share life with. No son to lean on. No one.

Compassion for this woman so moved the Savior that it welled up inside of Him, "Dear one, please don't cry." Then Jesus did something radical. He touched the coffin! He stopped the funeral and raised her son from the dead!

Amazingly, the widow made no request; there was no desperate plea. Jesus simply acted because He saw her hurt and it moved Him to action. Her pain moved His heart with compassion. This becomes our example of living as His ambassador in whatever vocation or calling we find ourselves.

Take the next few moments to meditate on the truth that what Jesus sees in the human heart moves Him to action, and He calls us to do the same.

Jesus, sometimes I can't always sense others' pain, but I want to do so as your ambassador. Holy Spirit, transform me into one who notices and cares.

M5. A Spirit-empowered disciple ministers God's life and love to the "least of these."

Day 5

Obedience Until Death

As growing young Christians, a group of us were asked the question, "Would you be willing to die for Jesus?" Immediately, many responded yes! Perhaps it was easy to respond in the affirmative because we never thought that we'd actually be called to go through with it. Or perhaps we didn't understand death.

As I grew older, I began to realize that though dying for Jesus could mean a physical sacrifice, it also meant giving up any rights to a life I thought I wanted to own. There are two ways to obey Christ until death: one is a literal physical death, and the other is to lose our lives every day in order to find them in Jesus.

As a young man with a promising future, Jim Elliot heard Jesus's call to the jungle. Many around Jim feared that he was throwing away his life, that he should stay home and stir up the church in America. On his first trip to Ecuador, Jim wrote in his diary, "My going to Ecuador is God's counsel, as is my leaving Betty [at the home base], and my refusal to be counseled by all who insist I should stay and stir up the believers in the U.S."[24]

Jim felt it more important to pursue that to which Jesus called rather than live a life of comfort in the United States. On the wall of his primitive hut was a sign that read: "You have to go out, but you don't have to come back." In January 1956, Auca Indians murdered Jim Elliot and four other missionaries.

Was there something unusual about Jim? No, except for his hunger for Jesus. Jim was willing to follow the words of Luke 9:23–24: "And he said to all, 'If anyone would come after me, let him deny himself and take up his cross daily and follow me. For whoever would save his life will lose it, but whoever loses his life for my sake will save it.'"

"You have to go out, but you don't have to come back."
– *Sign in the hut of missionary Jim Elliot*

Another of the missionaries was Pete Fleming. In preparation for working with the Aucas, Pete also kept a diary. Pete understood that though life was precious, it was worth dying to see others come to the saving knowledge of Christ. In his diary Pete wrote, "I am longing now to reach the Aucas if Jesus gives me the honor of proclaiming the Name among them. I would gladly give my life for that tribe if only to see an assembly of those proud, clever, smart people gathering around a table to honor the Son—gladly, gladly, gladly! What more could be given to a life?"[25] Only a few short years later, Pete, Jim, and the other three missionaries would be dead. What brought about the love and devotion of these men for a people they hadn't yet met? They prayed. They walked with Jesus intimately. They sought a life of purity and obedience. They realized the owner of their lives was Jesus, and not them.

With that, they were able to die to Christ as they lived and live with Christ as they died.

For most people reading this, Jesus hasn't called you to a foreign country to die as a martyr. He has, however, called you to give Him complete control over your life.

Revival Truths

- Jesus calls us to obey Him even until death.

- We can die to ourselves even while we are still alive on earth.

Lift up your eyes to the heavens, and look on the earth beneath. For the heavens will vanish away like smoke, the earth will grow old like a garment, and those who dwell in it will die in like manner; but My salvation will be forever, and My righteousness will not be abolished.

Isaiah 51:6 NKJV

Walking
in the Light
of God's
Word

Incredible Value

For You [God] meet him [us] with the blessings of goodness.

PSALM 21:3

Jesus's sacrifice on the cross served as a declaration of our immense value and worth in God's eyes. Because God created you and you bear His image, He has the right to declare your value, just as the government has the right to declare the value of currency that it produces and marks with its unique images. By sending Jesus to earth to die for you, God declared that you are worth the life of His only Son. How might you respond?

Imagine that these words are coming straight from Jesus as He talks with you:

- You are especially valuable to Me. You represent My thoughts, My personality, and what's important to Me. You are important to Me. I gave My life for you.

- You are especially valuable to Me because I cherish our relationship. I see how much love you have for others, and I smile when I think that it is only a fraction of the love that I have for you. After all, I gave My life for you.

- I would risk My life to save you. In fact, I did. I gave My life for you. I saw that you were in danger of being separated from Me forever, so I chose to die for you.

- You've been through so much. I want you to know that I love you and I'm here for you. You're not alone.

God's declaration of your worth is mighty, awesome, and powerful! It's personal—just for you. It's the best news we could ever hear!

Since God has declared your worth at Calvary and sent His Son to die in your place, how do you respond to Him? Could you give your life to the One who has distinctively placed His mark on you that reads: "Worth the gift of my

Son"? Could you follow a God like that? Could you declare by your sacrificial giving that you belong to Jesus?

Pause to move beyond any human pride in your achievements or success to humbly embrace the wonder of you being loved by Jesus. Respond with a yielded life.

God, I am humbled by Your declaration of my worth. Thank You for sending Your Son to pay my debt. I am in awe of Your goodness to me; my life and future are Yours.

L4. Spirit-empowered disciples rejoice regularly in their identity as "His Beloved."

Looking Forward

Obedience is a daily dying to our wills and desires as we follow Jesus wherever He leads. Sometimes God calls us to physically die out of obedience, but more often our call is to live in obedience, dying to ourselves every day. Next week we'll see how living an obedient life opens the gates for communication through prayer.

CHAPTER 5

Prayer AS RELATIONSHIP

What is prayer? The answer initially may seem obvious. Yet Jesus's disciples had already lived with Him for several years when they said, "Lord, teach us to pray" (Luke 11:1). They didn't ask, "Lord, teach us to witness"—even though they believed in evangelism. They didn't ask, "Lord, teach us to study the Scriptures"—even though they knew that was important. These disciples looked at the life of Jesus and identified the core of His relationship with His Father, so they asked Jesus to teach them to pray.

Prayer is two-way communication, and an obvious outpouring of the Holy Spirit comes from concerted and united prayer. E. M. Bounds noted that "God gives Himself to the praying ones, and that the measure of God's revelation to the soul is proportionate to the soul's longing, importunate prayer for God. Salvation never finds its way to a prayerless heart. The Holy Spirit never abides in a prayerless spirit. Christ knows nothing of prayerless Christians."[26]

Just as human relationships require constant connection through communication, our relationship with God needs and deserves the same. We cannot grow in our relationship with God apart from speaking to and hearing from Him. It's this depth in relationship that will lead to both personal and corporate revival.

Day 1

Prayer as Communication

Prayer is a simple means of communication. It began with Adam in the garden. When God first spoke with Adam and Eve, communication flowed unhindered from both directions. Those were the first prayers. After Adam and

Eve sinned, prayer became more of a spiritual discipline. Communication with God was now less direct, without seeing God face to face, but it still happened.

Prayer is nothing more than a spiritual continuation of God's face-to-face contact with Adam and Eve in the garden. Look at this conversation:

> And they heard the sound of the Lord God walking in the garden in the cool of the day, and Adam and his wife hid themselves from the presence of the Lord God among the trees of the garden. Then the Lord God called to Adam and said to him, "Where are you?" So he said, "I heard Your voice in the garden, and I was afraid because I was naked; and I hid myself" (Genesis 3:8–10 NKJV).

Sin entered the picture and became a barrier to communication. It will be important for you to deal with sin as you read this chapter. Sin brought shame, so Adam and Eve hid. Prayer is a way to keep us before God, to keep us from hiding.

In Laconia, Indiana, a small agricultural community across the Ohio River from Louisville, Kentucky, Richard had been the known "druggie" for years. Then, at age seventeen, he made a commitment to Christ. He quickly became a spiritual firebrand and witnessed door to door, seemingly every day. This young man would even visit different churches and challenge pastors right in the middle of their messages.

At the time, I was a twenty-two-year-old, full-time seminary student in Louisville and a part-time pastor in Laconia. I considered Richard a bit of a nuisance. Thankfully, he never interrupted me. But one day Richard did approach me and he asked, "Brother Tom, do you pray an hour a day?"

With regret, I answered, "No."

Then he confided how he prayed an hour a day on his knees in his bedroom after high school before witnessing. He said, "I could never have the courage to go out and talk with people about Christ unless I prayed an hour a day. I challenge you to spend an hour a day in prayer."

Richard's challenge seemed impossible. My days were filled. I managed a group of maintenance men for about 1,500 apartments in five complexes throughout the south side of Louisville. In addition to this full-time job, I took a full course load at seminary and pastored the church. In the basement of our rented old farmhouse, I studied each day late into the night. In the midst of that crowded schedule, I made a little time for my wife and our small daughter, Cara.

But I took this young man's challenge seriously and began to pray. Usually right before midnight, I would stop studying to begin praying for an hour. I started on my knees with a prayer list, then listened in silence for God to speak.

> **"Prayer is both one of the means and one of the fruits of union with Christ." – Andrew Murray**

One evening after supper, Ouida and I had another argument, and I stormed off to the basement to study. I could hear Ouida vacuuming loudly overhead and knew she was angry. In my prayers that night, I talked with God about our arguing. I was trying to justify myself before God by saying things like, "Lord, she's such a nag . . . ."

Suddenly His voice came into my mind telling me to be quiet. That voice spoke with authority and urgency.

I protested and wanted to argue with God at first. But then I heard His voice, shouting, "Shut up!"

After a few minutes of silence, I said, "Okay, Lord, now I've shut up. What do you have to say?" How arrogant I was!

God flooded my mind with Bible verses that asked me if I had been my family's prophet, priest, and king. Was I leading them spiritually? As I considered the question, I knew I was partially at fault. Then I inquired in prayer, "God, how much am I at fault?" Clearly, I was battling with pride. It was important for me to be right and win an argument—with Ouida or God.

The answer was clear: "100 percent."

That night I was a broken young man as I yielded my marriage to God. Tears flowed down my cheeks as I admitted my accountability to God for my marriage and my 100 percent responsibility as the husband and father. Prayer made me open to God's guidance. It wasn't a one-way diatribe. It was communication from me to God, and more importantly, from God to me. The challenge from the young man saved my marriage and changed my prayer life, now and forever.

Jesus frequently pulled away from the crowds and even his disciples to spend time alone with the Father. In fact, he prayed all night in Luke 6:12, and the next day, He chose the various disciples. Jesus knew that right decisions could only flow out of communion in prayer. To live a life of ongoing personal revival, you and I must learn to walk with God in the same way.

Revival Truths

- Prayer is simply communication with our heavenly Father.

- With conscious effort we can increase the amount of time we spend in prayer.

- God cannot change us if we hide from Him by not praying.

May He grant you according to your heart's desire, and fulfill all your purpose.

PSALM 20:4 NKJV

Walking in the Light of God's Word

God Is Excited to Be with You

The Lord confides in those who fear [reverence] Him.

PSALM 25:14 NIV

Can you remember sometime when you were excited to see a family member? Perhaps you were anxiously waiting to see your grandmother because her house was full of fun and special treats? Or maybe you've been excited to visit a friend who lived miles away, but the two of you managed to stay relationally close. Can you remember the anticipation you felt?

Can you recall times when a family member shared some exciting news with you or told you important information in confidence? How did it feel to know that this person trusted you? You undoubtedly felt loved knowing that this person opened his or her heart with you. Sharing time with people and opening our hearts through vulnerable communication promote the development of intimate relationships. These two principles are also true in God's relationship with us. He longs to visit with us and to reveal His heart. God can't wait to entrust us with the special parts of His life!

Scripture tells us that God longs to have this same kind of relationship with us (see Genesis 18). He wants to be able to spend time with you and stay relationally close. He can't wait to see you and hear from you. God longs to hear about what's going on in your heart and deeply desires to entrust you with the things that are on His. Allow the Holy Spirit to take this truth deeply into your heart as a powerful motivation to pray.

How do you feel knowing that you can have a relationship like this with God?

- I feel _____ when I consider a God who can't wait to see me, hear about what's going on with me, and even tell me what's going on in His heart.

God often entrusts us with the things that are on His heart through:

- His Word—When we read the Bible, God can talk with us.

- His people—By spending time with God's people, we can expect His revelation.

- Times of prayer and worship—By spending time in prayer and worship, God can speak to us.

God, thank You for being the kind of God who can't wait to see me, hear from me, and tell me what's on Your heart. I'm grateful and amazed!

L10. A Spirit-empowered disciple practices the presence of the Lord, yielding to the Spirit's work of Christlikeness.

Day 2

A Clean Heart

I've noticed that people are different in how they define the word *clean,* especially when it comes to their homes. Some people think their houses are clean when they've dusted and vacuumed, yet they never notice the stacks of newspapers, knick-knacks, ancient magazines, or other clutter in their houses.

They may have TV-dinner trays stacked on the kitchen counters—just in case they need them. Other people haven't dusted their houses in years, but they have wide-open floor space for the dust bunnies to roam because there is no clutter. I think both of these terms, *clutter* and *clean,* are important to consider when examining the cleanliness of our hearts.

David writes in Psalm 51:10, "Create in me a clean heart, O God, and renew a right spirit within me." David realized the value of an unhindered movement of God's spirit in his heart, and that unhindered movement required a pure heart. You can't purify your own heart. It's only through Jesus that you can receive such cleansing. That is why prayer is so important.

Sin is like the dirty house. There is dust covering everything. You need to vacuum the carpet and remove the trash. Prayer offers a time for you to confess your sins to God and for Him to forgive you. God wants to speak to you, but God's voice is difficult to hear if it is hindered by sin.

Take time now and pray. Ask God to reveal to you any area of your heart that is unclean. Perhaps you have unresolved anger or bitterness. Perhaps your thought life is not pleasing to God. Pray now to ask Him to reveal those areas to you and ask for His forgiveness. It is important to incorporate times like this into your daily prayer life. It's also important to be open to hearing God speak about these issues even as they occur throughout the day.

Worship Experience
Listen to "Clean," by Hillsong United: "Teach me. . . the joy of holiness that forms as You draw me close."

Our heart can also be cluttered. Maybe there isn't "sin" in the way we normally consider sin, but maybe our days are full of clutter or the noises of life that hinder our communication with God. If you allow your busy life to prevent you from taking time to kneel before the Lord on a daily basis, when does He have the opportunity to speak to you?

The great prophet Elijah searched for God's voice in 1 Kings 19:11–12, and he heard God saying, "Go out, and stand on the mountain before the Lord." The text reports that the Lord passed by, and a fierce wind raced into the mountains, breaking many rocks, "but the Lord was not in the wind; and after the wind an earthquake, but the Lord was not in the earthquake; and after the earthquake a fire, but the Lord was not in the fire; and after the fire a still small voice" (NKJV). The prophet heard God in the still small voice. With the noise in our world, it takes a commitment through prayer to hear God's voice.

Thoughts in Solitude by Thomas Merton is a valuable book to help us understand the value of solitude and time alone with God. We learn about such aspects as solitude's simplicity and the silence of solitude through which the quiet voice of God comes booming.

Yesterday, I described how young Richard challenged me to pray an hour daily in spite of a full life. Before you think my system for prayer was that of a spiritual person with no concerns, let me share that I had a serious problem during that time. Besides my duties as a pastor, maintenance man, and seminary student, my marriage needed attention. It was in terrible shape because I hadn't been hearing from God. I couldn't hear from God properly as long as arrogance and egotism and self-righteousness dominated my heart. These factors were dirt and clutter that hindered my relationship with God and my family.

How did I experience a breakthrough? It came from discipline over a six-month period of praying for an hour at the end of each long day. Those midnight until 1 a.m. prayer times were a discipline, but that's when God spoke to me.

Discipline to most is foreign, something that people often see as legalistic in our culture. Some people are disciplined about particular aspects of their lives. I have friends who golf on certain days each week. That's a discipline. Other friends fast one day a week. That's a different discipline. Each of us knows people who have a daily quiet time with God. That's another discipline. We have to discipline our tongue not to speak profanity or discipline our minds not to think evil of others. Discipline is a choice, a decision, and prayer is a discipline, a discipline best motivated by delight.

Make a fresh commitment to increase your prayer life. Pray again for God to reveal to you any further sin. Confess that sin. Listen for God to speak.

Revival Truths

- Our hearts can be unclean by either dirt (sin) or clutter.

- We cannot hear God speak through an unclean heart.

- We must have discipline to continually come before God and ask Him to reveal to us our sin.

Search me, O God, and know my heart! Try me and know my thoughts! And
see if there be any grievous way in me, and lead me in the way everlasting!

PSALM 139:23–24

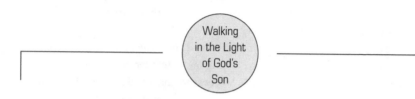

Walking
in the Light
of God's
Son

How's Your Posture?

And Jesus answered and said to her, "Martha, Martha,
you are worried and troubled about many things.
But one thing is needed, and Mary has chosen that good part,
which will not be taken away from her."

LUKE 10:41–42 NKJV

Physical posture seems to be important for physical wellness. During our
day-to-day life, it is helpful to frequently tune into our body, reminding ourselves to keep our spine straight, yet our other muscles relaxed. While we walk
around, let the muscles in our face, jaw, and shoulders relax. When we relax
our body, we find that our mind also relaxes. Likewise, spiritual wellness in our
prayer life depends on our posture before the Lord.

In the above biblical passage, we see a contrast between Martha, a follower
of Jesus who truly loved Him but made a priority of activity for Him, and Mary,
who loved and followed Jesus but made a priority of hearing from Him.

Consider the following questions. Ask the Holy Spirit to cleanse your life
from "clutter" that distracts. Consider also the implications for your priorities:

- What was Mary's posture? What is its significance to the principle
  of yielding to Jesus even before you hear from Him?

- Which priority does Jesus say is more important? Listening to
  Him? Or doing even necessary things for Him?

- The priority of hearing Jesus can guard us from earthly distrac-
  tions: What emotions seem to have filled Martha's heart? Mary's
  heart? What emotions often fill your heart?

- Martha demonstrated a measure of self-centeredness. In what ways might you demonstrate self-centeredness?

- This story shows evidence of "comparisons that lead to division in relationships." What comparisons have you been making? What divisions have resulted?

- This story reveals a "demanding attitude." In what ways have you demonstrated a similar attitude?

- How have "things" and activities crowded out your relationship with the Lord?

As you consider the implications for your own life, you will want to approach this encounter with the Lord in prayer. Pause and consider moving to "sit" before Him:

Lord Jesus, I want to sit at Your feet, listening, yielding, and loving You. Holy Spirit, prompt in me this lifestyle: "Speak Lord, for Your servant is listening" (1 Samuel 3:8–9).

L2. A Spirit-empowered disciple listens to and hears God for direction and discernment.

SPIRIT-EMPOWERED *Faith*

Day 3

More than One Way to Pray

Newsweek had an interesting front-cover headline on its January 6, 1992, issue: "Talking to God, An Intimate Look at the Way We Pray." The cover story revealed, "More than three quarters (78 percent) of all Americans pray at least once a week; more than half (57 percent) pray at least once a day."[27] More recent research done by Pew Research Center in 2014 shows nearly unchanged statistics: 76 percent of Americans pray weekly and 55 percent pray daily.[28]

Although the quality and depth of our prayers is somewhat unknown, apparently Americans recognize the need for prayer. "Prayer is the fundamental way we relate to God," Father Thomas Keating told the *Newsweek* reporter. Keating, who passed away in 2018, was a pioneering Trappist monk who led the Christian community in the silent, contemplative prayer movement. "Like any relationship, [prayer] goes through stages, from acquaintance to friendliness, then on to friendship, love and finally union," he explained.[29]

Prayer is communication with our heavenly Father. In a child-and-father relationship, it is well for a child to speak but wiser still for a child to listen when he or she is in the presence of the Father. Much can be said in a Christian's life, but how much better for God to do most of the speaking. Yet by what means do we increase our time and quality of prayer? Is there only one way to pray? Just as communication between people differs as relationships and circumstances differ, so does prayer with our heavenly Father. There are several different means to prayer.

First, you can be in solitude and alone before God. This discipline is the primary way you speak to Him and a way for you to quiet your heart and listen.

Second, you can pray with one or more accountability partners with whom you meet periodically. In chapter 2, I introduced you to Joe Leininger, one of my accountability partners. Everyone needs this type of prayer companion. Accountability partners can also be your spouse, but if not, then a same-gender accountability partner is recommended.

In *A Time to Pray,* Evelyn Christenson mentions that praying together with others, with triplets of Christians, was common in the Bible. Peter, James, and John were the triplet group when Christ prayed. Christ thought so highly of this group, He asked them to pray with Him prior to His arrest. Christenson rightly notes that "a threefold cord is not quickly broken." (Ecclesiastes 4:12). Evelyn noted six benefits of praying together. Such prayer:

- Forces a convenient location;

- Does not require expense, as these would be our friends who live close by us;

- Can be accomplished in just a few minutes a week;

- Has the accountability of others praying with you;

- Encourages joy rather than weariness;

- Builds close relationships among those who are praying together, horizontally as well as vertically with the Lord.[30]

Third, corporate prayer can be a meaningful way to commune with God and others. There are many variations and opportunities for corporate prayer. Participating in your local church and in Bible studies and cell groups will give you many opportunities for corporate prayer. It will also build relationships with your brothers and sisters in Christ.

You may have people at work with whom you can pray. For example, at the Billy Graham Evangelistic Association, our entire team meets daily before work and prays for specific parts of the ministry, for others, for the nation, and for God to bless our work that day. Also, there are smaller prayer meetings held by different groups in the mornings before work and during the week at lunch. Perhaps you are in a "secular" job but know other believers where you work. You could meet in the morning before work to pray together or meet at lunch.

A prayer summit is another way to pray corporately. Dr. Joe Aldrich, former president of Multnomah Bible College and Seminary, began a prayer summit ministry in the late 1980s, and pastors in several cities in the United States continue them annually to this day. He took fifty-two pastors from Salem, Oregon, to the Canon Beach Conference Center on the Oregon coast for four days of prayer and praise. They asked Jesus to show them how to minister to each other as pastors. While together, they spent time praising Jesus, praying, and sharing in community. During the week, the Holy Spirit fell in conviction on this group of pastors, and they were transformed. Individuals stood and publicly confessed to almost every known sin and received cleansing. This summit began a new approach for spiritual leadership: prayer. Today, through this movement and the leadership of Aldrich, the late Terry Dirks, and the Prayer Summit leadership, there have been over a thousand prayer summits for pastors in many different countries with thirty-eight thousand participants.[31]

> *"We have every reason to hope that God is willing, able, and ready to overthrow the status quo in answer to the united prayers of the saints."* – David Bryant

Fourth, you could participate in prayer walks. A prayer walk is just that—walking and praying. People walk around their towns or even drive around and pray for the needs of their cities. You could do this with a group or as an individual through your own neighborhood or other targeted area of your town. God has called some people to travel overseas and prayer walk through particularly spiritually dark countries for God to open spiritual doors.

Another creative way to pray is to simply ask someone to pray with you on the phone, over social media, or on a video call. Certainly, God wants us to pray directly to Him, and we can do it with others. The Lord told us that we would do greater things after Him (John 5:20; 14:12). Of course, He meant by the power of the Holy Spirit, but He could also see that technology was coming that would allow us to literally circle the globe in prayer via the Internet or phone lines.

God saw great collaborative efforts such as a substantive group of Nigerian women who now live in America, called Wailing Women, who have a 24/7, 365-days-a-year, never-ending, intercessory prayer call for revival in America. Their goal is to have this team of women praying every hour, every day across the nation. They're in the process of completing recruitment for this. They have shared that they believe America is vital to the spiritual health of our world and are praying for a true spiritual awakening in the United States so that righteousness here will bless other nations.

If you feel called to dive deeper into prayer and join a community of other believers seeking to do the same, another resource I have found is Project Pray. Founded by Pastor P. Douglas Small, Project Pray offers many great books on prayer for both churches and individuals. Doug also leads weekly prayer conference calls and even teaches classes on prayer via phone. You can find his website information on the resource page at the back of this book.

Revival Truths

- Prayer opportunities can be varied and creative, individual and corporate, using technology or incorporating prayer into the midst of other activities.

- We need to constantly be aware of the possibilities and then use some of these means as another way to spend time with God.

And rising very early in the morning, while it was still dark, he departed and went out to a desolate place, and there he prayed.

MARK 1:35

Walking
in the Light
of God's
Son

Jesus's Prayer List

He always lives to make intercession for them.

HEBREWS 7:25

Prayer isn't an obligation. It's an incredible privilege. We actually get to talk to the Creator in a variety of settings and situations. But here's another amazing truth: Jesus is praying for us! Scripture tells us that Jesus is in heaven praying for you! That's how He spends His day. The book of Hebrews says that Christ "always lives to make intercession for us" (Hebrews 7:25). Romans 8:34 explains that Jesus is at the right hand of God interceding and praying on our behalf.

Imagine that you awoke this morning. The house is quiet, no one else is awake. You walk toward the living room and only a small lamp illumines the darkness. Your eyes adjust; you can't quite believe what you are seeing, but there He is. Jesus is on His knees in your living room!

As you walk into the room, you can tell His lips are moving. You realize He must be praying. You're careful not to disturb the Savior, so you sit down softly beside Him. In the stillness of the morning, you're able to make out more of Jesus's words. Jesus is praying for you! He's praying for the concerns of your heart. He's praying to God on your behalf. It's as if Jesus is sitting beside His Heavenly Father, and He's carefully reviewing all the important parts of your day. He's rejoicing in the good parts and praying for you in the hard moments:

> Father, did you see the way that Your precious child
> has grown over the last few months? Did you see how he
> has become more like You? Isn't that terrific? Did you see
> how hard he/she worked this week at the new job and at
> home? What a diligent person! Father, please remember
> this child of Yours today. See the way his/her heart is anx-
> ious and fearful? I know You've seen the hurtful times and
> the pain-filled moments. I am hurting and I know You

are too. Please bring comfort and bring someone along to care for him/her. Bring reassurance that We are here and We love deeply.

Take the next few moments and join Jesus in prayer. He's praying for you. Could you meet Him there?

Jesus, I am grateful and amazed that You spend Your day praying for me. Thank you that . . .

L3. A Spirit-empowered disciple experiences God as He really is through deepened intimacy with Him.

Day 4

A Right Attitude

How's your heart before Jesus? Heart attitude is everything, for if you are going to pray and desire God to speak to you, then you want to be able to hear His voice. The following are some principles related to a right heart in prayer before God.

First, have the right perspective relative to who God is and who you are. Though God is accessible, we're not just talking to a human friend. When you pray, you enter the holy presence of the eternal God. Can you imagine?

As a believer, you are a high priest. Just as the Old Testament priest went through ritual washings and cleansings before he entered the temple, you approach God's throne with spiritual cleansings of praise, confession, repentance, and a plan to amend any wrongs you've committed. Now, with a clean heart, you're prepared to step into this spiritual relationship with God as the priest stepped into the Holy of Holies.

Second, you need humility of heart so God can speak to you. You can't approach God with pride or a haughty attitude—not if you expect to have a connection with the God of the universe. If you step humbly into the Lord's presence, then He can speak with you. First Peter 5:6–7 reminds us of this: "Humble yourselves, therefore, under the mighty hand of God so that at the proper time he may exalt you, casting all your anxieties on him, because he cares for you."

Third, be willing to listen. Listening to God is critical. We need to realize how much time we spend talking to God versus listening to Him.

God is always a gentleman; He isn't prone to speak at the same time I am. If I want to hear God, I have to give Him a chance to talk. One way to accomplish this is to combine prayer with fasting. I recommend Dr. Bill Bright's booklet, *7 Basic Steps to Successful Fasting & Prayer*.[32]

> *"In revival the town [Northampton] seemed to be full of the presence of God . . . So full of love, joy, and full of distress over sin." – Jonathan Edwards*

These three ingredients for prayer—the proper perspective, a humble heart, and a willingness to listen—are clearly seen throughout the Lord's Prayer. As noted previously there is only one case in Scripture where the disciples of Jesus asked for a specific teaching—and it's on the topic of prayer! We can learn a great deal about the ingredients of a heart attitude ready for prayer by studying Jesus's prayer for the disciples (Matthew 6:9–13).

Jesus began the prayer saying, "Our Father in heaven" (v. 9). Through these opening words, He acknowledged the authority and provision of God. He is our Father, to be respected. But He is also our Father whose watchful care is constant. If we enter God's presence with a humble heart, we acknowledge God as the Father, the One in charge.

"Hallowed be Your name" (v. 9). The name of God is most holy, and we should revere it. In Hebrew, the word for *name* means "the very essence of the being of the individual." When we use the words, "hallowed be Your name" it means the very person of God. If you study how people were named in the Old Testament, those names became the character of the individual. The Jewish people understood the reverence for the name of God, and the ultra-conservative Jews today will still not speak the name *Yahweh* out of reverence for the essence of God.

"Your kingdom come" and "Your will be done, on earth as it is in heaven" (v. 10). As we recognize our place, His will and desires become our will and desires. Often we approach God with our own agenda looking for Him to bless it, rather than humbly seeking His will. We must listen to God's voice to know His will. And we must seek Him to hear His voice. We submit to the Creator, rather than rebelling as the creation.

"Give us this day our daily bread, and forgive us our debts, as we also have forgiven our debtors" (vv. 11–12). We are to rely on Him for our sustenance, and we are to come to Him with a pure heart. Conviction, confession, and repentance are all important, but so is forgiving others. How can we hold grudges if we don't want God to hold a grudge against us? Because God forgives, we forgive. We must listen to hear God reveal to us our trespasses.

"And lead us not into temptation, but deliver us from evil" (v. 13). We come to Christ with a pure heart, but temptation can carry us away from a pure heart. We ask God to protect us from temptation and to prevent those initial steps toward evil. Satan is always tempting us, but God promises that His children are not tempted above what we're able to withstand (1 Corinthians 10:13). We ask Jesus not to just keep us from temptation, but to keep us from getting into things over our heads or things not in His plan for us at this time. Even "good" things can take us from "God" things. Only quiet listening and obedience will reveal the steps He wishes us to take.

"For yours is the kingdom and the power and the glory, forever. Amen" (Matthew 6:13). As we pray this, we recognize that God is the owner of all. It is *His* kingdom, it is *His* power, and it is all for *His* glory. We have ownership as God's children! We are blessed because He chooses to include us.

Revival Truths

- Heart attitude is critical to hearing God's voice.

- Humility and a willingness to listen are attitudes of a right heart.

- The Lord's prayer models how you are to have a consistent prayer relationship with your Heavenly Father.

Pray without ceasing.

1 THESSALONIANS 5:17

Walking
in the Light
of God's
People

Cultivating Joy and Obedience

But now I come to You, and these things I speak in the world,
that they may have My joy fulfilled in themselves.

JOHN 17:13 NKJV

Imagine Christ, as He stands with outstretched arms and prays to His Father. He prays on your behalf. The Gospel of John records His requests. Jesus prays the Father might protect you, sanctify you, and bring you to complete unity with the Lord and with one another. And all of these requests are motivated by His desire for you to experience His joy: "so that they may have the full measure of my joy within them" (v. 13 NIV).

Christ loved the Father through His joy-filled yielding. This was the inclination and attitude of His heart. We can also express our love to the Father in this same joyful way as the Holy Spirit within us prompts and empowers us. God wants us to experience more than willful, dutiful obedience. He desires that our obedience come out of the joyful wonder that we, the created, get to bring pleasure to the Creator!

But how will we cultivate this attitude? How can we become this joy-filled believer? Take time to read this list of ideas. Allow the Holy Spirit to prompt your heart with one or more of these points of action.

- Give frequent praise and thanks to God that you have received in the person of the Holy Spirit a yielding love to please Him.

- Make frequent declarations to God about how you long to please Him as you live in the fullness of His Spirit.

- Express joy for the simplicity of a life purpose that you are privileged to express His glorious presence and that He, through you, finds pleasure.

- "Exercise" yielding through submission in relationships with others.

Pause and pray with one or two others:

God, help me to complete one or more of these action steps. I want to express a sincere attitude of yielding in one of my relationships today, especially

_____.

W2. A Spirit-empowered disciple is a "living epistle." With reverence and awe, His Word becomes real in life, vocation, and calling.

Day 5

A Reminder That God Does Answer

Anyone who has gone to church has heard the pastor say that God does answer prayer; He always answers prayer. A friend of mine shared a string of possible responses from God. Perhaps He says no, meaning it will never be okay. Or He might say "Grow," meaning He'd like for me to grow more spiritually first. He might ask me to "sow" some seeds before my prayer is answered. Or He might say "Go"—it's a definite yes.

Regardless of which answer comes, He does answer: No, Grow, Sow, Go. It may not be the answer I wanted, but it is an answer.

Often we offer our prayers to the Lord with strings attached. Jesus tells us in John 15:7, "If you abide in me, and my words abide in you, ask whatever you wish, and it will be done for you." Jesus uses that little word *if* in a powerful way. Abiding in Christ means that we must be as connected to Him as a branch is to the vine of a plant. This is a mandate. In his book, *The Vineyard*, author Wayne Jacobsen wrote, "In the vineyards of this world, branches don't have freedom of choice. They are silent victims of whatever the farmer or his workers decide to be their lot."[33] In God's vineyard, however, we do have a choice. We can choose whether to abide.

As a leader within various Christian ministries, I have seen many kinds of people. Two different groups apply in this context. One group I have worked with often felt that no matter what they suggested, no matter what new thing they attempted in their jobs, it was not well-received. There was always a road-block to stop the idea from developing. Another group almost never had this experience. They made recommendations and changes that others appreciated and implemented. What was the difference? Perhaps the first group didn't abide in the organization. They were out of sync with the current needs and trends. They didn't seem to really understand where we were headed. Consequently, their requests don't fit with the bigger plan. The second group, however, had the pulse of what the ministry needed and where we were going. Their ideas were timely and necessary. They worked well with the purposes ahead. They paid attention to the whole picture, not just their individual parts.

I think this same concept is true for prayer. When we are abiding in Christ, He shares with us His desires which then become our desires. In John 15:14–15, Jesus has called us His friends and shared all that the Father has told Him. When we are connected to Christ, we just know what to pray.

Worship Experience
Listen to "Sweet Hour of Prayer," by William Walford:
"In seasons of distress and grief
My soul has often found relief
And oft escaped the tempter's snare
By thy return sweet hour of prayer."

It can be extremely difficult for believers to pray and feel as though God does not answer. *World Magazine* noted that media mogul Ted Turner stated he had received Christ as a young man at a Billy Graham Crusade but moved away from God when his sister died from an illness despite the prayers Ted offered.[34]

Did God answer Ted's prayers? Yes. Did he answer them in the way Ted desired? No. Does God know what is best in spite of how things appear? Yes. Though we mourn the loss of loved ones, Jesus assures us that heaven is truly our home, a much better place than earth.

Often believers end up feeling as though God didn't pay attention to them. It's difficult to realize that is a lie from the enemy. God's Word says that He never leaves us or forsakes us (Deuteronomy 31:6). It takes an act of faith to continue walking with the Lord even after disappointment. If we do, however, He will bless us in ways we could never imagine.

Revival Truths

- God always answers prayer. Always.
- To best know how to pray, we must abide in Christ.
- We can become discouraged if we believe the lie that says, "God doesn't hear us or answer our prayers."
- God will give us the desires of our heart if we delight in Him.

If you abide in me, and my words abide in you, ask whatever you wish, and it will be done for you.

JOHN 15:7

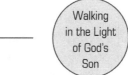

Walking in the Light of God's Son

Be Careful Not to Miss Him

"You search the Scriptures, for in them you think you have eternal life; and these are they which testify of Me. But you are not willing to come to Me that you may have life."

JOHN 5:39–40 NKJV

Life in a fallen world inevitably brings disappointments and misconceptions about God and "unanswered" prayer; fresh, frequent encounters with Jesus can confirm for us who He *really* is.

Being transformed by our encounters with Jesus means much more than amassing knowledge about Christ or mastering a systematic understanding of His life and teachings. The Pharisees pursued and accomplished great biblical knowledge—even memorizing the entirety of Jewish scripture and law, but they missed Him: "You have never heard His voice or seen His form, nor does His word dwell in you, for you do not believe the one He sent" (5:37–38 NIV).

Consider these portrayals of Christ as they reveal the true person of Jesus. Ask the Spirit to stir your heart as you imagine . . .

- The tear-filled eyes of Jesus as He weeps at Lazarus's grave (11:35).

- The saddened and gratitude-deprived heart of Jesus as He inquires about the nine lepers (Luke 17:17).

- The supportive and encouraging Jesus as He foreshadows Peter's betrayal (22:32).

- The accepting words of Jesus as He looks past the sinful nature of Zacchaeus (19:1–10).

- The Jesus who intercedes for us and the concerns of our heart (Romans 8:33–34).

Pause for a moment and consider:

Can you imagine the disappointment Jesus must have felt as the lepers failed to say thanks? Can you imagine the kind of Savior who is able to defeat the sting of death and yet is sorrowed by a friend's emotional pain? Have you come to know the Savior who knows you're going to fail and yet loves you anyway? Finally, have you known the Christ who not only died for your sins on Calvary but is now in realms of glory praying for your concerns?

Take the next few moments and reflect on this "kind of Jesus." Be careful not to miss Him! Now express your feelings for Him and to Him.

Lord Jesus, I want to "fellowship with Your sufferings" (Philippians 3:10 NKJV). You are a "Man of sorrows and acquainted with grief" (Isaiah 53:3 NKJV) and can sympathize with my struggles.

W5. A Spirit-empowered disciple meditates consistently on more and more of the Word hidden in the heart.

Looking Forward

Prayer is the channel of communication between the Father and His children. He is always ready to listen, always ready to speak. He always answers. In chapter 6, we'll see how He speaks, not just once or twice but on a continual basis, as we are in a continually growing relationship.

CHAPTER 6

KNOWING Jesus

In 1904, a young coal miner and Bible college student, Evan Roberts, prayed for God to bend his life, and the Holy Spirit touched him in a profound way. Evan went to his local pastor saying, "I have a message from God for the people." Initially the pastor tried to put him off, but Evan was persistent. Finally, the pastor agreed to allow Roberts to speak after the Monday evening prayer meeting. Seventeen people stayed, including the pastor.

His message was simple. "First, turn from any known sin. Second, put doubtful habits out of your life. Third, if you've harmed anyone, go and make it right. Fourth, obey the promptings of the Holy Spirit immediately, and fifth, tell other people about Jesus Christ."

His message wasn't unusual and certainly not unbiblical, and all seventeen people ended up on their knees before God—including the pastor. The pastor asked Evan, "Can you preach tomorrow night?" Evan preached every night for the next week. History records that by the second week you could hardly get through the crowds near the little church. And the results from Evan's prayers and call to a life in Christ? The great pastor James Stewart records:

> It was praying that rent the heavens, praying that
> received direct answers, there and then. The spirit of
> intercession was so mightily poured out that the whole
> congregation would take part simultaneously for hours!
> Strangers were startled to hear the young and unlettered
> pray with such unction and intelligence as they were
> swept up to the Throne of Grace by the Spirit of God.
> Worship and adoration [were] unbounded. Praise began
> to mingle with the petitions as answered prayer was
> demonstrated before their very eyes. Often when unsaved

loved ones were the focus of the intercession, they would
be compelled to come to the very meeting and be saved![35]

These events were the beginning of the Welsh revival, which lasted from
1904 to 1905. John Peters wrote, in the *Revival World Report,* "The Welsh
Revival was immensely successful, with over a hundred thousand conversions,
seventy thousand of them reported after a few months."[36]

Reverend J. V. Morgan tried to debunk the revival. His research claimed
that after five years, of the one hundred thousand who came to Christ, only
eighty thousand remained in the church. Sounds more like support of the
revival than a debunking!

From this spiritual awakening came a time of tremendous social change
in Wales—and it started with one man seeking God—Evan Roberts. It requires
solitude to hear the still small voice. God is not in the wind or the fire but in the
quiet heart that daily listens and obeys.

Our communion with God is not a one-time experience. In a growing
relationship, we will meet with Him regularly and hear His voice often. That
means planning for and protecting our time with Him. The goal is knowing
God better—a worthy goal indeed if He is to wholly use us.

Day 1

Our Spiritual Connection

As director of the 1984 Anchorage Billy Graham Crusade, I visited the
Alaskan bush, or remote regions, once or twice. It was amazing to see the
nine-foot satellite dishes near various frontier homes. The television dishes
would often be sitting on the ground, tilted nearly horizontally because of the
angle needed to connect to the satellite signals. To clear the way for the dish
signal, the Alaskans would cut a swath of trees away from their TV dishes. If
the homeowners had left the trees, they would have interfered with the signal.
Likewise, if anything grew back or was placed in a satellite's path, it too would
interrupt the signal.

In our lives, between our hearts and Jesus's, we need to continually clear
away anything that hinders our receptivity to that spiritual communication. To
hear God, you have to be an active receptor, a satellite dish tilted toward Jesus.
If you want to receive a satellite signal, you don't tilt the dish away from the sat-

ellite. The better the focus on the satellite, the stronger the signal. If you clean your heart before God in Christ, then you can tilt your heart toward God's throne and, as His words come down, the still small voice can center on your heart. This isn't a one-time event. It's a daily process.

Once you are connected with Jesus, your life as a receptor needs to keep a clear path. Just as God gave the Israelites manna for each day, we too must seek Jesus for our daily portion. We do that by:

- Planning time to be alone with Him.

- Seeking His face—daily.

- Talking with Him consistently.

- In solitude, stopping and listening to Him.

- Cleansing your heart through confessions.

- Surrendering your heart in purity.

Once we have done those things, we deal with issues of focus and truth: (1) Focus on who Jesus is; (2) believe in His guidance, that He knows what is best; (3) trust Him; (4) expectantly watch Him work in and through your life; and (5) live in the joy of your relationship.

Imagine eating your only meal on Sunday. Could you possibly eat enough to sustain you for the entire week? Not really, and certainly not with any amount of comfort. Just the thought makes my stomach long for food. And yet, that is how many people attempt to live their life in Christ. One to two hours of church on Sunday sitting passively in a pew is all the spiritual food some choose to eat. How sad, when Jesus offers so much more. If only we'll reach out and take it each day. There is more than enough for one day but not enough for more than one day.

We can't expect remorse without clear and consistent connection with Christ.

It's how He always intended our relationship to be. Each of us must choose in faith to be an active receptor to listen and hear the voice of God. Our first step is to actively seek a connection with God through Christ in prayer and a clean heart.

> *"Revival means the outpouring of the Holy Spirit that inspires the world and the church with the value of living Christianity." – David Andrews*

Revival Truths

- God wants us to be active receptors and listen to His voice.

- We must actively seek Jesus's presence in our daily lives.

- Revival requires a constant cleansing of our ability to hear from God.

I love those who love me, and those who seek me diligently find me.

PROVERBS 8:17

Walking
in the Light
of God's
Son

Be a Bethany

He is intimate with the upright.

PROVERBS 3:32 NASB

Bethany was a small town two miles outside of Jerusalem. The city was the home of Christ's friends, Mary, Martha, and Lazarus, but aside from that fact, the town of Bethany was pretty insignificant. It didn't have great historical, political, or even religious importance, but Jesus seemed to go out of His way to get there. He was intentional about going to Bethany, but why?

Bethany was a place of refuge for Jesus. It was a place where people He loved wanted to share moments of intimate fellowship with Him. Bethany was the place where Mary chose to sit a Jesus's feet and hear the vulnerable things of His heart. Jesus must have loved being in Bethany because it was a place where He could both give and receive loving care (See Luke 10:38–42).

Bethany was also a place of divine power and comfort. Jesus saw Mary and Martha's pain and felt their grief over their brother's death, and He wept. The human part of Jesus couldn't help but be moved by His friends' sadness. And then on that same day, Jesus brought divine restoration and life to Lazarus. Christ raised His friend from the dead, demonstrating His ultimate power and provision.

Jesus has the same desire for His relationship with you as you live out your personal revival. Imagine that Christ has these words to say, just for you:

> "Dear one, I am hoping that your life and your heart would be My Bethany. I am hoping to have a special, one-of-a-kind friendship with you. I want to share My joy with you. I want to share about the things that sadden My heart with you. Just like in Bethany—I want to lavishly give and receive from you. Just Like Bethany, I want to comfort you when you hurt because your pain moves My heart. I want to bring restoration to your life just like I did for Mary and for Martha. I want to see your family and your relationships revived, renewed, and full of life. And just like Bethany, even though I am your Savior and I am your God, I long to receive from you and spend time with you. I am ready to share closeness and intimate friendship with you."

God, I want my life to be like a "Bethany" for You. I'm grateful You want this kind of relationship with me because . . .

L5. A Spirit-empowered disciple lives with a passionate long-ing for purity and desire to please Him in all things.

Day 2

Knowing Jesus

We can compare a relationship with God to a marriage. Sometimes a man and woman date for two weeks and then marry. Other couples have known each other since elementary school. Then they complete high school and college before they decide to marry. Even though this second couple knows each other quite well, only through marriage can they enter a world of coexistence and interdependence, one previously unknown. Still, the marriage union will not give one person immediate omniscience about the other.

Because you are seeking a relationship with the Lord of the universe, when you step through the marriage veil of salvation, you receive just a glimpse of what God has to offer. Enjoying any aspect of His gifts hinges on knowing Him and growing in Him. What is amazing is that the knowing and growing never cease. There's great joy as we recognize that the opportunity to grow in our relationship with God is as infinite as the celestial system.

As a young boy in Mississippi, I often went outside during the early evening to help my mom hang clothes on the drying line. Under the starry sky, Mom taught me how to shake out the clothes properly, then hand them to her with clothespins so she could hang them faster. The heat would rise from the clothes in the cold night, warming our hands.

During those nights, as I looked up and saw the sky and stars, the vast nature of the universe would overwhelm me. A couple of autumn evenings in 1957, I watched the Russian spaceship Sputnik cross the horizon during its orbits. Though only 184 pounds, that glittering ball was easy to spot as it swept across the sky. At that time, scientists didn't know as much about the vastness of the universe. God is bigger and deeper and *more* than all we can see or imagine. He created it with the very breath of His words. And the Creator is always greater than the creation. It is the same with our relationship spiritually—there is no limit.

Have you ever heard someone say, "It's not what you know; it's who you know"? In a sense, it's the same in our relationship with Jesus. Not that we try to "use" Him, but knowing Him does bring us into the benefits of relationship with Him. Let's consider a few of the benefits of knowing Jesus:

- Eternal life (John 17:3)
- God in our midst (Isaiah 30:21)
- Understanding God's will (Ephesians 5:15–20)
- Acceptance of the events in our life (Romans 8:28)
- Wisdom of God (1 Corinthians 1:21–23)

Is it possible to really know God? In Ephesians 3:14–19, Paul talks about the "size" of God's love: "I bow my knees before the Father . . . that you . . . may have strength to comprehend with all the saints what is the breadth and length and height and depth, and to know the love of Christ that surpasses knowledge, that you may be filled with all the fullness of God."

We see from other biblical passages that God is infinite—the beginning and the end, the alpha and omega. Psalm 147:5 says that His wisdom is infinite. Given these characteristics, it seems likely that Paul's point was that there is no limit to God's love either. There is no limit to God. Even after an eternity with Him face to face, there will still be more to know.

Worship Experience
Listen to "Reckless Love," by Cory Asbury:
". . . the overwhelming, never-ending reckless love of God!"

Revival Truths

- God is infinite, and there is always something additional in knowing God.

- There are tangible benefits to a relationship with Jesus.

- The depth of our relationship with God is without confines or limitations.

Great is our Lord, and abundant in power; his understanding is beyond measure.

PSALM 147:5

Walking
in the Light
of God's
People

He Moved First!

I will remember the works of the Lord.

PSALM 77:11 NKJV

Can you think of a time when someone else's actions caused discomfort or trouble for you even though you did nothing to deserve it? Or can you recall a time when someone else's actions resulted in good things for you although you did nothing to deserve their kindness?

God's good news story is very much like that. In the Garden of Eden, Adam's one act of disobedience brought sin into the world and caused all of humanity to be separated from God. In beautiful contrast, Jesus's act of obedience at Calvary allowed each of us to enter into a loving relationship with God.

Imagine that God watched with a mixture of grief and sadness when you and I were born . . . because we were born into this world where He and Adam once shared a fantastic friendship. The world was perfect then—their relationship was perfect. But because of Adam's sin, the world became different.

Because God loved us even in our sinfulness, and because He knew that we were powerless to find our way back into a right relationship with Him, He took the initiative by sending Jesus to earth so that we all might receive life through Him. He wants to enjoy a deep closeness with us, so God took the initiative. He made the first move to show us His love!

How does it make you feel to consider what God has done for you? Is your heart moved that He:

- Has gone first to meet your need?

- Noticed your need?

- Took action because of His love for you?

- Was so moved with compassion that He died for you?

- Wants so deeply to relate to you?

Remember some of the things that the Lord has done for you. Pause with one or two others to tell Him.

God, You are great because You take initiative to give to us. You are great because You didn't wait until I noticed You; You gave first. I am amazed because You gave up Your Son so that I could relate with You. Holy Spirit, continue to deepen my intimate walk with Jesus.

L3. A Spirit-empowered disciple experiences God as He really is through deepened intimacy with Him.

SPIRIT-
EMPOWERED
Faith

Day 3

Submission

If I want an intimate, growing, spiritual relationship with Jesus, I will continually die to myself.

When I was forty-six years old, I was the director of counseling and follow-up both nationally and internationally for the Billy Graham Evangelistic Association (BGEA) as well as the Senior Crusade Director. For a person with the desire to touch the world for Christ through evangelism, this was one of the best jobs to have; yet I was somewhat uneasy in my spirit.

During that time, I turned to Ouida, my wife, and, relatively new in the director's position, told her: "Honey, I believe that I'm in training for something." Her response was somewhat like that of Sarah when Abraham, then age one hundred, told his wife they would have a child. Ouida said, "How can that be? You're forty-six years old. You have the best job in evangelism discipleship training and follow-up ministry that anyone in the world could want. You work with someone you trust explicitly, someone whose calling you can follow, someone whose calling is in direct line with the calling Jesus has put on your heart. How could you have any more?"

I don't know if she was disturbed by the possible impact on our family or just shocked that someone my age could be in training for something else!

Later, several opportunities for a change in ministry came my way. The least attractive one in stability was the most attractive in vision. International Students, Inc., a ministry headquartered in Colorado Springs, CO, and focused on reaching the more than six hundred thousand international students studying in American universities, had gone through a tremendous breakdown as an organization. Jesus had accomplished much through the leadership of the board of directors and others, but the job for me would obviously be strenuous. Though many individuals were still supporting ISI, the ministry itself had become weak in management and needed a lot of work. Was I the person Jesus could use? I was inadequate, but I had to trust, to submit to the authority and adequacy of Christ. Would I leave the strength and stability of the BGEA for an organization still reeling from massive change?

A tremendous pilgrimage began when I said yes to Jesus and this opportunity to trust Him. Andrew Murray said it so well. "You may not feel it, you may not realize it, but God takes possession if you'll trust Him. Such a life has two sides—on the one side, absolute surrender to work that God wants you to do; on the other side, to let God work what He wants to do."[37]

> *"Revival begins when men and women cry out to God."*
> – Barry Boucher

God answered my prayer to have an opportunity to mold a ministry, and I saw myself becoming the president and chief executive officer of International Students. I was thrilled with the possibilities.

But there was much to do. We had a wonderful team of people who remained at ISI—men and women who had done whatever it took to keep the ministry running. Also, one of the board members, Kirk Humphreys, had become the interim CEO for six months, flying from Oklahoma each week for three days in the midst of managing his own business. What a privilege to have such guardians of the vision.

The darkest days were to come as I moved from BGEA, one of the most prayed-for ministries on the face of the globe, to ISI, one that had virtually no prayer covering left. The hours were strenuous; during the first year, I would begin at seven in the morning and work until at least eleven at night (sometimes until 3 a.m.). On Saturdays I worked until 6 p.m. and often Sunday afternoons (though I did try to rest on Sundays). I reduced my exercise from daily to about once a week. Meals dropped from three a day to one or two. I had never experienced such a workload except in the middle of a Billy Graham crusade. Working the pace of a one- or two-week crusade for over a year was literally debilitating.

I would have traded those first few years with ISI for almost anything. I felt I had no one to turn to with my concerns and needs. The board had already been through so much. My spiritual mentor couldn't understand my position. My wife didn't need to hear about this all the time. Only Jesus, my Rock, could understand. I would walk Cheyenne Mountain at night for hours at a time crying out to God for His provision. The economics, the faith in ISI by the donors, the growth of the vision, the restructuring of the ministry, the leadership (certainly myself)—all needed His help, and so many other areas needed His help. It was beyond me to do this job.

We serve a God who is incredibly dependable and one who carries us when we are obedient far beyond anything we could ever ask or think. But in order for Him to carry me, I had to submit to His will. I had chosen to obey long ago when He first called me into ministry. I again had to choose to leave all that was safe and comfortable after many years with Mr. Graham. I had to daily submit to tough decisions and long hours at ISI.

I didn't always want to submit. I wanted to run sometimes. But as I submitted to where Jesus called me, He remained faithful to complete what He had begun. Today, He has turned around the ship of ISI from a floundering vessel to one worthy of battle. Christ is being honored. Submission is required in both big and small areas of life. It's required on an ongoing basis.

Revival Truths

- Submission is a daily act of obedience to the will of God.

- Submission is not always easy.

- God honors our obedient submission to His will.

> "Father, if it is Your will, take this cup away from Me;
> nevertheless not My will, but Yours, be done."
>
> LUKE 22:42 NKJV

To Protect and Provide

And forget none of His benefits.

PSALM 103:2 NASB

You have a God who has written down His laws to live by because He wants the best for you. He's not a God who wants to ruin your fun or control your life. He's a God who wants to protect and provide. You have a God who deeply desires to bring good things to your life and save you from harm as you yield to Him and His ways.

Remember a few of the times when you've seen God provide for you as you've submitted to His Word and His ways. Have you ever chosen to live by God's laws and sensed His peace? Experienced the relief of a clear conscience? The joy of a job well done? Or the gratitude of living a life with wise choices?

- *God, I am grateful that you've provided _____ as I choose to yield to Your Word.*

Now, remember a few of the times when you've seen God protect you as you've chosen to live according to His laws. Have you ever escaped negative consequences? Experienced relief from guilt or shame that may have resulted from poor choices? Felt protection from the pain of difficult relationships because you lived a life that aligned with God's laws?

- *God, thank you for your protection from _____, as I made decisions that yielded to Your Word. I am especially grateful for the time when . . .*

Spend the next few moments telling God about your gratitude for how He has provided for you and protected you. Thank Him for being the kind of God who is trustworthy and wants the best for you; renew your commitment to live submissively to Him and His Word.

God, thank You for being the kind of God who wants the best for me. I know You've given Your laws as a protection and a guide for me. That's one of the great benefits of my relationship with You! Help me to live a life of submission. Empower me to stand strong because of my trust in You!

W3. A Spirit-empowered disciple yields to the Scripture's protective cautions and transforming power to bring about life change.

SPIRIT-
EMPOWERED
Faith

Day 4

Practice the Presence of God

Born into poverty as Nicholas Herman in French Lorraine in 1611, at age eighteen he accepted Christ as his Savior. A few years later he became a footman—a servant who opened carriage doors and waited on tables. At age fifty-five, he entered a religious community called the Carmelites, located in Paris. Among these barefooted devotees to Christ, this humble believer and "lay brother" took the name Brother Lawrence. During his twenty-five years in this community, he served mostly in the hospital kitchen.

"He became known, within the community, and later beyond it, for his quiet and serene faith, and for his simple experience of 'practicing the presence of God,'" wrote Frank Laubach in his introduction to Lawrence's classic work, *Practicing His Presence*. "Eventually Brother Lawrence even received inquiries from people in other parts of France concerning how to have a similar reality in their own daily experience with Christ. Even church leaders sought him out for counsel and help."[38]

Is it possible to be in God's presence twenty-four hours a day? Brother Lawrence believed it was, and his life reflected that belief. Scripture as well indicates that we can remain in His presence. For instance, Psalm 139:7–8 declares "Where shall I go from your Spirit? Or where shall I flee from your presence? If I ascend to heaven, you are there! If I make my bed in Sheol, you are there!"

Scripture gives varying images of the presence of God. At Jesus's baptism, a dove indicated God's presence. In Philippians 4:5, we read that a spirit of gentleness accompanies God's presence. In verse 7, we see that peace indicates God's presence. Today, we know God's presence sometimes only through faith—because He has promised that He will never leave us or forsake us.

How do you recognize God's presence in your life? A core characteristic of God is omnipresence, or being everywhere. Regardless of where we are, in the depths or the heights or in between, God is there. And for the believer, there is greater intimacy with Jesus's presence, for He lives within each who calls Him Lord. In Genesis 28:16, we find Jacob recognizing that the Lord's presence was with him even as a fugitive. What we often lack is the recognition that we are in the presence of Jesus. It is not a warm, fuzzy feeling; it is a fact of who God is. He is in the still small whisper more often than the boom of thunder.

"How do I practice God's presence?" you may ask. First, look for it. Be open to it. Once you begin to recognize it, linger over it. Being in God's presence requires no special skills. It is a relationship and requires communication. We talk to God. We listen to God. He talks to us and listens to us. One way to open the door for recognition is through praise. Psalm 100:4 exhorts us, "Enter his gates with thanksgiving, and his courts with praise! Give thanks to him; bless his name!" Practicing the presence of God calls us to recognize His presence, walk by faith that He is there, and communicate with Him always. We are already in His presence; we need to live as such.

> *"I have tasted a thrill in fellowship with God which has made anything discordant with God disgusting."*
> – Frank Laubach

Think about a time when you had a very special guest over to your house, someone you esteemed greatly. How did that affect the way you cleaned your home? How did his presence affect your speech and behavior? Did you focus on the guest or yourself? That is not dissimilar from the results of being in God's presence. As we realize that we are in His presence, we become focused on Him. We are concerned about our behavior toward others; we are more cautious about how we live our lives.

As believers we have God living in us—His presence is with us always. It takes a daily recognition of His presence to begin to live in constant communion. I am convinced that when we really believe that we are in God's presence, that He in fact is in us, our hearts and our lives will change from the inside out. We have no choice but to be more like Him.

Revival Truths

- God is present with us always.

- We need to recognize His presence on a daily basis.

- As we recognize His presence and commune with Him, our hearts and lives will change.

Then Jacob awoke from his sleep and said, "Surely the Lord is in this place, and I did not know it."

GENESIS 28:16

Walking
in the Light
of God's
People

A God Who Reveals

"Abraham believed God, and it was counted to him as righteousness"—
and he was called a friend of God.

JAMES 2:23

Throughout Scripture, it is God's character to reveal. It is a part of His nature to disclose Himself to those who love Him. In fact, the book of Proverbs explains that we have the awesome privilege to become true friends of God as He "takes the upright into His confidence" (Proverbs 3:32 NIV).

Genesis 18 records an account of Jehovah God coming to earth to visit His friend, Abraham. This passage reminds us that we have a God who longs to relate to us as a friend. As the Lord God is about to leave to destroy the wicked cities of Sodom and Gomorrah, Jehovah pauses and asks Himself, "Shall I hide from Abraham what I am about to do?" (Genesis 18:17). In this story, God seemed to want to let Abraham in on what He had planned.

In the book of James, Abraham "was called a friend of God" (James 2:23). Likewise, God seemed to have a similar intimate relationship with Moses: "So the Lord spoke to Moses face to face, as a man speaks to his friend" (Exodus 33:11 NKJV).

Just as God deeply desired to relate to His friends, Abraham and Moses, God longs for a similar friendship with you and me. He wants to reveal His ways, His thoughts, His heart, and His character to each of us. He longs to disclose Himself to us and relate in meaningful ways. True revival flows through you and I as "friends" of God.

Consider now what a wonderful blessing it is to have a God who shows His love by revealing Himself to us! Pause with one or two others and allow your heart to be stirred with gratitude that God longs for you to know Him!

Write out a special prayer of thanksgiving to God for the wonder that His nature is to disclose Himself to you. Ask Him to "take you into His confidence." And then . . . be sure to listen!

Dear God, please speak to me. I wish to listen to You as I would a close friend. How might I more effectively live a life of personal revival? Speak Lord, I'm listening.

L2. A Spirit-empowered disciple listens to and hears God for direction and discernment.

Day 5

A Place of Rest

The word *rest,* in either Hebrew or Greek, does not mean to sit; it means to trust. Resting in Jesus is an attitude of trust, and we must foster this attitude daily. At the time of their conversion, people often experience a great sense of peace. This comes from a pure and innocent trust in Jesus. As we continue to grow in our relationship with Christ, it is important to renew that sense of trust in order to rest in Him despite the circumstances we face. God is the God of the impossible. What better place to rest?

Early in my ministry with BGEA, I worked as the assistant to Charlie Riggs, the director of counseling and follow-up. Charlie was an example to me of many attributes of Jesus, and resting in God was no exception.

The day before a Billy Graham crusade in Lubbock, Texas, in 1975, I attended a meeting to discuss the need for extra seating. Late in our preparations, we realized that there might be up to 10,000 more people attending the next night than we had originally planned. We didn't have enough chairs. We looked over a diagram of the stadium. Though I was young, I felt my opinion was valuable (could I have been a little prideful?), and didn't mind sharing that I thought it simply could not be done.

Charlie looked up at me and said, "Tom, God needs those chairs for people to hear the Gospel. It not only can be done, but it will be done."

Charlie had all the trust in the world that God would accomplish what He needed. We simply had to be obedient. Charlie was a man of action with a heart that rested in the Lord.

The following day, we worked like ants to move every possible kind of chair from the Lubbock churches. By the end of the afternoon, volunteers had perfectly placed ten thousand plastic, wooden, folding, and aluminum chairs!

Worship Experience
Listen to "Cecie's Lullaby," by Steffany Gretzinger:
"All you need, It's here inside my arms."

Our culture doesn't promote rest as God desires. We often confuse rest with laziness or a complete lack of responsibility. I often communicate to my team that we are to pray like it all depends on God and obey His leading like it all depends on us. That was the example I saw from Charlie Riggs.

Rest is an attitude of the heart. Charlie was one of the hardest working men I knew, but he was able to rest simultaneously. His attitude was that of obedience to Jesus for whatever He asked, not responsibility for the specific outcomes. Because Charlie could separate what Jesus was calling him to do from his human desire to control and manipulate situations for specific outcomes, Charlie could rest. It was God's train; Charlie was just along for the ride.

Rest is part of God's plan in creation, both physical and spiritual rest. Our bodies require sleep every night. Have you ever been around someone who hasn't slept well in a few days? Sleep deprivation is not a pretty sight. It interferes with judgment and reasoning, disrupts emotions, and leaves the body susceptible to sickness. Physical rest is important every day.

Mental rest is important also. There are times when we require a rest from our work, so we take a vacation. We may need a rest from any number of activities that we engage in on a regular basis. It's good for us to rest. It's part of God's plan. Even He rested on the seventh day of creation.

Rest is a normal part of our daily life, not something that should happen only occasionally. While we have specific times of physical and emotional rest, the Lord calls us to be in continual rest spiritually as we depend on Jesus.

Revival Truths

- Rest is part of God's plan.

- We need physical and emotional rest on a regular basis.

- It is possible to be in a state of continual spiritual rest as we trust in Christ.

Come to me, all who labor and are heavy laden, and I will give you rest. Take my yoke upon you, and learn from me, for I am gentle and lowly in heart, and you will find rest for your souls. For my yoke is easy, and my burden is light."

MATTHEW 11:28–30

Walking in the Light of God's Son

The Characteristics of Rest

Then Jesus spoke to them again, saying, "I am the light of the world. He who follows Me shall not walk in darkness, but have the light of life."

JOHN 8:12 NKJV

Resting in the Lord seems to be a characteristic of a life of personal revival, including:

- Celebrating with praises (*eulageo*): "Everyone was shouting, 'Lord, be our Savior! Blessed is the one who comes to us sent from Jehovah-God, the King of Israel'" (John 12:13 TPT).

- Casting out fear. "Then Jesus found a young donkey and rode on it to fulfill what was prophesied: 'People of Zion, have no fear!'" (vv, 14–15 TPT).

- Exalting Jesus: "All the eyewitnesses . . . kept spreading the news about Jesus to everyone . . . Isaiah said these things because he had seen and experienced the splendor of Jesus and prophesied about him" (vv. 17, 41 TPT).

- Drawing others to Him: "Now there were a number of foreigners from among the nations who were worshipers at the feast. They went to Philip . . . and they asked him, 'Would you take us to see Jesus?'" (vv. 20–21 TPT).

- Selflessness: "A single grain of wheat will never be more than a single grain of wheat unless it drops into the ground and dies . . . For I have come to fulfill my purpose—to offer myself to God" (vv. 24, 27 TPT).

- Growing faith: "Then Jesus told them, 'The voice you heard was not for my benefit, but for yours—to help you believe'" (v. 30 TPT).

- Spiritual awakening: "The ruler of this dark world will be overthrown . . . I have come as a light to shine in this dark world so that all who trust in me will no longer wander in darkness" (vv. 31, 46 TPT).

Share with Jesus your hope regarding your personal revival:

Lord, I'm hoping my walk with You will be characterized more by _____ and less by _____.

L6. A Spirit-empowered disciple consistently practices self-denial, fasting, and solitude rest.

SPIRIT EMPOWERED *Faith*

Looking Forward

As we grow in our relationship with Christ, there is a need for continual renewal. Revival in our hearts may begin at a specific point in time, but it never ends there. Daily God calls us to renewal through the presence of His Spirit. As we walk with Him and rest in Him, we open a connection through which He can work to bring revival to others. In the next chapter, we'll see how Jesus bestows gifts for us to use in His kingdom.

CHAPTER 7

REVIVAL within Your GIFTS

As you watch the news or read a newspaper, it's easy to become discouraged with the state of the world. You feel so small. Is it possible for one person to make a difference? God in His Word says yes!

He has endowed us with spiritual gifts to build up the body of believers, to help others know Christ, and to bring glory to Himself. From the time of creation, work was part of our being, and God designed that work to be purposeful in our daily lives. God gives each believer work and the gifts needed to effectively complete that work. Many believers fall into a false humility by claiming they are useless," or saying, "God can't use me." Some people don't acknowledge they have spiritual gifts at all. The circumstances of life have beaten their reasonable service down to the place where they don't know how or where to serve. This is not pleasing to God. In 2 Timothy 1:6, Paul urges Timothy not to be shy in using the gift God has given him, but to "stir up the gift" (NKJV), to grow in confidence, and use it.

In order to use our spiritual gifts, it's important for us to recognize them so we can increase our skills and see the service opportunities God has laid before us. When you've established an intimate relationship with God and have started growing in your faith, the natural outflow is to use your talents in the church, the local community, or wherever in the world God directs. Revival calls for all believers to fulfill their role in the body of Christ. And in our service, our lives can remain vibrant for God.

Since most believers have a combination of more than one spiritual gift, I will refer to them in the plural form as "gifts." In this week's studies, let's discuss spiritual gifts and how to use them in the local body of believers and in your community. While this information has a practical application, it will continue to emphasize *being* in Christ before you attempt to *do* anything. It's critical to continue to grow in your daily walk with the Lord.

Day 1

Discover Your Gifts

One of the most difficult people to evaluate is yourself. Certainly, you can look in a mirror and see your external features, but it's difficult to see character flaws. It is also a challenge to recognize your gifts. It takes even more work to find a place of service that provides great joy and satisfaction. Some people drift through their entire lives without this knowledge.

Scripture lists a variety of gifts—some say eighteen while others say as many as twenty-seven. While Scripture gives some specific lists, it also implies that other gifts are present through the actions of believers both in the early church and today. Intercession, for example, is not on a specific list, but it is evident through the lives of believers who spend countless hours in fruitful prayer for the needs of others. There are a variety of ways to list and categorize spiritual gifts, many of which are variations on the same theme. How does a believer learn about his or her spiritual gifting?

Abundant resources exist today to help the believer on the road to discovery. Books and inventory tests are plentiful. It's important to study several of these and choose one that is grounded in Scripture and helps you determine not just your gifting but how to best use your gifts. While this is not a comprehensive list, you can find some of these resources listed at the end of this book. I want to mention a few of them here.

C. Peter Wagner's book, *Your Spiritual Gifts Can Help Your Church Grow*, is an excellent place to begin the study of spiritual gifts. Dr. Wagner provides a list of twenty-seven spiritual gifts, from prophecy to mercy to giving. This is a comprehensive inventory to examine the expression of those gifts in your life as well as practical examples of how you can utilize those gifts. Wagner compiled his list primarily from Romans 12:6–8; 1 Corinthians 12:8–10, 28; and Ephesians 4:11. From elsewhere in the New Testament he has added the gifts of celibacy, voluntary poverty, martyrdom, hospitality, and missionary.[39]

Another helpful tool for individual use is Don and Katie Fortune's book *Discover Your God-Given Gifts* (Revell). These authors have separated spiritual gifts into three categories: the manifestation gifts, the ministry gifts, and the motivational gifts. Most helpful in this book is a description of not only gift characteristics but also the pitfalls of each gift. They give biblical examples of spiritual gifts in action.

A third set of materials available, and one that is good for groups to study, is *Network* (Zondervan). These materials, authored by Bruce Bugbee, Don Cousins, and Bill Hybels, look at spiritual gifts from three perspectives: determining where your passions lie, seeing what skills or spiritual gifts God has given, and determining your personal style for how to best put those passions and skills to work. These materials focus on the interdependence of believers to confirm our gifts and how to use those gifts.

As you can see just by this short description, there is a lot to read and study in the area of discovering your spiritual gifts. If you have not done so, I recommend that you obtain at least one of these resources and study more in depth the topic of spiritual gifts. It's important, however, not to make it too complicated. Beginning with these simple questions will help set you on the right course:

- What are the desires of your heart?

- Do others around you affirm this desire in you as something you can do well?

- Who has affirmed you and in what way?

- In what areas of service do you find joy?

- In what areas of service have you clearly known you were right where God called you to be?

The answers to these questions are a good place to begin to discover your spiritual gifts.

As you begin to understand your gifting, I have one huge caution: If people ask you to do things that are outside your area of gifting, don't hesitate to say, "No, thank you." Too often with other believers, we hesitate to say no, and the result is working outside of our abilities and gifts, perhaps with limited joy or productivity. Our daughter, Cara, is a physician. As she considered her gifts and how to use them to serve in her church, she felt drawn to the high school age group. Yet her church wanted her to work in Sunday school with younger children. This misplacement happens frequently in the body of Christ; so many people are not functioning where God has called them that there appears to be a shortage of workers. Churches are forced to continue the trend of misplacement to meet felt needs. Yet, if we all functioned according to our gifts, there would likely be just enough help to go around. It's important to discover your spiritual heart, and, when you find it, don't work in the wrong area—no matter how much pressure you feel.

Keep in mind that your strengths and abilities are from God. As you discover your passion and gifting, commit these into Jesus's hands and ask Him to show you how and where to use them. If you are resting in His guidance, then God will put the tapestry of your life together. As you understand your spiritual gifts, they can have a far-reaching impact on the world around you—in your local body of believers and your community at large. The first step is discovery.

Worship Experience
Listen to "I Give Myself Away," by William McDowell:
"I give myself away so You can use me."

Revival Truths

- God calls us to discover the spiritual gifts He has given to us.

- Your spiritual gifts, when exercised for Christ, will give you great joy and fulfillment.

- Others can help you identify your spiritual gift. Remember there is safety in a multitude of counselors.

Therefore I remind you to stir up the gift of God which is in you through the laying on of my hands.

2 Timothy 1:6 NKJV

Walking
in the Light
of God's
Word

Your Natural and Supernatural Bent

If any of you lacks wisdom, let him ask of God, who gives to all liberally and without reproach, and it will be given to him.

James 1:5 NKJV

Did you know that you have a "natural bent"—a unique, one-of-a-kind personality and view of the world? God created you that way. He didn't just pour one mold and call it a day. God uniquely designed you and then broke the mold! He then blessed you with the Holy Spirit and unique spiritual gifts. There is no one like you.

Why did God do that? He's a creative God. He loves to express Himself in exceptional ways. God creatively formed your DNA, your personality, your gifts, your talents, and your temperament. Secondly, God is a Creator who longs to relate to His creation. No one else can love God in just the way that we can. No one else can love others in the exact way that we've been designed to love. God created us with individuality and uniqueness because He delights in seeing us express that uniqueness in relationship with Him and others. Isn't that an amazing characteristic of our Creator?

Take time to celebrate this incredible characteristic of our God. How does it make you feel to know that God chose to create you with very individual gifts, talents, temperament, and personality? His intention was to create the "rare design" that could only be you!

- *I'm _____ amazed/grateful/surprised as I imagine that no one else can love God or others just like I can. This truth makes me feel _____ toward God.*

Take the next few moments and ask God to show you how He wants to involve you in making a positive contribution to the world. Ask God to reveal and confirm your spiritual gifts and how you can make a positive impact on others. Ask for His wisdom, knowing that He promises to give wisdom to anyone who asks.

God, show me how my spiritual gifts and talents can positively impact the lives of others. Please show me how my unique gifting can positively impact my ministry for You.

M7. A Spirit-empowered disciple faithfully shares time, talent, gifts, and resources in furthering God's mission.

Day 2

Developing Your Spiritual Gifts

Okay, so now that you've become familiar with the wonderful spiritual gifts God has given you, what's next? Sometimes I wish Jesus would just "zap" me into the finished product He intended for me to be, but He never seems to work that way. Our God is a God of order, and He likes to take us through the process of becoming a finished product. It is the same with the spiritual gifts He bestows upon us. Let's look at how we can take the knowledge of our gifts and learn to develop what we have discovered. This involves six steps: (1) present your newly discovered gifts, (2) plan how to develop your gifts, (3) know the pitfalls of your gifts, (4) personalize your gifts by studying their use in Scripture, (5) pray about your gifts, and (6) practice using your gifts.

> *"All the worry and fret of God's children would end if their eyes were opened to see the greatness of the treasure hid in their hearts . . . You carry God in your heart!"*
> *– Watchman Nee*

A good first step is to present your newly discovered gifts. Depending upon your church structure and lifestyle, you might share it with your pastor, a spiritual mentor, your accountability partner, or fellowship group. It is important to tell others, however. By telling what God is teaching us, we reinforce that information, and it helps us to grow. Sharing the information with your spouse is important, but also sharing it within the body of believers will provide a natural means of accountability. Pray for wisdom in discerning those with whom God would have you first discuss your spiritual gifts.

In telling others about your spiritual gifts, include an open door for accountability; it's a vital part of the body of Christ. Others can help you in following a plan for how to develop your gifts. As we continue in this section, we'll discuss ways to help you grow in using your spiritual gifts. Use those, and any other ideas you have, in your plan. Consider Proverbs 16:9 as you develop your plan: "The heart of man plans his way, but the Lord establishes his steps."

Telling others also means you can have valuable insight when you function outside of your area of gifting. For example, let's say you have the gift of leadership but not the gift of mercy. Your pastor has asked you to commit every Saturday to hospital visitation. Is that the best way to use your time, given your gifts? Probably not. But sometimes it takes an outsider's perspective to see that—if we're willing to listen.

Just a word about making decisions for where to serve. As believers, we have a general calling in Christ and a specific calling through our gifts. We are all called to tell others about Christ (general call), but not all of us have Billy Graham's gift of evangelism (specific). We never have an excuse to not help someone because we don't have the gift of "helps," or to not be kind to someone because we aren't merciful. Our gifting allows us to see where we can focus our time to serve; it doesn't give us an excuse to avoid something we'd rather not do.

While you don't want to become burdened with excessive information, it's important to take time to read materials written on spiritual gifts, such as some of those listed earlier in this chapter. A key element is knowing the pitfalls of your gifts. Don and Katie Fortune's *Discover Your God-Given Gifts*, which I mentioned earlier, is an excellent resource for spotting the potential pitfalls of spiritual gifts. Any strength, taken to its extreme, will become a liability. For instance, the person with the gift of exhortation runs the risk of being outspoken and opinionated. Take time to study the potential pitfalls associated with your gift. Ask Jesus to convict you in those areas and help you to change. None of us is perfect.

Be sure to personalize your spiritual gifts, recognizing them in biblical characters. Many believers forget that the individuals in Scripture were real people who had different gifts and callings. Study biblical characters to understand their strengths and weaknesses and to see how God used particular spiritual gifts. Again, the Fortune's book is an excellent resource showing biblical examples of gifts in action. You could also do a character study. Pick a character in Scripture with whom you identify and analyze the person according to spiritual gift inventories. It may take some time, and you won't always find one with "your gifts" right away, but it's a rich exercise worth the effort.

We've talked a great deal about prayer throughout this book. It is foundational. Next, pray about your spiritual gifts. Pray that Jesus would help you keep focused on using them for His glory and not your personal gain. Pray about the pitfalls. Pray about where God would have you serve in using those gifts.

Finally, practice using your gifts. This can sometimes be the most difficult and yet most fruitful way to grow in using our spiritual gifts. Basically, you can't develop your gifts until you use them. The rub lies in that while we are learning, we fail. Jesus is gracious to let us fail and teaches us through that process, but we humans usually avoid practice until we're perfect. (Or until we foolishly think we are!) This is where planning, under the direction of the Holy Spirit, is so helpful. Just as we exercise our physical muscles and they grow to allow us to do more challenging activites, if we exercise our spiritual gifts, we'll also grow in their use.

We'll often fail as we try. But if we continue to pray, to seek Jesus's desire, to step out in faith where He directs, we'll fail less and see fruit more. Don't forget that God works all things together for our good (Romans 8:28). Jesus uses us in His plan, but the fruit rests with Him.

Revival Truths

- After we discover our spiritual gifts, it's important to develop them for use.

- Spiritual gifts are for God's glory, not our personal gain.

- To grow in our spiritual gifts, we must practice using them.

And we know that for those who love God all things work together for good, for those who are called according to his purpose.

ROMANS 8:28

Walking in the Light of God's People

God Gives Good Gifts

In everything give thanks; for this is the will of God in Christ Jesus for you.

1 THESSALONIANS 5:18 NKJV

Think back to all the Christmas and birthday celebrations of your past. What gifts stand out as your favorite? Just as your family and friends have given you special gifts over the years, God has given you amazing gifts and talents. Your totally unique mixture of gifts and talents is just one of the ways in which God has demonstrated His ingenuity, creativity, and generosity.

God has given you certain abilities, talents, and passions that are related to your physical or mental abilities, such as athletic skill, artistic ability, academic excellence, or creative problem-solving. Think for a moment about some of the physical and/or mental gifts God has given you. (For example: You easily understand mechanical concepts, have some success in athletics, learn Spanish vocabulary quickly, etc.)

- *I'm grateful that God has given me the ability to . . .*

Because every aspect of your unique identity is a gift from God, each of these aspects has the potential to help others see God, experience His love, and respond to Him. Be sure to look for ways that might happen!

- *I feel _____ when I think about how my ability to _____ could help others see God.*

God also bestows upon us gifts that are spiritual in nature. Through the work of the Holy Spirit in our lives, God gives us certain spiritual gifts that reflect his character and His presence in our lives. Review these verses, asking for discernment: Romans 12:6–8; 1 Corinthians 12:7–11; 1 Corinthians 12:2–31. Has God given you one of these spiritual gifts?

- Teaching
- Exhortation
- Giving
- Leadership
- Mercy
- Compassion
- Prophecy
- Administration
- Discernment
- Faith
- Helping others
- Knowledge and wisdom
- _____ other

And remember, it's not so important that you are immediately and absolutely sure of the spiritual gifts but that you seek to discover and nurture the gifts as God reveals them to you.

Pause and pray with one or two others:

God, thank You for being so generous to me. You have given me so much. I'm especially grateful for how You've blessed me with the gifts of. . . . Confirm my giftings as I serve You and others.

L9. A Spirit-empowered disciple yields to the Spirit's fullness as life in the Spirit brings supernatural intimacy with the Lord, manifestation of divine gifts, and witness of the fruit of the Spirit.

Day 3

Serving in Your Church

As a young pastor in Mississippi, I tried to sing with the youth choir. I faithfully attended practice and sang with all my heart. I loved singing praises to God. One day, a member of the choir pulled me aside and said, "Pastor, we need to practice the special." Then he continued, most honestly I would add, "And your singing is so bad that we can't get it right." In other words, please be quiet. I heard the message, immediately gave up my position in the choir, and have never tried to enter that arena again. It's outside of my particular range of talents. Music brings me fulfillment, but I really have no ability in this area. My attempt to serve in an area where God had not gifted me was a hindrance to others who were serving where Jesus had called them. It's important for you to consider the body of believers with whom you worship.

How do your gifts match with the needs of your local church?

For the purposes of this discussion, let's assume that the church you attend is grounded in Scripture and reflects Christ. Have you considered less "publicized" needs, such as giving rides to those without a vehicle or cleaning up after a special event? Other less-known needs might include things your church hasn't done in the past but that you might be able to coordinate or provide.

For example, you might be able to fix cars. Most churches have plenty of single women or elderly people who would appreciate someone's ability to help with minor car repairs. The bottom line is, don't limit yourself or your church. If you're good at doing it, someone probably needs it!

Worship Experience
Listen to "Born for Such a Time," by Chris Burns:
"Hear the call, generation of God."

A caution about serving within the body of believers: Sometimes it's easy to notice the gifts and talents of others and begin to feel as though our gifts are "less important." This is especially true if we compare the more public gifts of teaching and preaching to the gift of helps—which often means behind-the-scenes work. We have been conditioned to see things this way. What is most important is not who has the most valuable gift because in God's eyes, they are all equally valuable but just have a different place in the body (1 Corinthians 12:18–27). It's most important that we keep our eyes focused on Christ and serve motivated by obedience to Him and Him alone.

Keep in mind that Jesus is the one who meets the needs of others. While He uses us in the process, He will be the ultimate provider. As needs arise in your church, be sure that you are ready to say yes. Being distracted by good things can prevent you from recognizing "God" things.

Revival Truths

- It's important to know the needs of your church.

- Match those needs with your spiritual gifts to determine your place of service.

- Consider both the publicized needs and those less publicized as areas of service.

- Be willing to start an area of service if you see a need that no one is meeting.

God arranged the members in the body, each one of them, as he chose.

1 CORINTHIANS 12:18

Walking
in the Light
of God's
Word

We All Suffer

If one member suffers, all the members suffer with it;
or if one member is honored, all the members rejoice with it.

1 CORINTHIANS 12:26 NKJV

God has designed you with a distinct identity. You have a one-of-a-kind set of talents, abilities, spiritual gifts, and personality traits. God has lovingly and generously given these gifts to you. As followers of Christ, these gifts are not ours to possess, guard, or even use as we please. They are gifts that God has given and gifts that He calls us to give back to Him and to share with others in return. As you come to more fully understand your strengths, abilities, and unique identity as God has created you, let your focus be this: How can I utilize all of these God-given gifts to *give* to others?

An important part of being a follower of Jesus is staying aware of what is going on in the lives of others and generously giving of ourselves. In so doing, we are allowing Christ to meet other's significant needs through us. If one person suffers, we can express Christ's love by suffering with them because we are all members of the same body of Christ.

Who do you know that might be suffering, feeling alone, or in need of support? What are some specific ways in which you can give of yourself and help that person feel Christ's love?

- A person who might be suffering is _____. I could share Christ's love with him/her by . . .

- A person who might be feeling alone is _____. I could share Christ's love with him/her by . . .

- A person who might need support is _____. I could offer my help by . . .

God's Word reminds us many times that when Jesus came across people who were hurting in some way, He was moved with compassion (Matthew

9:36). If Jesus were to see the people you have just named, how might He respond? Jesus would be so moved with compassion for the people you've identified that He couldn't help but respond. He would demonstrate love in action. What emotions well up in you as you reflect on a God who is moved by our suffering, aloneness, and need for support?

God, when I consider that You are moved with compassion by our struggles, I feel _____. Move my heart with Your compassion and help me demonstrate love in action as I call upon the Holy Spirit's prompting, gifts, and power.

M7. A Spirit-empowered disciple faithfully shares time, talent, gifts, and resources in furthering God's mission.

Day 4

Serve Your Community

Though we often begin serving in our local church, your gifts may be useful beyond those four walls. It's important to remember that we are gifted to build up the body of believers for a purpose—"to equip the saints for the work of ministry, for building up the body of Christ" (Ephesians 4:12). We need to remember that the non-believers outside our church walls are counting on those works of service as a demonstration of Jesus's love. But because of perceived needs in the church, we often neglect the needs of the community. I say "perceived" because there are times when a particular program or plan creates work without building up the body. In this section I will encourage you to become involved in your community.

> **"Sometimes the best way to love God is by loving His children, 1 John 3:11-20."**
> **- Todd Pierce, Riding High Ministries**

In Scripture, we see that Jesus was involved in His community. He attended social events, such as weddings, and participated in the religious ceremonies of his day. In Matthew 25, Jesus brings us into a social aspect of the Gospel, and we see that we are to care for the least one in need as if they were Jesus Himself. Though food and shelter are specific ways we can help others, there are many ways to serve in your community besides a homeless shelter or food bank. But how do you find out where you can serve? Consider civic groups and clubs that have objectives that match your goal to serve. Look at the news sources you use daily. What kinds of stories grab your attention? Do any of these stories give you ideas for how you might get involved and serve?

Some believers have separated themselves from society. Jesus does not give us that example. He fully participated in social and cultural events, in fact. He performed His first public miracle (as recorded in John) at a wedding. Jesus attended funerals and feasts. He was part of the society in which He lived. He even worked at a "secular" job as a carpenter before beginning full-time ministry.

Don't be afraid to participate in your community. Jesus is counting on you to touch the lives of those who don't know Him. That's impossible if you don't move beyond the four walls of your church. You are Jesus with skin and may be the only Jesus some people ever see. Let Him serve through you.

Revival Truths

- Church is not the only place where we can serve.

- Jesus calls us to be involved in our communities.

- Non-believers in the community can see Jesus's love in action through us.

I was hungry and you gave me food, I was thirsty and you gave me drink, I was a stranger and you welcomed me, I was naked and you clothed me, I was sick and you visited me, I was in prison and you came to me.

MATTHEW 25:35–36

Walking
in the Light
of God's
Son

He Notices

A new commandment I give to you, that you love one another:
just as I have loved you, you are to love one another.

JOHN 13:34

Jesus confirmed our need for attention, or to be "noticed" in many ways. First, Jesus often ministered to large crowds of people, but He also frequently took the time to show attention to specific individuals, including Nicodemus (3:1–21), the lame man at the pool (5:15), the woman with the issue of blood (Mark 5:25–34), and Bartimaeus (10:46–52). God continues to demonstrate His care and concern for each of us by giving us His undivided and unlimited attention when we speak to Him in prayer.

Scripture also tells us that God knew each of us in the womb (Psalm 139:13) and knows our innermost thoughts (v. 2). Philippians 2:6–8 confirms that God wants to spend time with us. God thought it was important to know what it's like to be in our world because Jesus left heaven to enter our world and live here on earth. He wanted us to know that being a part of our world is a priority to Him.

Think about the people who are in your life right now. Who might benefit from receiving your attention and the ministry of your unique gifts and talents?

Meeting someone's need for attention might look like:

- Spending time with a person so that you find out about their struggles, joys, and dreams.

- Entering another person's world—going to or being involved in their interests and activities.

- Listening and observing another person in order to discern their emotions, gain understanding, and show care.

- Being a listener who gives good eye contact, appropriate feedback, and hears a person before responding.

- Spending time with another person doing what they enjoy doing.

How might you meet another person's need for attention this week? How could you give first?

- I think _____ (give a specific name) could benefit from my attention this week. I plan to give him/her attention by . . .

Lord Jesus, thank You for entering my world. Help me to do the same for others. Holy Spirit, lead me this week to open my eyes to those around me that I might give witness of Jesus, utilizing the gifts and talents You have blessed me with.

M3. A Spirit-empowered disciple champions Jesus as the only hope of eternal life and abundant living.

Day 5

Sacred or Secular Walk

The observant editor of *Discipleship Journal*, Sue Kline, once wrote a column about her visit to a snowboard shop. The attitude of one young employee there, complete with body piercings and tattoos, impressed her. The snowboard shop guy treated people with cheerfulness and respect, and loved helping his customers—all attitudes of Christ. The author revealed that on the same day she visited the snowboard shop, she struggled to be like Christ in her "sacred" work. She was impatient, complaining, and gossipy . . . while working in full-time ministry. Her question to the reader was "Which work was secular and which was sacred?"[40]

In the American church, Christians typically place their work into two distinct categories. One is the secular; the other is the sacred. Traditionally, sacred work is defined as within a church or a parachurch organization, performing full-time Christian work as both their ministry and livelihood; or in the case of a missionary, serving with little or no pay. So, we have Christian musicians, Christian booksellers, and Christian websites, operated, of course, by Christian entrepreneurs. In contrast, secular work is anything outside of a full-time ministry. But are any of these former jobs better just because they have a "Christian" label? What makes one Christian and the other not?

I used to live in Colorado Springs where more than one hundred Christian ministry organizations operate. It was easy to bump into other ministry folks, and the community was well aware of the vast number of "Christian workers." What could be distressing, however, was that sometimes there was no difference between the attitudes of the believers and those of the non-believers. Or even worse, those proclaiming Christ through full-time service behaved *less* like Christ than unbelievers did. For example, one local pastor admonished his church about their behavior in restaurants after the Sunday morning service. Several restaurant workers disliked working on Sundays because the "church people" were so cheap. They lingered at tables for hours, the pastor explained, keeping the tables from other hungry customers, and then left meager tips. That's hardly an attitude of Christ.

As you discover and develop your spiritual gifts, you may feel a call into full-time service with a church or other Christian agency. If that's from God, that's wonderful. Be obedient. Go where He leads. But you may also feel confirmation to stay in your job outside the Christian arena or even to move from a job with a Christian agency to one with a secular organization. That's great too because from God's perspective, there is no separation between sacred and secular. All of His creation is whole.

Paul exhorted the church, "Whatever you do, work heartily, as for the Lord and not for men" (Colossians 3:23). God created us for work. In Genesis 2:15, we see the first work God commissioned was farming—tending the garden. This would not be considered a "Christian" job today—unless you worked as a church groundskeeper! Jesus has called His followers to be salt and light to the world (see Matthew 5:13–16), a clear indication that we should bring the flavor of God to those who don't know Him.

What is most important, what makes work secular or sacred, is not the work itself, but the attitude of the heart. How do you treat others? What kind of attitude and work ethic do you carry? Don't get caught believing that one calling is higher than another. Get caught exemplifying the fruits of the Spirit as you use the gifts of the Spirit wherever Jesus has placed you.

Someone serving in a Christian ministry when Jesus has not called him or her there is not doing sacred work but rather is working in the flesh. It is a temptation to base our worth on our work, and so it sometimes feels more "godly" to be in Christian service. This is a lie from the enemy. Jesus will use your spiritual gifts perfectly in the place to which He has called you. Revival depends on believers touching the lives of unbelievers. That's impossible if we don't even know any unbelievers. Listen to His voice and obey. Wherever Jesus is—that's holy and sacred work.

Revival Truths

- Our work is secular or sacred because of our attitude, not our job.

- The fruits of the Spirit are a measuring tool for the "sacredness" of our work.

- We are to work where Jesus calls us, using our spiritual gifts to glorify Him.

- Our value comes from Jesus, not our work.

Let your light shine before others, so that they may see your good works and give glory to your Father who is in heaven.

MATTHEW 5:16

Walking
in the Light
of God's
Word

Answering God's Call

Then the Lord put forth His hand and touched my mouth, and the Lord said
to me: "Behold, I have put My words in your mouth. See, I have this day set
you over the nations and over the kingdoms, to root out and to pull down, to
destroy and to throw down, to build and to plant."

JEREMIAH 1:9–10 NKJV

Jeremiah finds himself living in a time when God's people are distant from
God and have been for a while. They abandoned God and worshiped false gods
(Jeremiah 2:13). No one was genuinely seeking God (5:1–2). They were sin
happy (9:2–3). They wronged each other (v. 5) and rejected God's Word (11:10).
If Jeremiah were alive today and living in the western world, he would find
himself in a very similar situation! Whether in a sacred or "secular" context,
God is still calling modern-day Jeremiahs.

It was in this context that God called Jeremiah to be a difference maker
while impacting his culture. Let's look at Jeremiah's calling.

- First, God communicated to Jeremiah that God had known him,
  set him apart, and appointed him before he was even born (1:4)!
  God had a specific mission for Jeremiah to accomplish.

- Second, Jeremiah faced obstacles that provided an opportunity for
  him to avoid God's calling on his life. It is understandable to see
  why he was nervous (v. 7): he was young, the content of the message God wanted him to deliver was very difficult (v. 10), and he
  didn't have prior experience to lean on as this was all new territory.

- Third, God encouraged Jeremiah that not only is He bigger than
  all of the obstacles Jeremiah faced, but He would be with him every
  step of the way until the mission was completed (v. 8).

Jeremiah took the above three elements to heart as He answered God's
calling on his life, and he became a major difference maker in his day. Our

world is desperate for modern day Jeremiahs. Be encouraged to answer God's call today!

God, thank You for giving me a life mission, for setting me apart, for being bigger than my obstacles, and for being with me. Help me to answer Your call and to make an impact on this world in a way that honors You.

M6. A Spirit-empowered disciple bears witness of a con-fident peace and expectant hope in God's Lordship in all things.

SPIRIT-
EMPOWERED
Faith

Looking Forward

Functioning within the spiritual gifts Jesus has given you is a vital component for revival in our lives. The body will be sick and ineffective unless we're all doing our part. In chapter 8, we'll see how using our gifts gives the opportunity for evangelism with great results.

CHAPTER 8

AN Evangelism EXPLOSION

The word *evangelism* originated from the Greek word *euangelion*, which translates to "the Gospel." Within the structure of this word *euangelion* is the word *evangel*, which means "good news." The early English called it "God's Spell." They said that the good news of God will put "God's spell" on the person who would receive it. This is good news—God's nature, purpose, power, and love incorporated in the human vessel.[41]

Followers of Jesus desire to know Him and to make Him known—to share the good news of spiritual rebirth through Jesus Christ. In marriage we reproduce offspring; similarly, as Christians, our calling is to spiritually reproduce. The faith by which we live is transferable from one person to another. That's evangelism.

Often people say about me, "Tom's heart is revival." My heart is really evangelism, but the heartbeat to get it there is revival. For mass numbers to make commitments to a relationship with Jesus, it will take a renewed and revived church. Each person's fire must be rekindled. That leads to explosive evangelism—through the cleansing of the church and the unhindered flow of the Holy Spirit. The goal in revival is to see evangelism explode as it has historically during and after other great awakenings.

Evangelism is what revival is all about. Many think that revival is evangelism. No; revival is preparing the church for evangelism. It's the process for preparing the church for the reproduction Jesus intends.

Will you be one to tell others? Do you want to be?

Day 1

A Burden for Others

At the time of our salvation, as we begin our walk with Christ, most of us are burdened only for ourselves. We focus on our relationship with Jesus. We've read about it and heard about it, and people from history have talked about it. And so, we want it. Our burden is for our own soul.

Then, as we understand the preciousness of our relationship with Christ and the wonder of daily grace and mercy, we look around at our loved ones and say, "They need to know Jesus." Soon we begin to notice those outside our family and relatives as well, those we know well and those we know little or not at all. We see emptiness. We realize that without Christ all that waits is an eternity in hell. We rightly conclude, "Everyone should have a chance to know Him."

How do you develop this passion for others? First, recognize it's not a human passion. It's an eternal passion that comes from the heart of Jesus. In the natural flesh, our only burden is for self, but, as the Spirit renews us, we walk in an intimate relationship with Jesus. He begins to show us others.

The hymn "Lead Me to Some Soul Today" by Will H. Houghton reflected the heart of D. L. Moody, who witnessed to someone every day. If you can take a minute, search for this song on YouTube and listen to it. There are stories of Moody getting out of bed at 11 p.m. and telling his wife, "I forgot to witness today." He went onto the street and buttonholed the first person he encountered, who often responded, "Who . . . oh, Dr. Moody?" The people in his neighborhood knew Moody and his love for the souls of others. On a consistent basis, Moody led people to a personal relationship with Jesus Christ.[42]

Worship Experience
Listen to "Lead Me to Some Soul Today," by Will H.
Houghton:
"Lord lead me to some soul today.
O teach me, Lord, just what to say;
Friends of mine are lost in sin
And cannot find their way.
Few there are who seem to care

And few there are who pray;
Melt my heart and fill my life.
Give me one soul today."

One day, after singing "Lead Me to Some Soul Today," I told Jesus, "Here I am in seminary learning how to tell others about you, and I don't tell people about you every day. Lord, I'm going to make a pact with you. If you will bring somebody into my path every day for two weeks, I'll witness to them." It happened through Jesus—not an engineered deal forced in my flesh. Each day He brought someone whom I could tell about Him.

At the end of those two weeks, I said to the Father, "Lord, this has been wonderful and it has not been embarrassing. There has not been pressure on me or on these people. They've just been there and ready to hear. It's been absolutely incredible." Then, in prayer, I asked, "Daddy, where have these people been before?"

God spoke to my heart and said, "Tom, they've been there all along. Where have you been?"

I was so busy and caught up in being Tom that I never saw them. Business with my family, my full-time job, my church on the weekends, and my full-time student work at seminary kept me walking past people who were separated from Jesus. I was studying to tell others the truth of Jesus and His salvation, but I was so task-oriented that I ignored the privilege of "relationship proclamation"—telling those whom I meet, including those with whom I have only a casual relationship, about God's love through Christ. I'm not suggesting that you witness to every person you meet, but is your heart right to hear Jesus when He directs you toward someone in your path? Is your heart in a place to hear from Jesus on a moment-by-moment basis?

Maybe you've never shared Christ's story with someone before. Maybe you don't have a burden for others. You are not alone. Jesus will grow that desire as you ask Him to do so. Here are some tips for you to begin to gain this burden for souls.

First, study the Word of God to see His heart for evangelism. In 2 Corinthians 6:2 we read: "For he says, 'In a favorable time I listened to you, and in a day of salvation I have helped you.' Behold, now is the favorable time; behold, now is the day of salvation." Second, pray and ask Jesus to show you the needs of the people around you. As we see others through God's eyes, their need for Him becomes clear. Third, remember that you are sharing the most important aspect of your life. It's interesting how people will behave like screaming maniacs during a football game and yet be embarrassed to share about the God of the universe. Keep it in an eternal perspective. Are you really embarrassed of Jesus? Fourth, remember God has called you and me to be "witnesses." We are only expected to share what we have seen Jesus do in our own lives. We are not required to know every answer to every question. Relax. You know the miracles Jesus has performed in your life.

Three ways to prepare for sharing your faith are: (1) take a class on witnessing or apologetics, or even an overview of the Bible to help you gain confidence in sharing with others; (2) find a tool that will help you share your faith. (On the resource page, you'll see a booklet entitled *Steps to Peace with God*; it provides a simple means to present Christ.); and (3) if you have plans to share with someone, ask others to pray for you during that time.

Jesus promises that He will finish what He has begun (Philippians 1:6). While we often feel pressure to get "results," remember that although you may present the Gospel, only Jesus can save. Our heavenly Father is like the shepherd who searches diligently for the lost sheep. We can help guide the lost who are near us.

Revival Truths

- A pure heart helps us see others through Jesus's eyes.

- It's important that we are not so busy doing our own thing that we miss Jesus's direction to share with others around us.

The Son of Man has come to save that which was lost.

MATTHEW 18:11 NKJV

Walking
in the Light
of God's
Word

Just Like You

Your testimonies also are my delight and my counselors.

PSALM 119:24 NKJV

Jesus understands. The real God is One who came to earth and lived among us in the person of Jesus. And because He did that, Jesus is able to understand and relate to all of our human experiences and emotions. The Bible clearly reveals that Jesus knew what it was like to be hungry, thirsty, and tired. He knew what it was like to be criticized, misunderstood, betrayed, and abandoned. Crowds of people frequently ridiculed Him, and He faced unimaginable physical pain on the cross. He knows what it's like to hurt, both physically and emotionally. Identifying with the Savior allows the Holy Spirit to deepen your gratitude for His love and to deepen your burden for others who need to know Him.

This particular truth can be comforting for us, especially when we are in the midst of painful circumstances ourselves. During these times, it's often helpful to realize we have a Savior who is praying for us and that the One who is praying for us understands our world. He's experienced the same feelings that we have. Although Jesus hasn't experienced the same set of circumstances, He has felt the same emotions. Just like you and others around you, Jesus has suffered:

- Rejection by his own people (Luke 4:14–30; Mark 6:1–6).

- Abandonment by His disciples (Mark 14:43–50, 66–72).

- Disappointment by people closest to Him (Matthew 17:1–5).

- A lack of acceptance by family and friends (13:57).

- Criticism by the religious leaders (Luke 20:17–20; 22:1–6).

- Great loss and sadness after losing a friend or loved one (Matthew 7:1–5).

- Feeling unappreciated even after meeting other's needs (Luke 17:11–19).

It can bring comfort and delight to us to know that we have a God who understands. Meditate on the amazing truth that Jesus can relate to the emotions you and others are going through. He rejoices during your successes and sympathizes during your struggles. Take a few moments to live out Psalm 119:24. Let the testimony of Christ be your delight.

- *It means the most to me that Jesus experienced* _____ *because I . . .*

Now, express your wonder and gratitude to the One who understands:

Jesus, I feel grateful/hopeful/amazed and filled with delight when I think about how You experienced _____. Thank You for being the kind of God who lived here on earth so that You can identify with me. Holy Spirit, make me the kind of person who can bear others' burdens and thus fulfill the law of Christ—the law of love (Galatians 6:2).

M2. A Spirit-empowered disciple expresses and extends the kingdom of God while sharing compassion, justice, love, and forgiveness.

SPIRIT-
EMPOWERED
Faith

Day 2

Indicators of Revival

The evangelist Charles Finney noted seven indicators of a coming revival. Many of these are components that lead us to evangelism. Let's examine each of these signs since their presence may indicate an awakening. Are these signs operative in your life?

1. Revival comes when the sovereignty of God signals a revival is at hand. Do you sense a movement of the Spirit of God in your own life? Is your spirit drawing to God's Spirit? Do you have a desire to be intimate with Jesus Christ?

2. Revival comes when wickedness grieves and humbles Christians. Does the wickedness of the world distress you as a follower of Christ? When you read the newspaper or look at television or the internet, does this information grieve you? Have you reached a point as you pray about this wickedness that your own wickedness grieves you? Your own pet sins? Your own lack of faith or of love? Your own lack of obedience to Jesus?

3. Revival comes when followers of Christ pray for revival. Do you pray for Jesus to awaken His church in this country? Do you pray that an awakened church will reach out and touch the souls of men and women spiritually and socially?

4. Revival comes when ministers especially direct their attention toward revival. Have you noticed your pastor is preaching and teaching more and more about the need for an awakened nation? An awakened church? As a lay minister of the Gospel, are you praying for and interested in an awakened heart? An awakened body of Jesus?

5. Revival comes when Christians begin to confess their sins to one another. Is this indicator operative in your life? Are you conscious of sin in your life? Do you have a desire to confess your sins to Jesus and those you offend? Do you have an accountability partner or group?

6. Revival comes when followers of Christ are willing to make the sacrifices necessary to carry on the movement God has started, regardless of the personal cost. Are you at a point where you see that nothing is more important in your family, your city, your state, this nation, or the world than a relationship with Jesus? Are you willing to sacrifice if Jesus should ask? Are you willing to say to God, "God, I love You and I trust You so much. You are my Daddy. I will give You everything I've got, and You can use it any way that You want." Are you willing? Are you willing to be willing?

   Bill Bright is a good example of someone willing to sacrifice for his relationship with Jesus. As a wealthy young businessman with international concerns, Bill listened when Jesus spoke to him and his wife, Vonette. They got on their knees and turned everything over to Christ. As a young man, he had promised his wife an expensive home in Beverly Hills, yet they turned it over to Jesus and signed a contract to give everything to God. They presented their lives as a living sacrifice, and the Lord blessed them in a fabulous way through the ministry of Campus Crusade for Christ (now named CRU). Jesus is not your employer. He's your Lord. Are you willing to be His slave? Sometimes we think sacrifice is a big deal, but it's really just a daily choice.

7. Revival comes when ministers and laity are willing for God to promote spiritual awakening by whatever instrument He pleases. For example, are you willing for Jesus to use you to promote this movement? Will you allow Jesus to use your children, or do you

have plans for their future that wouldn't permit them to follow His call? The Lord does not call everyone into full-time vocational ministry, but He does call all into full-time service for Him.[43]

> *"Revival is no more a miracle than a crop of wheat.*
> *Revival comes from heaven when heroic souls enter the*
> *conflict determined to win or die—or if need be, to win*
> *and die!"* – Charles Finney

Revival Truths

- The seven indicators of a coming revival are: (1) God's sovereign moving in the church, (2) grief and humility over wickedness, (3) prayers for revival, (4) pastors focusing on revival, (5) Christians beginning to confess sins to each other, (6) Christians willing to sacrifice, and (7) pastors and laity willing for God to promote spiritual awakening by whatever instrument He pleases.

- Jesus is our Lord, and He calls on us to present our lives to Him as living sacrifices.

Will you not revive us again, that your people may rejoice in you?

PSALM 85:6

Face to Face

You, O Lord, are a God full of compassion, and gracious,
longsuffering and abundant in mercy and truth.

PSALM 86:15 NKJV

Take the next few moments to imagine the character of the real God and
how He might relate to you. The psalmist tells us that the real God is overflowing with compassion for you and then longs for you to be a source of comfort
and witness to others.

Imagine one of your most difficult days. Think about one of those days
when conflicts with family, work pressures, or relationships with friends were
at their hardest. Imagine a day when nothing seems to go well; you're overwhelmed and feeling very alone.

At the very moment, when things seem their worst, imagine that you come
face to face with Jesus. Are you afraid He'll lecture you or tell you how you
could have done things better? Are you afraid He'll shake His head in disappointment and say, "How many times have I told you . . .?" Are you worried
that He'll walk past you and not even notice the stress on your face or the sadness in your eyes? Or perhaps you're scared that He might notice those things
but just not take the time to care.

The real Jesus would be full of compassion. He would look at you with the
kindest eyes and warmest smile. He would give you a warm embrace and ask
about your day. Jesus would listen as you tell Him about your struggles. He would
be attentive and genuinely want to know how you feel. Jesus would reassure you:

- I'm not going to inspect you or tell you what you've done wrong.

- I want to provide for you.

- I want to give you strength and encouragement for this day.

- I'm not distant or uninvolved. I care deeply about what you're
  going through.

- I was with you every moment of today—laughing when you laughed, crying when you cried.

- My heart hurt each time you experienced something difficult. I was present with you then and I am here for you now.

- I'll never leave you because I love you. I'm not disappointed in you. I feel great compassion for you.

- I want my compassion to give you the stamina to face the day. My compassionate love for you is unwavering, unchanging, and never-ending.

From a grateful heart, ask the Holy Spirit to lead you to those struggling and alone.

God, thank You for Your compassion. Thank You for being to me "the God of all comfort" as I yield to the Holy Spirit's prompting and power that I might "comfort others with the very same comfort" (2 Corinthians 1:2–4). Lead me in sharing both the Gospel and Your compassion with others in my life.

M2. A Spirit-empowered disciple expresses and extends the kingdom of God while sharing compassion, justice, love, and forgiveness.

Day 3

A Prepared Heart

Many years ago at the Forest Home Conference Center in California's San Bernardino Mountains, a young Billy Graham knelt down by a stump with his Bible. He knew that intellect alone couldn't answer his questions about the authority of Scripture. He needed to have faith in his heart that God's Word was true. Billy prayed, "Oh, God; I cannot prove certain things. I cannot answer some of the questions . . . people are raising, but I accept this Book by faith as the Word of God."[44] He was making a commitment to go proclaim God's Word faithfully, and he knew that in order to do that, his heart had to be prepared by faith.

A daily openness for evangelism comes first with a daily openness to Jesus. Each of us must be able to pray, "Jesus, I'm open to You today. I want to be obedient to whatever You put before me." If our attitude isn't right, we can't be available for Him to work through us. We need to remember that no matter what we have planned, our day—each day—belongs to Jesus.

> *"Revival is . . . God's quickening visitation of His people, touching their hearts and deepening the work of grace in their lives." – J. I. Packer*

Sometimes I get so caught up in the "work" of God that my heart attitude is one of production rather than people. When I get on an airplane, it's often the first time I've had time alone in quite a while. My flesh says, "Oh, Jesus, don't let anybody sit by me who will take my time." I know that's not an open attitude, but sometimes I really feel that way. I'm sure I can trust Jesus completely to know my needs and care for me, but my flesh is selfish. He knows when I need time to remain alone, and He knows when I need to share His Word with others.

Perhaps the key to a prepared heart is in how you start your day. We see the example of Christ making time in the early morning to be alone to pray (Mark 1:35). What is your attitude in starting your day? Do you get a jump-start on your to-do list, or do you first consult the Master of the universe about *His* plans for you? Are you willing to get up in the morning and say to Father God, "I'm your slave. I want to have an intimate relationship with You today. I want to sense Your presence all day long. I know I have plans, but I want to be available for Your plans. I want You to guide me to a soul today—someone who needs You as much as I needed You before I came to know You."

If you begin the day with this heart attitude, you will be prepared for whatever Jesus brings across your path. Though you may not directly speak to someone today, you will still share Christ in your actions because of your open-heart attitude. The key attitude is openness toward Jesus, to whomever He leads you to and for whatever reason. Once you open your heart, keep it open during the day. Paul calls believers to "pray without ceasing." By having this open heart during the day, you will hear Jesus's direction.

Many people are afraid to share their faith—mostly because they're afraid they won't have the right words to say. Yet Jesus promises in His Word that He will supply all our needs (Philippians 4:19), and He also promises to give us the words to say when we need them if we have an open heart to hear. His words do not come back empty (Isaiah 55:11). Today, make a fresh commitment for God to direct your life and use it to tell others about Jesus.

Revival Truths

- Our attitude needs to be open to Jesus's daily will for our lives.

- If we are open to Jesus, He will direct us to those with whom we can share.

- Openness to Jesus begins at the first part of the day.

In your hearts honor Christ the Lord as holy, always being prepared to make a defense to anyone who asks you for a reason for the hope that is in you; yet do it with gentleness and respect.

1 PETER 3:15

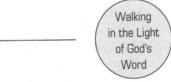

Walking
in the Light
of God's
Word

Just for You!

As each one has received a gift, minister it to one another,
as good stewards of the manifold grace of God.

1 PETER 4:10 NKJV

Imagine a beautiful, many-sided diamond, brilliant in color and clarity. This is the image that Peter has in mind when he speaks of God's "manifold"–– many-sided grace. Just as a diamond has many facets that reflect light in a unique and stunning way, God's grace has many aspects. Each side of his grace becomes visible when we experience His love in our lives and then share His love with others.

God offers this multi-faceted diamond to you as a gift, with each side of the diamond representing the grace you need at various times in your life. He offers you loving acceptance when you're feeling unlovable or different, affection and care when you're lonely or need reassurance, appreciation for your efforts, approval as His beloved child, and comfort when you are in pain. He wants to give you the gifts of encouragement when you are down, respect for you as an individual, security in the midst of uncertainty, and support for when you are overwhelmed. These gifts He lovingly offers to you. You've done nothing to deserve them and nothing to earn them. That's God's grace!

Take the next few moments to remember a time when you felt discouraged and God encouraged you through His Word, a song, a family member, or a friend. Or remember a time when you felt overwhelmed, and He gave you a sense of peace and security or brought someone along to support you.

- *God, I remember a time when I felt _____ and you offered your grace to me by . . .*

Be sure to thank Him for this gift. He gave it just for you, and as you celebrate His love and grace, it sensitizes your heart to freely give this same love to others.

God, thank You for Your grace. Your love and grace have so many facets. I am thankful that You freely share them with me. Thank You for being a God who is generous to meet my needs as You prompt and empower me to startle people in my life with this same love. Lead me today to someone I can impart Your love and hope to.

P2. A Spirit-empowered disciple startles people with loving initiatives to give first.

Day 4

An Available Day

David McKenna, former president of Asbury Theological Seminary, wrote, "We are a generation of spiritual doers who do not have the time or patience to exercise the spiritual disciplines of 'being.' As an evangelical activist myself, I realize . . . [that we] minimize prayer and maximize planning." Later, he added, "Jesus' example of working with His disciples and Paul's emphasis on the Body of Christ refute this notion. Our 'being' and 'doing' require mutual accountability in the Christian community as well as personal accountability to God."[45]

How do you plan your time? Do you plan your own time or do the events and urgency of the day plan it for you? Or do you just let it happen—in response to Jesus? How flexible are you to the moving of the Holy Spirit? It is possible for our days to become so tightly packed with activities that there is no time available to allow a move of Jesus.

Consider how you make decisions about whether to commit to something for yourself or your family. When an opportunity arises, do you stop and ask God's opinion, or do you just say yes because it might sound like a good idea? I'm not talking about hours on our knees, but even just a quick prayer, "Jesus, is this okay with you?" Doing so will give a check in your spirit about His plan.

I've heard this saying: "If the devil can't make you bad, he'll make you busy." We have bought into productivity hook, line, and sinker. Not that being productive is bad. And not that doing good things is wrong. What causes problems is that we're so tied up doing things we thought were a good idea but were outside the will of Jesus, that we have no time to respond when He calls us to a specific task. We don't like to wait on God. In our waiting, we often feel "lazy." So we fill our time. But at what expense?

> *"Revival is nothing more than a new beginning of obedience to the Word of God." – Charles Finney*

The Lord told Ezekiel, "And I sought for a man among them who should build up the wall and stand in the breach before me for the land, that I should not destroy it, but I found none." (Ezekiel 22:30). God deeply desires you to stand in the gap for your family, your friends, your neighborhood, your city, your country, and your world. The question is, are you available?

Jesus is looking for men and women to stand in the gap for their neighbors and loved ones. How are you standing in the gap? Or how could you be standing in the gap? You can pray, "Today, Lord, I want to stand before you. I want to be intimate with you. I want to stand in the gap today. Order my steps so that I am always doing exactly what you want me to be doing."

Do you think Jesus was lazy? Probably not. And yet, He often appeared to take His time in situations we would see as requiring immediate action. Consider the story of Lazarus in John 11. One interesting point in this story is that while Lazarus was on his deathbed, Jesus remained away two more days. The events of those two days are so insignificant that John didn't even record them. We know now how the story ends, but at the time it actually happened, no one knew except Jesus Himself. Jesus was available to be where the Father directed, regardless of the circumstances around Him and what *appeared* to be right. How available are you?

Revival Truths

- Our day can be random or planned.

- It is our responsibility to be available for Jesus's use, regardless of our own plans.

- Our availability often depends on how we consult Jesus before we make a commitment of our time.

For my thoughts are not your thoughts, neither are your ways my ways, declares the Lord. For as the heavens are higher than the earth, so are my ways higher than your ways and my thoughts than your thoughts.

Isaiah 55:8–9

Walking in the Light of God's Son

I See You

He looked around to see who had done this thing.

MARK 5:32

Jesus was a busy guy. He was always involved in the lives of people. On one particular day, He was hurriedly moving through the crowd because of the impending death of a religious leader's daughter. Jesus was occupied. He was taking care of "important" business. But if we were able to look closely, we would see that Jesus didn't miss a thing. The need of just one, simple, unassuming lady got his attention and His lavish provision.

There she was, on the outskirts of the crowd. She was someone whom no one had noticed. She was outside all the hustle and bustle of life but was still overwhelmed by the weight of her need. She'd tried to fix the crisis. She'd tried to solve the problem. She'd tried all that she could, but her need, her pain, and her struggle had only gotten worse.

Sometimes we try to solve things on our own. We try to fix the crisis, but things only seem to get worse. Some of us, like the lady in Mark 5, are on the periphery of the crowd. We're spectators, watching Jesus take care of the "big things," and wonder if He notices *our* need.

Picture yourself in the scene of Mark 5. You're the one who's tried to fix things. You've tried to solve the challenges of life, but things have only gotten worse. You're the one who is surrounded by people, but those people haven't been sensitive to your needs. You might be standing on the edge of the crowd and have a growing sense that people in your life haven't noticed your needs, much less been a part of meeting them.

Now imagine, in the midst of that scene, the crowd suddenly stops. And Jesus, who's been heading in another direction, turns around and looks at you. He looks into your eyes, looks deep into your heart and then speaks with tender words: "Dear One, You just touched me. Your pain, your need, the weight of your struggle has just touched Me." Jesus takes the next few moments to speak to the issues of your heart. He comforts the pain you feel. He calms every fear. He soothes every disappointment and addresses every need, and now He sends you to do the same for others!

Jesus, thank You for noticing me and my needs. Thank You for not being too busy. Freely I have received Your attention and notice, Your love and care; empower my sharing the same with those in my life (Matthew 10:8).

M8. A Spirit-empowered disciple attentively listens to others' stories, vulnerably share their story, and is a sensitive witness of Jesus's story as life's ultimate hope.

Day 5

Full-Cycle Evangelism

Have you ever noticed the motley crew Jesus had as followers? Most of them were poor peasants—generally farmers and fishermen. He had Judas, a money-grabbing traitor; Peter, a swaggering, egotistical braggart, always getting his foot in his mouth when he should have been silent; James and John, ambitious boys who eventually would try hard for the top seats in the kingdom. He also had Matthew, a despised Roman tax collector. He even had at least one prostitute as well as some other women of questionable reputations. What a hopeless group on which to build a kingdom of purity, modesty, humility, and holy principles! Not a one with any moral sense.

Who would have expected anything but ignominious defeat and disastrous ruin of this group once it lost its charming and powerful leader? But Christ welded this disparate crowd into a Spirit-filled, power-baptized, evangelizing, crusading, martyr-making, world-shaking organization. The group would conquer kingdoms, lifting putrid civilizations out of their despair and ruins onto the high plateaus of nobility and usefulness. Eventually, His followers through the centuries would redeem people by the millions!

Jesus expects no less from us, broken sinners that we are. As Peter and John carried the message of Christ, we too are called to carry the message of Christ. Our purpose to share the good news is for salvation, but there is a second purpose. In Matthew 28:19, Jesus tells us to make *disciples* of all nations.

> *"Revival and evangelism, although closely linked, are not to be confused. Revival is an experience in the Church; evangelism is an expression of the Church."* – Paul S. Rees

Often, the word *disciple* can be even more intimidating than the word *evangelism*. Part of the reason is discipleship takes a bigger commitment, something we are often reluctant to do. The word *disciple* means "learner." It's impossible to learn from someone without an investment on the part of both the pupil and the teacher. Jesus's example was one of total devotion to those who would believe and follow. Does He ask any less of us?

Full-cycle evangelism is helping those who accept Christ to grow in maturity so they can share their faith with others. We are saved not just for our benefit but to share with others. As people make commitments to Christ, we must love them enough to say, "Could we meet once a month (or once a week) to simply go through a basic Bible study together?" Some great Bible studies are available to use in follow-up. (See the Resource page for several.) Someone who is brand-new in the faith can use these studies to help someone else grow in their relationship with Christ.

You need to be willing to sacrifice. Remember the sixth point from Charles Finney: to sacrifice whatever God requires (see day two of this chapter). That sacrifice most often is in the form of time and love.

Revival Truths

- Jesus uses unlikely characters to spread His Gospel.

- God calls us not just to evangelism but to discipleship.

- Discipleship requires sacrifice and commitment.

For "everyone who calls on the name of the Lord will be saved." How then will they call on him in whom they have not believed? And how are they to believe in him of whom they have never heard? And how are they to hear without someone preaching? And how are they to preach unless they are sent? As it is written, "How beautiful are the feet of those who preach the good news!"

ROMANS 10:13–15

Walking
in the Light
of God's
Son

The Source of Love

Let us love one another, for love is of God;
and everyone who loves is born of God and knows God.
He who does not love does not know God,
for God is love.

1 JOHN 4:7–8 NKJV

We see daily evidence that people are having trouble loving. Gang violence, the increase in divorce, racial tensions, and hate crimes all point out that loving one another is often harder than we think.

How about you? Are you having trouble loving? Do you have difficulty showing love to any particular person or type of person?

In 1 John 4, we read that love is from God. He's the source of all love. It comes from Him. So if we're running out of love, we have to look to Him for the supply. Secondly, the verse tells us that if we do not love, we have not come to know God. If we're having trouble loving someone, especially those who do not yet know Jesus, then we haven't come to truly know God or deeply experience His true love. Here's what that might look like:

- If we view God as a stern, inspecting dictator, we may tend to inspect other people. We might have a hard time giving grace to others, giving second chances, or offering forgiveness.

- If we view God as one who is always disappointed, then we may come to believe that others can never measure up. We might have trouble seeing the positive attributes in ourselves and other people.

We might have trouble being grateful for God's blessings or appreciative of others' care for us.

- If we view God as distant or uninvolved, we may come to believe that God doesn't notice our needs, so it may be hard to notice anyone else's. We may find it hard to trust other people. We may have trouble getting close to other people.

In contrast, if we view God as one who looks forward to being with us and is excited to love us, then we can respond to others in the same way. We can be free to notice other's needs. We are able to give care, love, grace, and forgiveness because we have experienced those attributes in our relationship with God (Matthew 10:8).

Lord Jesus, here am I—"send me" to those who need You. Please help me to experience more and more of Your love so that I am free to love others well.

P9. A Spirit-empowered disciple demonstrates God's love to an ever growing network of "others" as He continues to challenge us to love "beyond our comfort."

SPIRIT-
EMPOWERED
Faith

Looking Ahead

As we see the results of revival—evangelism—we see a little more of our part in God's plan. In chapter 9, we'll discover how God uses the past, the present, and even the future to work together for His unfolding plan.

CHAPTER 9

A KEY TIME in Revival History

At the end of the twentieth century, twenty years ago, Campus Crusade (now called CRU) President Bill Bright pointed to four elements coming together for a worldwide movement of God's Spirit and worldwide evangelistic outreach. Those four have never existed in prior Christian church endeavors, according to Bright. They are: strategy, resources, technology, and people.[46]

1. Strategy. We have a plan for worldwide evangelism that has come from prayer and evangelistic movements, including AD 2000 and Beyond, and Mission America.

2. Resources. We've got more money in Christian hands than ever before. In the United States alone, for funding Christian ventures, $13 trillion will change hands in the next decade from one generation to the next, Bright reported. Also, in the midst of this potential funding, the resourcing agencies and individuals are gathering together to more effectively distribute their funding. These groups meet regularly, meet the mission and ministry agencies, allow them to share what they are doing, and then proceed to invest. Never before has this occurred in the history of the Christian church.

3. Technology. We've never had the opportunity to communicate around the world so inexpensively and so quickly. We can spread the claims of Christ quickly through television, radio, and the internet.

4. People. Many Christians are coming together in vocational service to God. For example, since 1998, men and women have attended the Finishers Conferences, designed for workers who

want to move from success to significance with their lives. Those attending have arrived at midlife of their career and are considering a move to using their skills with Christian agencies. A good tool for you to learn more about how to make this movement in your own life is Bob Buford's book *Halftime.*

Bill Bright was describing several key elements that are now converging and expanding in Jesus's church today. These converging elements can bring about the greatest spiritual awakening the world has ever experienced, for these converging revival streams are more powerful than any seen previously. God is fanning the flames of a great awakening. Dr. Bill Bright's insights were and are like a spiritual fulcrum for such a time as this.

Day 1

Lessons from the Past

In 1858 the United States was in turmoil. The economy was weak. One of the major political parties was dissolving over the slavery issue. Civil War was imminent. Detractors believed, with good cause, that America would not survive.

During this time, one of the old churches in New York City, the old North Dutch Church, was also in a desperate condition. The church had lost its people. They had moved away. The leadership of the church could not even find an ordained clergy to pastor the fleeing congregation.

A New York businessman named Jeremiah Lanphier was invited to lead the church. Not knowing what to do, he developed handbills and distributed them throughout the area to businesspeople, inviting them for prayer on Thursdays. The initial meeting began at twelve o'clock, and no one arrived until twelve-thirty. By one o'clock, six people had become a part of this meeting. The next week twenty gathered, and the following week, forty. Within six months, thousands of people were gathering at lunch to pray for the nation. The newspapers covered the meetings. The press accounts flowed, and the stories were inspiring. Here are two, as recounted in *America's Great Revivals.*

> One time a man wandered into the Fulton Street
> meeting who intended to murder a woman and then
> commit suicide. He listened as someone was delivering

a fervent exhortation and urging the duty of repentance. Suddenly the would-be murderer startled everyone by crying out, "Oh! What shall I do to be saved!" Just then another man arose and with tears streaming down his cheeks asked the meeting to sing the hymn, "Rock of Ages, Cleft for Me." At the conclusion of the service both men were converted.

Another time an aged pastor got up to pray for the son of another clergyman. Unknown to him, his own son was sitting some distance behind him. The young man, knowing himself to be a sinner, was so impressed hearing his father pray for another man's son that he made himself known to the meeting and said he wanted to submit to God.[47]

Within two years, one million people had made commitments to Christ through this lay-led prayer movement that spread from New York into other cities in the nation, often filling every public building at lunch day after day, Monday through Friday. Professional ministers were on the sidelines. People were experiencing the heart of God.[48]

> *"In revival the things of heaven become all important, the things of earth of much less importance." – Anonymous*

Yet, surprisingly little has been written about Jeremiah C. Lanphier. At a time of national turmoil and uncertainty, Jesus chose a most unlikely prospect and a most unlikely church to lead one of the greatest works in the history of this nation.

God uses "the foolish things of the world to put to shame the wise," the apostle Paul wrote (1 Corinthians 1:27 NKJV). Although you may feel foolish or unworthy to be used by Jesus, history is clear that God will use unlikely people to bring about great change. Do not underestimate the power of Christ to work His will in His own way. The Prayer Revival of 1858 was a climax of great political, social, economic, and spiritual desperation. The concerted prayer aligned our nation to receive an outpouring of heaven. God brought those two circumstances—a time of desperate need and of concerted prayer—together for revival among the people, and He used an ordinary man in the process.

Are you willing to trust Jesus to use you in any way He desires?

Revival Truths

- God's ways are different from our ways.

- Jesus chooses unlikely people to carry out His plan.

- We choose to submit to God's desire to use us.

God chose what is foolish in the world to shame the wise; God chose what is weak in the world to shame the strong.

1 CORINTHIANS 1:27

Walking in the Light of God's People

Great Reward

The law of the Lord is perfect, converting the soul; The testimony of the Lord is sure, making wise the simple; The statutes of the Lord are right, rejoicing the heart; The commandment of the Lord is pure, enlightening the eyes; The fear of the Lord is clean, enduring forever; The judgments of the Lord are true and righteous altogether. More to be desired are they than gold, Yea, than much fine gold; Sweeter also than honey and the honeycomb. Moreover by them Your servant is warned, And in keeping them there is great reward.

PSALM 19:7–11 NKJV

When we move from knowing the Word to actually allowing the Word to shape our choices, we are promised significant benefits now as a disciple of Jesus. David tells us that when we live in accordance with the Word of God our souls are restored, we receive wisdom and enlightenment, and we are filled with joy—in short, "there is great reward" (v. 11). In addition, the psalmist notes that God's Word serves to warn us, helping us to avoid choices that might have tragic consequences. When we live out God's Word in our everyday actions and decisions, we enjoy a clear conscience before God, are enabled to pursue right relationships, and are filled with the joy and peace that come from knowing that we are making wise choices. The call to discipleship is for us to see other Jesus followers enjoy these "Great rewards."

Can you think of an occasion when you helped another believer make an important choice that was influenced by the Word of God? What was the outcome? How might the outcome have been different if this person had made a choice that God's Word had not influenced?

How does your heart respond in knowing that God has called you to serve others to live out their convictions, aligned with His Word, so that they will have great reward? What does that do to your heart to know that God's ultimate desire is for you to be a part of making disciples who make disciples?

- I feel _____ when I consider that God wants me to live out my biblical convictions and then help others do the same.

Pause to pray with one or two others, celebrating God's heart for great reward, the provision of His Word, and the privilege of joining Him to make disciples.

M9. A Spirit-empowered disciple pours life into others, making disciples who in turn make disciples of others.

Day 2

The Current Climax

When we talk about the move of the Holy Spirit today, consider the following recent headlines and reports:

- "Faith-based Movies are 'Exploding' in Hollywood and 'Changing Lives"[49]

- "59,000 Gather to Wage War against Spiritual Inaction at The Send"[50]

- "Holy Spirit over Iran: Revival results in 3 million new believers today from just 100,000 in '94"[51]

- "Revival hits army base with 1,459 receiving Christ"[52]

- "PureFlix's Pro-Life 'Unplanned' Movie Takes 4th Place in Weekend Box Office"[53]

- "Over 19,000 Saved in Manila after Billy Graham's Grandson Preaches at Historic Gathering"[54]

- "Franklin Graham's 'Festival of Hope' Reaches 94,500 Colombians, Venezuelan Refugees with Love of Christ"[55]

We didn't hear of such powerful news events happening like this thirty years ago. Of course, opposition to the Spirit of God still thrives. It's happening all over the world, from arrests of house church leaders in China, where hundreds have been arrested in recent years—some were tortured; others were sentenced to labor camps—to even here in the United States. Consider just this headline: "Supreme Court won't hear case of HS football coach fired for on-field prayer." The accompanying story explained that on January 22, 2019, the US Supreme Court refused to hear the appeal of Joseph Kennedy, the assistant coach of a high school football team from Washington state. In 2015, school officials fired Kennedy from his coaching job at Bremerton High School when he refused to comply with their orders to discontinue his habit of praying on the field at the end of each game. The case made national headlines.[56]

Consider your world today. Is there an open door for the move of God's Spirit, or is opposition seemingly keeping the door closed? Is your heart open to the move of God's Spirit, or do you have roadblocks? Pray that Jesus would show you how to overcome those roadblocks. There are five signs that suggest America is ready for spiritual revival:

1. The Holy Spirit is being poured out in obvious ways.

2. Prayer is increasing in significant numbers and frequency.

3. Unity is sweeping biblical Christianity.

4. Brokenness is spreading among believers.

5. Among the church population, more people are becoming warriors for Jesus.

> *"Revival is . . . nothing more than a return to Apostolic Christianity."* – John Morgan

The twentieth century will be known as "The Martyrs' Century," as several mission agencies have reported that more people have lost their lives for their Christian faith during the century just concluded than in the previous nineteen centuries combined. Most of those martyrs were not Americans. And yet, we in the United States often see ourselves as "superior, more spiritual" Christians because of our culture and lifestyle. If we are children of God, following God's Word with the Holy Spirit as our guide, then we have to die to our own traditions that lift up our egos and self above others.

The Table Coalition (formerly Mission America Coalition) is a good example of Christians coming together in unity in America. This group is composed of more than six hundred general committee members spanning over eighty-one denominations and more than three hundred national, parachurch, and citywide ministries. The coalition includes over seventy national ministry networks involving over three thousand parachurch and citywide leaders. It meets several times a year at both local and national gatherings to put Gospel relationship into action in areas such as prayer, evangelism, discipleship, and justice.

Several years ago during a major prayer conference involving more than one hundred organizational leaders, Bob Reccord, former president of the mission board of the Southern Baptist Convention, stood up and said, "I pray as we come in these doors today, we have left our logos and our egos at the door because we come here as servant leaders of this nation to bow before God almighty and ask Him to move through us in unity to reach a lost and dying world."

Never before have all of these points converged into a single stream of activity—resources, people, strategy, or technology. God has promised a "new thing" and He is pouring out His Spirit now. Get under the downpour. Today, make a fresh commitment to increase your awareness of how world events are coming together in a unique fashion. Ask Jesus to reveal this awareness to you.

Revival Truths

- Jesus is working in a fresh way to bring together the course of human events for His Kingdom.

- There is both openness and opposition to the move of God's Spirit.

The Lord will wait, that He may be gracious to you; and therefore He will
be exalted, that He may have mercy on you. For the Lord is a God of justice;
blessed are all those who wait for Him.

ISAIAH 30:18 NKJV

Walking
in the Light
of God's
People

It Is the Lord

This was now the third time that Jesus was revealed to the disciples
after He was raised from the dead.

JOHN 21:14

Jesus is still making Himself known today! He may not be revealing
Himself with nets full of fish, but He is clearly making known His presence and
witness. He can reveal Himself through Scripture, or He can reveal Himself
through a testimony, the beauty of a summer day, or even in still and quiet
moments. Think about the moment when you surrendered to Jesus Christ.
How did God reveal Jesus to you? Was it through the example of a family member or a friend? Was it in a sermon or through the Scriptures? Was it through a
testimony? Did He meet and reveal Himself directly? How did you "hear" Him
and come to know Him?

- God revealed Jesus to me through _____

  _____.

- My yielding to Christ involved _____

  _____.

Pause quietly to give Him thanks: *Lord Jesus, receive the gladness of my
heart as an expression of my love.*

The disciples yielded to Christ's words to "cast the net on the right side" (v.
6), and similarly this is the role of each Christ follower. Christ reveals, and His
followers are to yield.

Now with one or two others, reflect on your own yielding to the revelation of Jesus: *Holy Spirit, prompt and empower my walk of yieldedness.*

M3. A Spirit-empowered disciple champions Jesus as the only hope of eternal life and abundant living.

Day 3

Hope for the Future

Interestingly, recent headlines in various newspapers and magazines have been most encouraging as we begin to see a shift in our nation. Perhaps, as George Gallup told a gathering of Christian leaders in Colorado Springs two decades ago, "The pendulum in America has already begun to swing, from materialism to spirituality, but it's a free-floating spirituality looking for a place to light."[57]

Hope for the future lies in the relationship that today's young people are developing with Jesus Christ. We see youth today standing up for Jesus, even to the point of death. The Columbine High School shootings remain a vivid example. On April 20, 1999, two high school students killed twelve students, one teacher, and themselves. How could Jesus work in this situation? Through this tragedy that rocked the nation, Christian students like Cassie Bernall and John Tomblin Jr. stood firm in their faith in Christ. Gunmen who professed to follow satan had targeted Christians and others.

"Do you believe in God?" one of the shooters asked Cassie Bernall. "Yes, I believe in Jesus Christ," she replied.

"Why?" he asked. The gunman murdered Cassie before she could reply.

But physical death did not shut the voice of this young martyr. Weeks and months later, students wore T-shirts with Cassie Bernall's picture, inscribed, "Yes, I believe." These students said, "We'll take our high school back for God." They're answering the question which the misled young executioner asked, a question parents and adult society have not adequately responded to: "Why?"

There is hope that though Cassie and her classmates may be the beginning of a new wave of Christian martyrs in the United States, a new generation is gripping the message of Jesus in a way the current generation never imagined.

In 2015, I met another example of the work of Jesus in the upcoming generations. At the Billy Graham library, I ran into David Marino, a young, slender man in his early twenties. He said that he wanted to go to Greece and share Jesus's love and salvation with Muslims there. Four years later, in March 2019, he was back in America and came to have lunch with me at the Billy Graham Evangelistic Association. He is now married, and his beautiful young wife is originally from Iran. They live in Athens and daily go out into the public square, playing board games with Muslim refugees (becoming champion competitors), telling them about Jesus, inviting them for meals, sharing Jesus's love and truth about salvation. To date, they have seen over 100 immigrants to Greece from the Middle East put their faith in Jesus as personal Lord and Savior. They have a house church with about twenty members who have come to Jesus in complete hope and rest. Their lives are full of tremendous joy as they meet together in prayer, praise, Bible study, and worship.

Worship Experience
Listen to "Fall Afresh," by Kari Jobe:
"Holy Spirit, fill this heart again."

Age is not a factor when it comes to living a Jesus-life. Timothy was a fellow traveler and official representative for the apostle Paul even though he was much younger than Paul. Paul exhorted Timothy to continue with the ministry, to be bold regardless of his age (1 Timothy 4:11–16). Despite being shy and reserved, Timothy was faithful and obedient. The question for adults today is: Can we willingly pass the torch to this new generation? Will we walk alongside them training, supporting, and encouraging them in what Jesus has called them to do? Are we willing to humbly step aside and allow God's future to come to pass?

On any Sunday at New Life Church, the largest church in Colorado Springs (with an average weekly attendance of about twelve thousand), hundreds of youth stand at the altar during the praise-and-worship part of the service.[58] These youth not only praise Jesus openly, but they also live each day in the same manner. These are not timid children who sing "Jesus Loves Me" once a week during a youth meeting. These are bold teens leading Bible studies in their schools, studying Christian apologetics, and sacrificing for the cause of Christ. Some have made trips to closed countries in order to drop Gospel tracts; others have fed the hungry, helped the disabled, and reached out to the lost youth in their city.

It's true, the youth of today don't look like the youth of my day. Their hair is sometimes purple, and they have earrings in places I couldn't imagine. Does it mean they love Jesus less? I don't think so. Does it mean they have a lesser calling into His service? No. No more than it meant John Wesley had lost his faith by rewriting "bar" tunes of the day with Christian lyrics. Jesus moves in each generation. Perhaps we would better serve today's youth to come alongside them to support their ministry. While they can learn from us, we can also learn from them.

The next generation is taking up the cross of Jesus with an intensity and purpose unmatched. We can have hope in our future.

Revival Truths

- God will continue to work in the future as He has worked in the past and present.

- Today's youth are committed to Christ.

- Adults can walk alongside the youth to support them in their ministry.

- We have hope for the future because of the youth of today.

And it shall come to pass afterward, that I will pour out my Spirit on all flesh; your sons and your daughters shall prophesy, your old men shall dream dreams, and your young men shall see visions.

JOEL 2:28

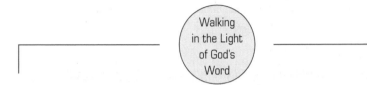

Walking in the Light of God's Word

Sharing the Glory of His Grace

Receive one another, just as Christ also received us, to the glory of God.

ROMANS 15:7

Imagine someone giving you a multi-faceted diamond with many aspects to its brilliance and worth. God's grace is just such a priceless multi-faceted gift!

Picture that one facet or "side" of His grace is His acceptance, and we have the opportunity and privilege to share it with others. "Accept one another, then, just as Christ accepted you, in order to bring praise to God" (Romans 15:7 NIV).

Who are some of the people in your life who might need a measure of God's acceptance shared through you? Maybe someone recently rejected? Someone who recently "failed" in some way? Someone struggling with relationships? Specifically reflect on how *different* millennials and Gen Z are from your generation—and then the Holy Spirit's challenge from Romans 15:7.

Acceptance might look like: giving another chance when someone has done something wrong; allowing the other person to think, act, or feel differently from you; loving that person anyway, in spite of offenses. Acceptance might sound like: "What you did was wrong, but I still love you and want a relationship with you; We do think differently on that issue, but I still want to be your friend; No matter what you do, I'm always here for you; We all mess up at times, but you can count on me as you work through this."

Consider several practical ways that God might want you to express His acceptance to others around you, especially next generations, maybe even in your own home. Share at least one of these demonstrations of His grace to another person today.

Dear Lord Jesus, please lead me to someone today who is feeling rejected, or to a person who feels like a failure, or to someone who is experiencing conflict in a relationship. Send me to someone very different than me. May I take initiative to embrace that person unconditionally and sacrificially, expressing Your acceptance toward him or her.

P3. A Spirit-empowered disciple discerns the relational needs of others with a heart to give of God's love.

Day 4

What Does God Promise?

During an International Student, Inc., youth retreat in Austin, Texas, I chatted with a twenty-seven-year old with a Ph.D. in computer science. He had returned from China, where he had been making $100,000 a year with a Chinese company—an extraordinary amount in that country. Five weeks before the retreat, Mr. Zhao accepted Christ, quit his job, and came back to the US to study the Bible with the goal of taking the Gospel to China. Talk about choice. I sat with this young Christian, mesmerized at his faith in the promises of Jesus.

Zhao told me, "I can see only about a year into my future, but I know my God can see the rest of my life." He had been sleeping on a couch in an apartment with two other believers in Austin, wanting to get into a Bible college or seminary and learn about Jesus. This man had come from nothing, achieved worldly wealth and success, and then made a choice to give it up to serve the Lord.

What does God promise Zhao? What does He promise us? Consider just a few of the promises of God:

- *He is worthy of our trust.* "Commit your way to the Lord; trust in him, and he will act" (Psalm 37:5).

- *He gives mercy.* "He saved us, not because of works done by us in righteousness, but according to his own mercy, by the washing of regeneration and renewal of the Holy Spirit" (Titus 3:5).

- *He offers forgiveness.* "Bearing with one another and, if one has a complaint against another, forgiving each other; as the Lord has forgiven you, so you also must forgive" (Colossians 3:13).

- *He has great love.* "We love because he first loved us" (1 John 4:19).

- *He gives strength.* "I can do all things through him who strengthens me" (Philippians 4:13).

- *He protects us from fear.* "When I am afraid, I put my trust in you" (Psalm 56:3).

- *He gives guidance.* "Your word is a lamp to my feet and a light to my path" (119:105).

- *He will never forsake us.* "For he has said, 'I will never leave you nor forsake you'" (Hebrews 13:5).

- *He gives peace.* "And the peace of God, which surpasses all understanding, will guard your hearts and your minds in Christ Jesus" (Philippians 4:7).

Mr. Zhao was willing to step out in faith, to test Jesus to see if He was true. His reward of knowing the faithfulness of Jesus will be great. If we are not willing to step out in faith, to go wherever Jesus leads, we may never know the depth of His promises for us. God's promises are precious to us; we need to know them and walk in them.

> *"Revival is . . . above everything else, a glorification of the Lord Jesus Christ, the Son of God. It is the restoration of him to the centre of the life of the Church."*
> – Martyn Lloyd-Jones

Jesus promises that all will have the opportunity to know Him. In the Muslim world, dreams are greatly respected. One woman had a dream that troubled her. When this woman was a teenager, her father had been a Christian but in the subsequent years, had left his faith. Several years later, this woman had a dream in which a being appeared who called himself Issa (the Arabic word for Jesus), saying, "Follow me."

The next day, the woman went to her father and asked, "Who is Issa?"

He said, "Well . . . that's God."

"And this Issa told me to follow him. What does that mean?"

"Well, that's God speaking to you."

Not satisfied with his answers, the woman persisted in seeking Jesus for years. Finally, she went to a Christian man whom she knew and asked about her dream. He explained the story of young Samuel who served in the temple. When the Lord called to Samuel, the boy called out and said, "Speak, Lord, for your servant hears" (see 1 Samuel 3:8–10). This Christian advised the woman to follow a similar course of action. The dream never occurred again, but in the following months, this woman came to believe in Jesus Christ because she knew about Issa. God keeps His promises.

Revival Truths

- God's promises are precious and true.

- We must step out in faith to see the deep faithfulness of Jesus.

> For all the promises of God in Him are Yes, and in Him Amen,
> to the glory of God through us.
>
> 2 CORINTHIANS 1:20 NKJV

Walking
in the Light
of God's
People

From Head to Heart

> I have come to judge those who think they see and make them blind.
> And for those who are blind, I have come to make them see.
>
> JOHN 9:39 TPT

Like a map, God wrote the Scriptures to point to eternal life through Jesus. Yet, the religious elite of His day would not go down the path.

- They memorized, but it never went from the head to the heart.

- They tried to act out other scriptures, but the words never changed their lives.

- They sought God but not the great gift of eternal life they said they pursued.

This is also true in the church today. There is so much study but little sanctification. There are many translations but not much transformation. The words of Jesus are not only for us to read, memorize, and sing about on Sunday morning, but they are for us to experience and practically walk out in our daily lives.

Get out of your head and into your heart. Jesus gave us the Holy Spirit that we would never be alone (14:16–17). When we read His Word, the Holy Spirit is with us to direct us so the external word becomes the internal word that results in the directed path for life today.

Listen to His voice instead of just reading the words. Is there a path, a direction, or step that He is leading you to take today?

Pray with one or two others and ask the Holy Spirit to speak to you from John 9, and then read the chapter. What biblical passage has He impressed on your heart? Now verbalize the lesson back to God in prayer: "Lord, I see where you showed great grace to the blind man. I need that grace today . . . I see where many people ignored the man but that you sought him out . . . I see where religious people read but never obeyed."

Now respond to what you *see* by doing what Jesus would do. Read His words, listen to His voice, and experience the blessing of practical obedience in your life today:

Jesus, You promised that Your Holy Spirit would lead me in all truth (John 16:13). I want to now follow in experiencing Your truth. Today, allow Your Word to go from my head to my heart. I commit to obey Your instructions.

M1. A Spirit-empowered disciple imparts the Gospel and their very life in daily activities and relationships, vocation, and community.

Day 5

Façades

Have you ever visited a movie set or seen the backside of a stage set? What looks like an actual building from the front you soon realize is nothing more than a façade. There is no real house or western street. There is no security or shelter in a façade—just a painted front held by a few two-by-fours for the duration of the play or movie. It doesn't take much to knock it over once the production is complete. It wasn't real to begin with.

Many believers today hold onto façades in their lives. Even though they have seen Jesus at work in the past and see Him at work today, they are not able to hold onto His promises for a new generation and the future. Consider some façades you might cling to: control, self-preservation, an "I can do it myself, thank you" attitude, self-competence, an unhealthy dependence on a relationship, your income level, the neighborhood in which you live, your kid's school, the kind of car you drive, the church you attend. The list goes on.

Perhaps there are façades in your life. Think about it for a moment: What do you cling to in place of Christ?

> *"I have learned to know beyond the shadow of doubt, that the will of God is the most delicious and delightful thing in the universe." – Hannah Whitall Smith*

"Sue" came to work in a ministry organization after a successful job where she supervised more than one hundred people and earned a substantial salary. She left a ten-year career and financial success because she felt a call to full-time ministry and wanted to obey. In the process, she saw her income take a nosedive, and her position of responsibility diminished. Though she felt at peace, there was a raw ache within her.

Eventually, Sue realized that she had derived all of her worth as a person from her job, her income, her position of control. She depended on a façade of stability when she needed to depend on Jesus. Through Sue's prayer and honesty with God, He showed her a better way. He reminded her of Ephesians 1:3–6, which declared that God loved her and chose her before He laid the foundation of the world. It didn't matter whether she was a top executive or a janitor. What mattered was Christ's love for her and her obedience to His call. Jesus had broken down the façade. He could build a real structure now.

Revival is possible only when we are focused and devoted to Jesus. Any façade we hold creates a form of idol worship, and revival cannot come without our hearts worshiping Christ alone.

Revival Truths

- We often depend on façades rather than the power of Jesus.

- Christ cannot work through us when we cling to façades.

- Jesus is willing to help us expose and remove those façades.

Everyone then who hears these words of mine and does them will be like a wise man who built his house on the rock.

MATTHEW 7:24

Walking
in the Light
of God's
Word

He Is Good

Teach me good judgment and knowledge,
for I believe Your commandments . . . You are good and do good.

PSALM 119:66–68

The Bible is more than rules and regulations. It's more than nice stories and parables. The Bible is like a love letter from God. God has written His letter, and He's hoping that we'll read it and respond authentically.

- We know that God's Word shows us what to believe about life.

- We hear how the Bible reveals how we should live our lives.

- But the often missed (and sometimes most critical) role of God's

Word is that it invites us into an intimate relationship with the Savior where we can be real, no façades, no fakes.

Here's a prime example: We all know that church leaders regularly emphasize the importance of the Ten Commandments. Remember those? Here are four of them.

- You shall not murder.

- You shall not steal.

- You shall not commit adultery.

- Honor your father and mother.

We're challenged to live according to the Ten Commandments and believe the critical insights about God's character and holiness. But when we study the Ten Commandments and don't experience the heart of the compassionate Father who gave us those commandments, we don't see the God who is love. We miss the message of compassion behind the Ten Commandments when we see only the "thou shalt nots" without recognizing the heart of love that lies behind them.

To live life beyond any façades, we need to explore: Why did God give us these commandments? Was it to raise a standard of moral behavior? Yes. Was it to give testimony of a righteous God? Of course. But Deuteronomy 10:13 also speaks of God giving these commandments for our own good. Evidently, our loving Father gave us these commandments because He didn't want His children to hurt themselves or one another. It's this type of heart intimacy with the Lord that prompts and empowers us to "get real."

Take the next few moments and consider how God has given us His Word (even His commandments) for your good. He has written down the Scriptures in order to keep you from harm. He loves you and does not want to see you hurt. It's this heart connection with the Lord that frees us from "pretending."

- *As I consider the Lord's care for me and how He wants good things for my life, I feel . . .*

God, thank you for giving us Your love letter in the Bible. Thank You that You have written everything that's contained in Your Word because You want what's good for me; You provide a safe place for me to be real!

W8. A Spirit-empowered disciple lives "naturally supernatural" in all of life as His Spirit makes the written Word (logos) the living Word (Rhema).

SPIRIT-
EMPOWERED
Faith

Looking Ahead

Jesus is always at work. He never sleeps. He has worked in the past, is working in the present, and will continue to work in the future. Ours is to embrace His will and work. Let's look ahead to Christ's specific work in our nation.

CHAPTER 10

JESUS REVIVED in Our Nation

Our nation has few spiritual moorings left. In 1962, a US Supreme Court decision removed prayer from the public schools. Today "Merry Christmas" has become "happy holidays." We rarely hear the name of "Jesus Christ" other than as a curse. The politically correct movement even replaced A.D., which stands for *anno Domini,* "in the year of the Lord," with C.E., or "of the common era," to show the current year. Yes, we are a country with minimal spiritual anchors. Charlie Jarvis, an attorney and the previous executive vice president of Focus on the Family, echoed the Russian writer Fyodor Dostoyevsky, saying, "If God is gone, all things are permissible."

The Bible says, "Righteousness exalts a nation, but sin is a reproach to any people" (Proverbs 14:34). God put this in place at the foundation of the world, knowing loving, biblical principles would be the best help to people in their relationships with each other and with Him.

In 1998, researcher and trend forecaster George Barna spoke to nearly two hundred pastors in Colorado Springs. One of the pastors asked George what he thought was going to happen in our nation. The noted commentator and author thought solemnly for a moment and then responded, "We are either going to have revival within the next ten years, or we are going to have anarchy."

After a moment of thoughtful silence, the pastor asked, "George, which do you think it will be?"

"I believe it will be anarchy," Barna replied. There was complete silence throughout the room as the pastors wondered at his response. Barna believes in Jesus and in revival. He even wrote the preface for my previous book, *Revival Signs.* Why would he choose anarchy?

The pastor pressed George for a reason.

"I'm not God," the pollster responded. "Revival is in the hands of God, and only He can see what He is going to do, but, if He doesn't intervene in the affairs of this nation, we shall have anarchy."[59]

Is God breaking through?

Twenty-one years after George Barna's prediction that we must either experience revival or anarchy, we are seeing grassroots revival. True to James Burns's laws of revival, which reveal that each revival is different in variety, this grassroots revival is not quite like any of those we have before seen. Tiny sparks of revival are lighting up simultaneously and seemingly disconnected all across America. Only in the last year, we have begun to see the Lord gather the sparks together and bring His body into oneness in Jesus.

The shift toward revival in the body of Christ in America over the last two decades has been subtle, almost like watching a baby grow. When my children were babies, I didn't realize how quickly they were growing when I was with them every day. But if I went away on a trip and then returned home, I could see little things had changed. One day, I blinked, and they could walk! This is how the current revival in America is growing.

Revival happens one person at a time. Because of that, the fate of the nation may literally hinge on how Christians maintain their walk with Christ. God can flow to the lost through His church. As others come to Christ and begin to grow through consistent time in God's Word, His truth will speak to the renewed heart and increase a burden for social justice. Remember, society is changed from the inside out to conform to God's Word. Revival is the precursor to explosive salvation of the lost, and that is the precursor to social justice.

Day 1

Who Is in Charge of the Nation?

William Penn once talked about the fact that if you won't have God, you will have tyrants. In the midst of the darkness of our nation, we wonder if it is spinning out of control. What do we believe? Is Jesus in charge? Consider just a few of the ills our country faces:

- We see a general disrespect for life through abortion, child abuse, and euthanasia.
- The abuse of opioids is epidemic.
- Crime remains a serious problem.

- High divorce rates destroy family stability.

- Inner cities are in chaos and decline.

- Workplace ethics are questionable at best.

- Truth is relative.

- Moral foundations, once embraced, now are crumbling.

The pessimist would look at our nation and say we don't have a prayer. The truth is that prayer is all we do have. It's our hope.

> *"Study the history of revival. God has always sent revival in the darkest days. Oh for a mighty, sweeping revival today."* – **Adrian Rogers**

And yet, people in the United States have a growing and intense interest in spiritual matters and biblical prophecy. On January 1, 2019, the YouVersion Bible App received more than one million new subscriptions in a single day—a 62 percent increase from January 1, 2018. Developers of the app currently have thirteen thousand devotional Bible-reading plans available in at least fifty languages.[60] Consider these article titles from the pages of America's leading news magazines:

- "Watch Billy Graham's 5 Greatest Sermons," from *Time Magazine*[61]

- "What the Bible Says about Secrets," from *The New York Times*[62]

- "Science Finds God: The achievements of modern science seem to contradict religion and undermine faith. But for a growing number of scientists, the same discoveries offer support for spirituality and hints of the very nature of God," from *Washington Post/Newsweek*[63]

When considering the dawn of a new millennium, Bill Bright, President Emeritus of Campus Crusade, wrote, "I'm standing on tiptoe with anticipation to see a great spiritual tidal wave sweep our land and envelope our whole globe. Our Lord came to seek and save the lost."[64]

Yes, Jesus is in charge, just as He always has been. Consider the ministry of Habakkuk. For decades, this Old Testament prophet prayed for his nation only to see it slip further into a moral abyss, spiritual lethargy. But God reminded Habakkuk of His involvement and promised His ways would continue: "For the earth will be filled with the knowledge of the glory of the Lord as the waters cover the sea. . . . He stood and measured the earth; he looked and shook the nations; then the eternal mountains were scattered; the everlasting hills sank low. His were the everlasting ways" (Habakkuk 2:14; 3:6). God was—and is—in charge. In the midst of corruption, God is still in command.

In contrast, Isaiah did not doubt the mighty hand of God: "Oh that you would rend the heavens and come down, that the mountains might quake at your presence—as when fire kindles brushwood and the fire causes water to boil—to make your name known to your adversaries, and that the nations might tremble at your presence!" (Isaiah 64:1–2). Are you convinced in your heart that God is in charge of all situations?

As a nation, Americans have not turned their hearts toward Jesus; because of that, we suffer consequences. Jesus's power to redeem, however, is never diminished. In the midst of our chaos is His peace and hope. In 1994, two Christian leaders were part of a private briefing with the President. Walking across the White House lawn after the meeting, one said to the other, "If God doesn't send revival, nothing else really matters." He meant that spiritual renewal for the country is necessary. Otherwise, we're hopelessly lost.

The other leader responded, "And, if God does send revival, nothing else really matters."[65] A spiritual awakening of America can and will turn this nation upside down.

Revival Truths

- Jesus is moving in a fresh way in our country.

- God is in charge, despite negative circumstances.

God my King is from of old, working salvation in the midst of the earth.

PSALM 74:12

Walking
in the Light
of God's
Word

Will the Real God Please Stand?

Can a woman forget her nursing child, and not have compassion on the son of her
womb? Surely they may forget, yet I will not forget you. See, I have inscribed you
on the palms of My hands; your walls are continually before Me.

ISAIAH 49:15–16 NKJV

No matter how dark the hours seem, what kind of God do you have?
How do you view Him? We all have different perceptions of God's character, a
slightly different view of Him and how He relates to us. Some of us see God as
more of a policeman, a guiding shepherd, a school principal, a well-meaning
doctor, a dictator, a stern but loving father, or a disinterested spectator. What's
your view of God?

Do you have an inspecting god? It's almost as if he has a heavenly tally
sheet and carefully records everything we do. This kind of god inspects our
every move and then relates to us according to how many good marks or bad
marks our tally sheet shows.

Do you have a disappointed god? He looks down at us and never likes
what he sees. He notices our attempts at living a good life but ultimately
shakes his head in disappointment. This kind of god might shrug his shoulders
because he's given up on us; he's just sure we won't get it.

Do you have a distant and uninvolved god? This kind of god is often too
busy to notice our small concerns. He hears us as we talk to him, but he sits
behind that big desk in heaven and gives us his half-hearted attention. He's nice
to us, but he often seems detached or maybe too distracted to care.

The real God is much different, and it's the kindness of the Lord that
prompts repentance and revival in our day. He is attentive and caring. He
doesn't look down from heaven with a tally sheet or sit behind a desk.

- The real God's care is so deep and so strong that even a mother's
  love pales in comparison.

- He thinks of you so often and is so excited about the possibility of a relationship with you that He's "tattooed" your name on the palm of His hand.

- He's not inspecting you; He's admiring His creation in you.
- God is not disappointed in you; He is excited to love you.
- God's not uninvolved; He is with you every moment of every day.

Pause to pray in celebration that He will not forget you:

God, help me to see and share the real You in our day. I want to know You more intimately so that as I better sense Your love for me, I can respond with deepened love for You and others, living out my part in personal revival.

L3. A Spirit-empowered disciple experiences God as He really is through deepened intimacy with Him.

Day 2

Living Like Jesus Is in Charge

Our country has reached a critical juncture, and it's time for courage, boldness, and speaking the truth. You may feel insignificant, but you'll never know how Jesus will use you until you obey the burden He places on your heart. If we believe Jesus is in charge, then we respond to His call, knowing it is to accomplish His purpose.

Each of us can and should respond. For Carolyn McKenzie and Marnie Ferree, the responses came to the ongoing threat our country faces from pornography and sexual addiction. These women didn't lead any organization or rise from a position of national power. They simply responded to a concern through the power of Jesus.

A public health nurse, Carolyn organized protests and filed complaints with the district attorney about the porn shops and strip clubs in suburban Memphis. Some people called McKenzie a hypocrite because she was fighting to close places she had never been inside. To handle this objection, McKenzie asked a vice cop to escort her through the rougher areas of Memphis. This policeman took her to "modeling agencies" and topless clubs. "I felt so discouraged," Carolyn recalled, "like there was no way I could ever begin to affect this industry." It was then she noticed the dancers. "I was surprised to find out many are actually clean-cut college or career girls. A lot of them are doing it simply because they need the money."[66] So she started leading these young ladies to Christ and helping them find other options to escape the sex industry.

"I look at these girls as the daughter I never had," she said. She organized a group called the Citizens for Community Values (CCV) of Memphis, led by Carol Wiley today. This organization partners with local churches to provide mentors to assist women with finding their way out of the industry. This often means providing basic resources, such as money to pay their bills, assistance finding new jobs, and medical care. It may also mean arranging for free legal representation and drug counseling. Today this grassroots ministry has helped over six hundred women in varying degrees by giving them an opportunity to leave the darkness of the commercial sex industry to come to the light of Christ's love and forgiveness.

Meanwhile, Marnie Ferree of Nashville works with sexually addicted women. Once caught in the web herself, Marnie has created a twelve-step support group to help heal the addiction. "There really is such a thing as sexual addiction. It's not just a male disease." Her addiction cost her her marriage. "I kept doing what I didn't want to do," she explained. That's the classic definition of addiction, and she traces the root of her sexual addiction to early childhood when a twenty-year-old family friend molested her (Marnie was only five at the time), and the abuse continued for years. As a teen, she became promiscuous and later married. Through the help of a Christian therapist and a twelve-step support group, she returned to Jesus.

"I came to know and serve the God who has changed my life. It's only through dependence on God that I'm able to assist these women." Marnie now has a master's degree in counseling and, through a workshop program she first established in 1997, works professionally with people struggling with sexual addiction. At the time, it was the first such program in existence for women. It now serves participants from all parts of the United States and into Canada. In 2001, Marnie's program received its official name, Bethesda Workshops, and added counseling opportunities for men and couples. Marnie has become a licensed marriage and family therapist with a reputation across the country as a pioneer in recovery from sexual addiction, especially for women. "For me, it's a visible sign of God's grace: He's taken my pain and sin, and He's using me to help others."[67]

Another woman making a difference in her world is Erin Fox-Clough. Erin works through a group home in Charlotte, NC, to reach out to the severely disabled and indigent. "I was plopped in the middle of all these beautiful, unique people," she shares. "They just wanted to make friends, be engaged, and be a part of life like everyone else." Erin is a singer, so she began using her gift to teach her new friends to sing and taking them to her church to lead music. "I could tell God was using my friends to soften hearts and to open eyes; they just needed a platform to do so," explains Erin. Jesus soon positioned Erin as a music teacher in an art center for adults with special needs. Every step of the way, the Lord was in charge—He provided the transportation and resources that Erin needed to share His love, using music as the vessel.[68]

Like these women, we can participate in Jesus's plan. When we do, we, too, will see the Spirit of God actively at work, and we will know He is more powerful than the evil we fight in the world.

> *"I am only one; but still I am one. I cannot do everything, but still I can do something. I will not refuse to do the something I can do." – Helen Keller*

Revival Truths

- We are to live our lives knowing God is in charge—it is difficult or even impossible to stand against evil if we don't trust Jesus.

- Jesus uses individuals who walk by faith to make a difference in their world.

- We make a difference by obeying Jesus and reaching one person at a time for Christ.

By faith we understand that the universe was created by the word of God, so that what is seen was not made out of things that are visible.

HEBREWS 11:3

Walking
in the Light
of God's
Word

Two Kinds of Love

He who has My commandments and keeps them, he it is who loves Me.
And he who loves Me will be loved by My Father,
and I will love him and manifest Myself to him.

JOHN 14:21

While we live in a time when it seems love is growing cold, we have received by way of the Holy Spirit's indwelling both the Father's love and the Son's love as the standard of all other love relationships. Herein lies the hope for us and our nation.

You may have never considered this before, but our Heavenly Father demonstrated love very differently from the Son.

- Throughout Scripture, God loves the Son by revealing all things to Him: "For the Father loves the Son and shows Him all He does" (5:20 NIV). It is the Father who commands, sends, and commissions as He demonstrates His love for the Son by showing Him all things. At the moment of your salvation, the Holy Spirit placed within you this same self-disclosing love of the Father. You have within you One who is longing to reveal to you eternal things!

- In response to the Father's revealing love, the Son loves the Father by yielding to His will. As a demonstration of His love for His Father, Jesus always yields to His Father. "I can do nothing on My own initiative" (v. 30 NASB). "I love the Father, I do exactly as the Father commanded Me" (14:31 NASB).

- In response to the Father's revealing, the Son's yielding is so complete that Jesus said, "Anyone who has seen Me has seen the Father" (v. 9 NIV). He perfectly represents His Father's will, ways, and heart because He and the Father are one.

- You have within you the One who is inclined to yield and longing to please the God who has revealed Himself to us. You have within you the One who longs to express and extend God's glory through a yielded life.

The very same love that Jesus and the Father experience with one another is now in us. Jesus lives within you, and He is in charge, empowering you to yield! Tell the Lord about your gratitude and humility, asking Him to engage you in a walk of revival.

God, I feel _____ when I consider that You live in me and want me to know You. I am especially grateful that the Holy Spirit prompts and empowers me to walk in Your wisdom, Your Word, and Your ways. I yield to Your leadership of my life. You are in charge!

M6. A Spirit-empowered disciple bears witness of a confident peace and expectant hope in God's Lordship in all things.

Day 3

God's Power in Our Nation

Historically, we have seen God's Spirit in our nation. These outpourings of God's Spirit and power are revealed in a pattern from history and give us reason to anticipate revival. The current events in our nation show the spiritual darkness that cloaks us. In the middle of this darkness, people are looking for light. The soul of a man or woman can find that light in a relationship with Jesus Christ. Many people are looking for such a relationship because they have had a cracked or broken relationship—out of the brokenness of the world.

The First Great Awakening in the United States prior to the American Revolution (during the early 1730s through 1760s) remains an example of national renewal and revival. Repentance, fasting, and prayer drew the nation to the Lord, releasing mercy, grace, and a withholding of judgment. Later, during the early 1790s, most denominations were shrinking in numbers, and alcoholism was rampant even in children as young as age eleven. This preceded the Second Great Awakening, again triggered by repentance, fasting, and prayer.

As we examine the heritage of our nation, especially the founding fathers, we see that they came to this country for freedom to worship Christ. American President John Adams said, "The general principles in which the fathers achieved independence were . . . the general principles of Christianity. Now I will avow that I then believed and now believe, that those general principles of Christianity are as eternal and immutable as the existence and attributes of God." Benjamin Franklin said, "Whoever shall introduce into public affairs the principles of primitive Christianity will change the face of the world." And the patriot Patrick Henry, best known for declaring, "Give me liberty or give me death," also said, "It cannot be emphasized too strongly or too often that this great nation was founded not by religionists, but by Christians, not on religions, but on the Gospel of Jesus."[69]

Clearly, our nation has strayed from this Christian foundation. Its citizens have adopted personal gain as their modern creed. For instance, in an article entitled "The Cheating Game," *U.S. News & World Report* writers concluded that when it comes to cheating, "Everyone's doing it."[70] Divorce is common and often easily obtained. One in four or five children (22 percent) live in homes with their mothers only—no fathers—according to the US Census Bureau.

The family unit is in disarray. The American Association for Marriage and Family Therapy reports the findings of national surveys showing that 25 percent of married men and 15 percent of married women have cheated on their spouses.[71] Spousal abuse, both emotional and physical, is increasingly common, as is child abuse. The violence that children witness (and at times are victims of) in the home or in the media has taken its toll. The FBI reported that of the 17,251 homicides in America in 2017, 17 percent of the killers were age twenty-two or younger.[72]

> *"The appearance of revivals owes nothing to chance; they are a witness to God's sovereignty."* – *James Burns*

In spite of all that seems wrong with our country, I believe grassroots revival is not just coming but is here and growing. As we discussed in other sections of this book, we see:

- A return to the centrality of Jesus and the cross.
- A return to the Bible devotionally for faith and practice.
- An explosion of witnessing and telling others about Jesus Christ.
- A movement of social justice as people begin to obey the Scriptures.
- Prayer for the power of Jesus to continue to work in our nation.

We are also now seeing confession and repentance on a corporate level in our nation for national sins. Just as Jesus uses personal repentance to bring about personal revival, He will use national repentance to bring us into national revival. After attendees finished repenting of personal sins at the sixty-sixth Annual National Observance of the National Day of Prayer in Washington, DC, Dr. Ronnie Floyd led those gathered in the capitol building in confessing our national sins, including: denying the one, true, living God; no longer fearing God; believing the prosperity of our nation is because we are great; succumbing to the pressure of pluralism; thinking we do not need God; greed and debt; national addictions to sex, alcohol, and drugs; marginalizing truth; and mainstreaming lies. God began to release His light around the room as men and women fell to their knees on behalf of our nation.[73]

Revival Truths

- While we have many things wrong with our nation, Jesus is displaying His power.
- God calls us to pray for the power of Jesus to continue to work in our nation.
- National repentance will release national revival.

I urge that supplications, prayers, intercessions, and thanksgivings be made for all people, for kings and all who are in high positions, that we may lead a peaceful and quiet life, godly and dignified in every way.

1 TIMOTHY 2:1–2

Walking
in the Light
of God's
Word

Search Me, Lord

*My own sheep will hear My voice and I know each one,
and they will follow me.*

JOHN 10:27 TPT

Hearing Jesus is critical to following Him in personal revival. His voice is not unclear or uncertain, but often it's our hearing that is impaired. To follow Him faithfully requires freedom to hear.

Be still before the Lord and offer the same prayer that David prayed as you seek to put away things that might hinder you from hearing God: "Search me, O God, and know my heart; test me and know my anxious thoughts. See if there is any offensive way in me and lead me in the way everlasting" (Psalm 139:23–24 NIV).

- Search me, O Lord, for sins that hinder me from hearing You. Free me from all moral filth, evil, malice, deceit, hypocrisy, envy, and slander. Free me to have a cleansed heart and mind. Speak now, Thy servant listens. I need to put away . . .

- Search me, O Lord, for unresolved emotions that keep me from hearing You. Free me from any guilt or condemnation, any anger or bitterness, any fear or anxiety. Free me to live each moment "in the present" with You. Speak now Thy servant listens. I need to put away . . .

- Search me, O Lord, for childish things that distract me from hearing you. Free me from rationalizing my behavior and blaming others, from idle chatter and self-focus. Free me to practice personal responsibility before you and others. Speak now, Thy servant listens. I need to put away . . .

- Self-initiative prevents me from hearing you. Free me from my thoughts, my ways, my ideas, and my goals. May I instead embrace

Your thoughts, Your ways, Your ideas, and Your goals. Speak now, Thy servant listens. I need to put away . . .

Pause and wait before the Lord. Listen as He reveals what you need to put away. Now yield to Him, even though you may not fully know all that will be necessary:

Lord, I sense the need to put away _____
_ *in my life. Even before fully knowing all that you may require of me. I yield to You. I long to hear You. Remove this from my life so that I can more freely hear what You reveal to me. In Jesus's name. Amen.*

L2. A Spirit-empowered disciple listens to and hears God for direction and discernment.

Day 4

Unparalleled Unity among Christians

In the United States, God is bringing about a unity within the Christian body as never seen before. While we are united in many ways, I want to focus on three specific aspects of unity. We are united in desperation, united in prayer, and united in desire to seek Him.

True believers are united in desperation—socially, politically, economically, and militarily. We are desperate for leadership. We are desperate because of sin. There is so much sin in our nation that we've redefined sin. More than forty years ago, Karl Menninger, in his classic book, *Whatever Became of Sin,*[74] showed that when a person has so much sin that he doesn't know what to do with it, he finally redefines it so it's not sin anymore. That has now happened.

A former United States president, when talking with congressmen several years ago, discussed "the fudge factor," a policy in which a leader does not tell the entire truth. A notable national Christian leader responded to this concept, saying, "It's unimaginable to me that a president of the United States would even suggest that he would lie to avoid carrying out a law that he disagrees with. . . . If we (shrug this off), . . . we would be announcing that we accepted a president who mocks the law."[75]

Today, unbelievable sin is socially acceptable. Examples abound: sexual impurity, the destruction of marriage, abortion (which is the actual taking of the life of unprotected, unborn, or newly born infants with their own DNA and individuality), lying, cheating, greed, and corruption. These sins abound both personally and in high places of government, politics, and yes, even religion. Justice breeds injustice, and equality breeds inequality. Though these and other sins are socially accepted in parts of society, they are unacceptable to God. Proverbs 14:34 reminds us, "Righteousness exalts a nation, but sin is a reproach to any people" (NKJV).

In the midst of this desperation, a movement toward Jesus in concerted and united prayer among the Christian community has been underway. Lou Engle and other charismatic leaders in The Call have carried forward the national prayer and evangelism anthem. Seeking Jesus in massive, unified prayer through both stadium events and social media, The Call has become a spiritual forerunner for a new Jesus movement. The goal is a step of faith, especially among young people, to pay whatever price is necessary to see Jesus lifted up and God the Father move through the power of the Holy Spirit. There is a growing emphasis and belief for a lightning strike from God that will ignite a cataclysmic prayer movement and explode evangelism in an immense, spiritual tsunami.

In early 2019, The Call issued into The Send in Orlando, Florida, where 59,000 young people came together utilizing Luke 1:17, "And he will go before him in the spirit and power of Elijah, to turn the hearts of the fathers to the children, and the disobedient to the wisdom of the just, to make ready for the Lord a people prepared." The revelatory shift from The Call into The Send is a movement from fully committed prayer and fasting, a voluminous cry to the Creator God, into the initiation of a Jesus movement of evangelism with the uncommitted receiving the saving love of Jesus as Lord and Savior.

Amazingly, God is also moving so distinctly in love and forgiveness for unity in my home state of Mississippi that outsiders would little expect such a movement. Unite Mississippi has developed a very close union between African American, Hispanic, and white pastors in Jackson, Mississippi, for all of society to come together in Veteran's Stadium on April 27, 2019, calling that region to prayer, worship, and evangelism, especially for youth. Mississippi is historically one of the most segregated states in the United States of America, but now God is bringing unity and prayer out of her heart!

This has been an amazing pilgrimage for the entire community with hundreds of churches and thousands of volunteers involved. From all accounts, there has been united prayer and fasting in Brandon, Mississippi, for several years, and it has been the seedbed for this formal outreach. Chip Miskelly is a local furniture business entrepreneur who with his brother Tommy, began his business with a small loan in 1992. Jesus has blessed them and they in turn have honored their community. Chip's daughter went to a Passion weekend with Loui Giglio in Atlanta and came home saying to her father they needed to reach out to the youth of Mississippi. That's all it took!

Have we ever known such boldly unified prayer and evangelism? We are unified in seeking. We are unified in our desire to know Him intimately. We are unified in the early stages of prayer for revival. We are seeing John 17:21, "That they may all be one, just as you, Father, are in me, and I in you, that they also may be in us, so that the world may believe that you have sent me."

> *"It is not possible to exaggerate the importance of your fellowship with your fellow Christians." – John White*

Today, we see people hungry for righteousness and with a desire to be filled with Christ's love like never before. In Jeremiah 3:3, the Bible discusses God's showers and rain. When God poured out His Spirit at Pentecost in Acts 2 and began to empower the church for the work of the Great Commission, it was the early rain. Today God is pouring out the latter rain. As a farm boy, I knew the early rain came after planting to germinate the seeds. A planted seed is hard and dry, but the rain penetrates the soil to soften and enlarge the seed. Within each seed, the starches change to sugars, and the roots go down. Then shoots go up, and the plant bears fruit. If the latter rain doesn't come, the shoot may come up yet may not become rich for harvest, bearing little or no fruit.

In 2018, I was in California supporting Franklin Graham in the Decision America Tour, calling the West Coast of the United States to prayer and to Jesus Christ as Lord and Savior. As I was driving through the verdant orange groves on my way over to I-5 North, I noticed that the oranges were quite small. Eventually, I stopped at a roadside shop and talked to the proprietor. When I inquired as to why the oranges were so small, he told me there had been a drought and noted I must not know much about orange trees. I replied that he was correct. He went on to tell me that in the drought the trees conserve the water in their taproots for survival to maintain as much life as they can. So, the normal amount of water does not go to increase the size of the fruit. If a late rain comes in time, the fruit might still grow to the right size before market. If not, they would not be able to sell oranges in the normal size.

Back driving on I-5 North, Jesus opened my mind to the truth of this metaphor. The orange trees were just like the crops on our family farm growing up—they needed the latter rain to bear fruit. Many churches in America today are in the same drought spiritually, not receiving enough moisture, they conserve their energies into their taproot, inside the four walls of the church. But, when the latter rain of God's Spirit as mentioned in Joel 2 and Acts 2 comes, not only will touched churches be full of rain and joy and praise flowing into the fruit itself, but the rain and joy and praise will draw people outside the four walls of the church to come in. After receiving Jesus's love, the newly redeemed will be drawn to the Bible, to the devotional life, to sharing their faith in Jesus with others. Together, we will express hope and joy that will flood unified throughout our planet. I rejoiced in the car so much that I actually shouted as I thought of what God would do when the latter rain falls, which is imminent in my opinion.

God says in Joel 2:17, "And it shall come to pass afterward, that I will pour out my Spirit on all flesh." Today we are seeing a special rain, an outpouring of God's Spirit. It softens and breaks the outside kernels of our hearts to produce much fruit and a great harvest. People who have been in the church for years are saying, "I want more out of life. I want to increase my service to Jesus." Like the plants, the insides of people are changing from hard hearts to ones soft toward Jesus. The Lord is bringing people from various parts of the church of Jesus Christ together in a new fashion.

Revival Truths

- There is unprecedented unity among believers in today's church.

- We are especially unified through desperation, prayer, and a desire to seek Him.

The glory that you have given me I have given to them, that they may be one even as we are one, I in them and you in me, that they may become perfectly one, so that the world may know that you sent me and loved them even as you loved me.

JOHN 17:22–23

Walking
in the Light
of God's
Son

Harmony Makes Him Happy

I do not pray for these alone, but also for those who will believe in Me through
their word; that they all may be one, as You, Father, are in Me, and I in You;
that they also may be one in Us.

JOHN 17:20–21 NKJV

Think about how crucial each of our body parts is to life. Your heart, lungs,
and spinal cord have very specific functions. In order for the body to function
properly, every part must perform specific tasks in concert. The failure of even
one small part can lead to serious illness or even death of the human body.

Just as every body part has a specific function to perform in the human
body, you also have a specific function that God has set aside for you within the
Body of Christ. Your distinctive, God-given identity makes you uniquely suited
to serve the Body of Christ. Just as an eye is not meant to help us hear and a
nose is not meant to hold a tool, we are each called to serve the body of Christ
in specific ways, ways in which others may not be suited to serve.

God's desire is that His children would form a single body, united by a
shared purpose and driven by a shared commitment to Him. Jesus hopes that
you and I will be an expression of His life and His unity with the Heavenly
Father, and it impacts Him deeply when there is conflict among members of
His body. How do you think it makes Jesus feel to see His followers divided?
How do you think Jesus feels when He sees His people being critical of one
another, judgmental, harsh, unloving, insensitive, disrespectful, or dishonor-
ing? How does Christ's heart respond to see the Body of Christ hurting itself or
to see His family in conflict?

- When Jesus sees His followers divided, it must make Him feel

  _____ .

Pause with one or two others for a few moments and reflect on the heart
of Jesus. The One who created you and died for you, hurts when He sees the

conflicts between those He loves. His prayer is for the witness of our unity to speak of Him in a watching world.

God, please use me to be an agent of unity and harmony with Your people. Show me one specific person whom I could better love this week. Move me beyond descension to walk in the revival testimony of oneness.

P8. A Spirit-empowered disciple takes courageous initiative as a peacemaker, reconciling relationships along life's journey.

Day 5

How Individual Actions Can Affect Many

Once a virtuoso cellist said, "If I miss one day of practice, I know it. If I miss two days, my teacher knows it. If I miss three days, everybody knows it."

I have found this true about my quiet time. If I miss one day, I feel dry that day. If I miss two days, I'm not relating to my wife as I should. If I miss three days, then I begin to be irritated and an irritant. I look at the world differently because I haven't been letting the light of Jesus Christ fill me—through prayer, quiet time, and meditation. My openness to Jesus diminishes; I am less willing to obey His daily call.

As we see Jesus moving in our nation, we must be in continual relationship with Him. We must be devoted to a life of prayer, fasting, Scripture study, and obedience. If we are not, He cannot work through us to bring revival and heal our land. We are the vessels through which Jesus works. Our lives affect others, even those we've never met.

Worship Experience
**Listen to "So Will I" (100 Billion X), by Hillsong Worship:
"For if everything exists to lift You high, so will I."**

In the 1990s, Jesus personally touched a successful university football coach, Bill McCartney. He had a vision to begin a men's movement in the nation and left a big-time program at the University of Colorado to answer God's call. The movement began with a few men coming together to pray and grew into millions praying, worshiping, and reaching out through an organization called Promise Keepers. Coach McCartney saw a need. He sought God's power through prayer. He became part of the solution to an identified problem.

You can become part of the solution too. Intimacy with Christ will give you the stepping stones to understanding your role. It's between you and Him. Stop now and pray. Say to Jesus, "I'm just one human being, but what can I do? I know that You love me. How can I let You share that love through me?"

Ask the Holy Spirit to show you where you are part of the problem. Our response is to be faithful and obedient to Jesus's daily call. We begin this journey by trusting Him completely. God honors our obedience.

Social historian and critic Allan Bloom once wrote about George Washington:

> [His] life reflect[ed] his profound faith in God. . . . He directed his men to be punctual in attendance for worship services and to refrain from cursing. He realized that God was not likely to grant victory to an army that profaned His name. . . . In his own hand, Washington wrote, "Direct my thoughts, words, and work, wash away my sins in the immaculate Blood of the Lamb, and purge my heart by Thy Holy Spirit. . . . Daily frame me more and more into the likeness of Thy Son, Jesus Christ."[76]

If we follow God in every step of our lives, then God will do what He designed for us. Each piece of our life is part of a mosaic that God assembles for His glory. It's our job to obey; it's God's job to bring results.

Revival Truths

- Our lives affect others, even those we don't know.

- We are to live faithful lives in relationship with Christ.

- Jesus wants to use us in His plan.

- Our response is to be faithful and obedient to Jesus's daily call.

How precious to me are your thoughts, O God! How vast is the sum of them!

PSALM 139:17

Walking
in the Light
of God's
Son

Action of One

The Father has an intense love for me because I freely give my own life—
to raise it up again.

JOHN 10:17 TPT

"I lay down my life that I may take it again!" This action of one has changed the world. Although the Jews did not grasp the significance of Jesus's words, each of us as Christ followers understands them (v. 19). He has made us partakers of His divine nature through the life He laid down: "God made Him who had no sin to be sin for us, so that in him we might become the righteousness of God" (2 Corinthians 5:21 NIV).

Pause and consider Christ's cry to His Father from the cross: "My God, my God, why have you forsaken me?" (Matthew 27:46). As Jesus took our sin on Himself, the Father, in His holiness, had to turn away. Then Christ, through the Holy Spirit would take up His life again! Reflect once more on being born again. Why did Christ become sin? Even more personally, for whom did He do it? Who will benefit from His resurrection?

Quietly listen to His Spirit whisper the words to your soul: "He did it for you. He did it for you!" The One who knew no sin became sin (2 Corinthians 5:21). If He did not need to die for any other person in the whole world, He would have died for you—and He did die for you. You are the one individual through whom He longs to work His work of revival.

Allow yourself to respond to this glorious truth. He was raised for you. Meditate on the thought, or even whisper the words, "He did it for me." Is your heart moved with wonder, humility, and joy? Does gratitude and praise fill your soul? Does calling and yieldedness grip you?

Now share your heart with God. Give thanks for His initiative in manifesting His glory and presence to you. He laid down His life—and took it up again—for you!

Lord, I am so grateful that _____ .
Revive me, send me.

L2. A Spirit-empowered disciple listens to and hears God for direction and discernment.

SPIRIT-
EMPOWERED
Faith

Looking Forward

As we grow personally and reach out to others, we have the potential to see Jesus revived as King in our nation. But our impact extends beyond that. As we shall see, we can also impact the world.

CHAPTER 11

Vision for World AWAKENING

The world is a big place, and the concept of touching more than two hundred nations for Christ sounds overwhelming. Yet Scripture tells us to proclaim His truth throughout the world, to every person.

- "Declare His glory among the nations, His wonders among all peoples. . . . Let the heavens rejoice, and let the earth be glad; and let them say among the nations, 'The Lord reigns.'" (1 Chronicles 16:24, 31 NKJV)

- "Declare His glory among the nations, His wonders among all peoples" (Psalm 96:3 NKJV).

- "Oh give thanks to the Lord; call upon his name; make known his deeds among the peoples!" (105:1).

How we view the world can make all the difference. Do we see it as a world created and owned by God, full of people who don't know they're called to be His children? Do we see the world as one family divided by sin? Or do we see differences in skin color, cultures, and lifestyles that cause us to hesitate in accepting our part in reaching the world for Christ? Let's consider our worldview and how we can touch and love the world for Christ.

Day 1

This Is My Father's World

In the beginning, there was nothing, according to Genesis 1:2. Everything was without form and void. We learn that God *bara*—made out of nothing—the world. The world came from the heart of God. Why? Because He's a creative God, and He wanted a place for His creation. The planet is for those who would be in fellowship with Him. Unlike angels, who are obliged to have fellowship with the Lord, mankind was created to choose fellowship with the Father. God wanted something to love, so He spoke man into being. God made the world as part of His creation, and He made it perfect. By giving humans a free will, He marked creation with the potential for imperfection. Mankind couldn't be perfect if the potential for imperfection didn't exist.

God created us for fellowship, love, and worship. Revelation 4–5 and 7:9–17 describes the activities of heaven—God receiving honor, praise, and worship. Part of the spiritual fall on earth was the separation of our "belongings" from us. Now we have to receive back through Jesus what was already ours. Our purpose for existence became clouded. Initially God created us for fellowship with Him, but without redemption, we often seek work as a reason for living instead of resting in the completed work of Christ. We miss the greatest activity possible—to love God. Revival is about this process of returning to the reason for our existence.

People ask questions like, "Why am I here? What's my purpose? What's the reason for my being?" The answers were clear before the Fall. Now we must seek and find them. We must *choose* to return to God. Our God is jealous; He wants people who are made in His image to love Him out of their own desire.

Worship Experience
Listen to "For the Beauty of the Earth,"
by Folliott S. Pierpoint:
"Lord . . . to thee we raise . . . our hymn of grateful praise."

When I was twelve years old, Mom drove me to downtown Corinth, Mississippi, for shopping. We covered those seven miles from our farm in

Kossuth in a 1951 green Studebaker, and on the way, I thought about the story I had heard in Sunday school the week before. My teacher, Gerald Wegman, a mechanic, had helped the children study the story of the Tower of Babel. I found the story intriguing. If God made the world and everything in it, why was this tower so perverse? The story made it clear that though mankind was united, they left out the need for God. Instead of giving God the glory, they were going to build a tall tower to get as high as possible—to be like God. The Lord looked down and gave them different languages so they couldn't communicate to finish the tower.

As I rode with my mother, I reflected on what had happened since then: People have not lived together in harmony and don't speak the same language. Suddenly I thought, *Wow, look at the United States! It's a nation that came together to seek Jesus Christ for freedom to worship God without the force of a state religion. And the whole world lives here with immigrants from every country of the world. And essentially the US uses the same language.*

"Mom, is it possible that the United States of America is an experiment by God to reverse the Tower of Babel and see if we as a nation can live together and love each other under Jesus Christ? Is it possible?"

My mom was taken back by the question. She said, "Son, I don't know. That's an interesting thought."

In my heart, I began to understand the special nature of this country. The United States is special not because the people or the government or the land is special in itself but because of God. Even on our coinage, the words are printed, "In God We Trust."

It is possible as a nation to live together in harmony. But each of us must work to bring about truth as an objective anchor from which we can work to develop the best relationship possible with each other and the Lord.

Today Christ is the unifying factor in our spiritual life. English is the predominate world language. Could the United States be the cap on the dynamite stick to bring about a worldwide return to Him? We should pray to that end.

Revival Truths

- God created the world for His pleasure.

- God created us to be in fellowship with Him.

- We are a part of the world awakening as individuals and as a country.

He has made from one blood every nation of men to dwell on all the face of the earth, and has determined their preappointed times and the boundaries of their dwellings, so that they should seek the Lord, in the hope that they might grope for Him and find Him, though He is not far from each one of us.

ACTS 17:26–27 NKJV

You're His Beloved

As I have loved you, so you must love one another.

JOHN 13:34 NIV

With this one verse, Jesus was reminding the disciples about all of the ways that He had loved them as well as foreshadowing His upcoming display of love on Calvary. Christ's reminder of how He loves is without comparison. And in this same verse, Jesus also gave us a clue about how His love is supposed to impact our lives and the world in which we live. He wants us to soak up His love deeply and personally and then demonstrate that same love to others in our day. The verse from John reveals the basics of Christianity: Receive His love and then show it to others.

How has Jesus loved you? Take a moment to reflect on just a few aspects of His love:

- God has shown His love to you by sending His Son to die for you. While you were still going your own way and an enemy of God, He sent Jesus to die just for you. His love is without condition, demand, or expectation. It is freely given because you are the "loved of God" (Romans 5:8).

- God has shown His love to you by being present with you at every moment of every day. Nothing can separate you from His love. Nothing you do can change His love. His love cannot be lost, lessened, or diminished. It is forever yours because you are the "loved of God." It's who you are because of what He has declared as true of you (8:38–39).

- God has shown His love to you by sending His Spirit to live inside of you. The Scriptures say He has poured out His love to you. Like a fountain or a spring of living water, a relationship with God means daily refreshment, eternal well-being, and a continual filling of His love because you are His "beloved" (Ephesians 3:18–19).

These truths are most meaningful in a world desperate for hope. Reflect on who God has declared you to be and how you can make a difference in your world:

- I am especially thankful for the truth that God loves me by _____ because . . .

God, I want to deeply experience Your love for me. I want to fully embrace my identity as Your "beloved." Let my love for others be a reflection of how You have loved me.

L4. Spirit-empowered disciples rejoice regularly in their identity as "His Beloved."

Day 2

My Vision of the World

What is your vision for the world? Is it a big place or small? Do you see the world as a place God made and is trying to bring back to Himself? Or do you see the world as two-hundred-plus nations and thousands of groups of people who can't live in harmony?

Do you see the world as full of children whom God loves and about whom He cares equally? Or is your vision narrower, and do you believe one group is better than another? Do you see the world as having the potential of being unified? Is that good or bad?

Ultimately, is the world God's, or is it man's? Or is it satan's? Do you regard God as the creator and sustainer of all? Your beliefs about the world impact what you think about God and yourself.

Is the world a good place or bad place? Are we related to each other biologically or even as part of God's family? Do you care about the other countries and people groups in the world? Do you see that as part of your place in the kingdom of God?

Why does your world view matter?

Consider Jesus's words in Matthew 23:37, "O Jerusalem, Jerusalem, the city that kills the prophets and stones those who are sent to it! How often would I have gathered your children together as a hen gathers her brood under her wings, and you were not willing!" Jesus grieved for His own city; He loved His people and desired that they would know the truth of God. That is very clear. Then, in Matthew 28:19–20, we also see that Jesus's heart is for the entire world—He tells us to make disciples of all nations. There is a time and place for us to focus on home, and there is also a time and place to focus outside of our country into the world. God is the God of the entire world, not just the United States.

International Students, Inc., for example, has held evangelistic and discipleship conferences for mainland Chinese students and scholars. Through these events, we have seen many come to know Christ for the first time, others receive baptism, and others make commitments to full-time service in China for Christ—to take the truth of Jesus Christ and His salvation to China.

One of the greatest blessings is to hear the testimonies of those students and scholars who have felt Jesus's call to return to China as indigenous (or native) missionaries. They leave profitable careers in the United States in fields of science, medicine, technology, and education to serve Christ in China. The Great Commission fuels their fire. Many feel that China will become the largest missionary-sending country in the world, and they want to be a part of it. Their burden is not just for China but for the world.

When we look at the world through spiritual eyes, we should be able to visualize, as the prophet Ezekiel did, a valley of dry bones. Spiritually the world is dry, and God wants to raise these bones to life. First, Jesus moves the church in revival, then among the unconverted, awakens them to their lost condition and the hope of salvation through Jesus Christ. Dry bones can live!

> *"Revival is . . . the inrush of divine life into a body threatening to become a corpse." – D.M. Panton*

Revival Truths

- Our vision for the world should mirror what Jesus wants for the world.

- Jesus's desire is for all people to know His truth.

I will put my Spirit within you, and you shall live, and I will place you in your own land. Then you shall know that I am the Lord; I have spoken, and I will do it, declares the Lord.

EZEKIEL 37:14

Walking in the Light of God's People

Fresh Work

A thief has only one thing in mind—he wants to steal, slaughter, and destroy. But I came to give you everything in abundance, more than you expect—life in its fullness until you overflow!

JOHN 10:10 TPT

The promised abundant life is His life expressed through us in personal revival. Abundant life comes through the Christlike character of Jesus and is much needed in our world. Quietly listen before the Lord as His Spirit speaks of needed Christlike character in your life. Ask the Lord to give you discernment and direction as you respond to the following:

- *Lord, I sense a needed fresh work of servanthood in me, particularly toward _____.*

- *Holy Spirit, I long for the humility of Christ to be more real in my life through my dependence upon You, my vulnerability before You and others, and my approachability.*

- *Lord Jesus, I need a strengthening of Your faith in me, that I might believe You for great things. Particularly, I want to trust You for . . .*

Now, in today's world, stand in faith against the "thief" who seeks to steal and destroy your witness in today's world.

- *Free me, Holy Spirit, from all of life's anxieties so that my heart might rest secure in You. Help me to cease any attempts to fearfully and selfishly take that which You've promised to supply.*

- *Lord forgive me, as there have been times that I have taken Your grace for granted. As I am committed to personal revival, I want Your Spirit to stir within me a sensitive and grateful heart. Overwhelm me with a deep awareness of my identity as the beloved of God. Constrain and control me through the grateful wonder of Your love.*

Now share with one or two others at least one of the ways that His Spirit might want to make changes in you. Pray together, with each of you asking God to change you in these ways. Ask Him to deepen your servant's heart and to humble your walk before Him and others. Implore Him to strengthen your faith, casting out all of your anxiety. Ask His Spirit to fill you with the gratitude for His wondrous love as He empowers your witness.

W4. A Spirit-empowered disciple humbly and vulnerably shares of the Spirit's transforming work through the Word.

Day 3

My Place in the World

Your whole world begins with you. Your world does not begin with your spouse, or your children, or your best friends. It doesn't begin with your neighborhood, or with your pastor, or your church. It doesn't begin with the leaders of your community, city, state, or nation. Your world begins with you.

Is there anybody who impacts your world more than you? No and yes. No—if you have not totally surrendered to Jesus Christ, and you are not intimate with Him. Yes—if you have an intimacy with Christ, and you give yourself to Him every day as Lord. In that case, Jesus impacts your world through you.

For example, if I am a free man, no one impacts my world more than I do.

But if I'm a slave and have an owner, who impacts my world more—me as a slave or my owner? The owner.

Who owns your life? Whoever owns your life will impact your world the most.

Do you own your life? Or does Christ own your life?

If you own your life, then your focus will be to impact the world for yourself. If Christ owns your life, then your life will have two desires for impact— first for Him and then for others. Interestingly, Jesus always cares for our needs in the process of serving Him and others. To reach our world for Christ, our focus must be on others, not on ourselves. Do you belong to Jesus? If you belong to Jesus, how can you set your agenda? When we read God's Word, we can determine the Lord's agenda.

Jesus leaves no room for negotiation in Mark 8:34–35: "And calling the crowd to him with his disciples, he said to them, 'If anyone would come after me, let him deny himself and take up his cross and follow me. For whoever would save his life will lose it, but whoever loses his life for my sake and the Gospel's will save it.'" Every person innately wants to save his or her own life in a sense and make his or her own decisions. Each of us must deal with the independent, me-first attitude.

> "Revival is . . . always the action of God. It is not man. It is God pouring out His Spirit." – *Martyn Lloyd-Jones*

Have you noticed how individualism is a key philosophy in America? For example, we don't prefer mass transit; one person per car is the typical morning commute. Frank Sinatra, the gifted and independent-minded singer, made his anthem, "I did it my way." Of course, there is no question that each of us is an individual, yet our culture has taken this individualization to the extreme. There is no meaning in life outside of "my box." If you learn to handle only what is inside your box or realm of influence, you will miss Jesus's call to be part of a greater plan.

Our place in this world is to be part of the body of Christ. That body is located across the world, not just within our individual churches, or even exclusively in the United States. The Bible says that when one part of the body weeps, we all weep. When one part rejoices, we all rejoice. Do you weep with persecuted believers across the world? Do you see them as part of the same body?

Jesus gives us the command to turn and seek God, saying in Matthew 6:33, "But seek first the kingdom of God and his righteousness, and all these things will be added to you." In our culture, we have internally paraphrased this verse to become, "I'll seek my way first and see if I can get to my end." In marriage and family life, this individual bent has had its toll on our children. As syndicated columnist Cal Thomas wrote, "Too many parents are divorcing. Too many children think they are unwanted and unloved, that they disturb our comfort, rob us of pleasure, and cost us money, which we regretfully spend on them."[77] It's all *my* desire and *my* own way.

To have the greatest return on our existence, we as a nation must seek Christ's will. As we follow God's principles, we will experience the greatest blessings of life. Hebrews 11:27 declares, "By faith he [Moses] . . . endured as seeing him who is invisible." Notice the element of faith in Moses, and it's the same for us. Faith carries us like nothing else. Even though our faith is invisible, if we trust Jesus, we will have the result that we want in our lives—fulfillment and joy—as each of us finds the place He has created just for you, just for me.

The apostle Peter wrote, "Arm yourselves also with the same mind, . . . that he no longer should live the rest of his time in the flesh for the lusts of men, but for the will of God" (1 Peter 4:1–2 NKJV). What is our motive—to do our thing or the will of God? If our foundation is self, there is no power. We will be making our way by ourselves, often at the expense of others. If our foundation is in Christ, there is power. The Bible tells us in Romans 6:19 that we are weak in our natural self. John 3:6 says, "That which is born of the flesh is flesh; and that which is born of the Spirit is spirit."

Revival Truths

- Jesus has created a special place for me in the world.

- God calls me to a selfless rather than a selfish life.

- I am connected to all believers in the body of Christ throughout the world.

When He was asked by the Pharisees when the kingdom of God would come, He answered them and said, "The kingdom of God does not come with observation; nor will they say, 'See here!' or 'See there!' For indeed, the kingdom of God is within you."

LUKE 17:20–21 NKJV

Walking
in the Light
of God's
Word

Special Delivery

Freely you have received, freely give.

Matthew 10:8 NKJV

It's no surprise, but none of us can really see God. But the crazy truth is that although people cannot see God with their eyes, when we demonstrate love for others, people *can* see God. Jesus wants our world to know and experience Jesus. People see God in us when they experience His truth and love lived out through us. In fact, you may be the most important expression of God that some people will ever see.

Reflect for a few moments on how you have experienced God's care through the life and love of another friend or family member. Think about those times when God brought someone to help you, listen to you, support, or encourage you at just the right time. Remember the moments when God sent a friend or family member to pick you up when you were sad, hang out with you when you were lonely, or give you a hug when you were down.

- *I'm grateful for the time that God sent _____ at just the right time, because . . .*

- *I'm so glad that God brought _____into my life when . . .*

It is our gratitude for receiving God's love through other people that can prompt us to show love in our world. When we regularly remember how God has brought other people in our lives to love us well, we will be motivated to do the same for others.

Who are some of the people around you who might especially need to feel some of God's love right now?

- _____ (name a specific person) probably needs to experience some of God's love right now because . . .

How can you show love to this person using the unique personality traits, gifts, and abilities that God has given you?

God, thank You for sending people to "deliver" Your love at very important times in my life. Holy Spirit, help me to do the same for others. I want people in our world to see the Real God in me.

M2. A Spirit-empowered disciple expresses and extends the kingdom of God while sharing compassion, justice, love, and forgiveness.

Day 4

The Light of the World

In 1988, Benazir Bhutto became the first woman to lead a Muslim nation in modern times. Before Benazir went to college at Harvard-Radcliffe, her father, Pakistan's Prime Minister Zufikar Al Bhutto, gave her a beautiful copy of the Qur'an. He told her, "You will see many things that surprise you in America, and some that may shock you. But I know you have the ability to adapt. Above all you must study hard. Very few in Pakistan have the opportunity you now have, and you must take advantage of it. Never forget that the money it is costing to send you comes from the land, from the people who sweat and toil on those lands. You will owe a debt to them, a debt you can repay with God's blessing by using your education to better their lives."[78]

Benazir's first encounter with American students at Radcliffe was an eye-opener. She wrote about those early college days in her biography, *Daughter of Destiny:*

> "Pak-i-stan? Where's Pak-i-stan?" my new classmates asked me when I first arrived at Radcliffe.
>
> "Pakistan is the largest Muslim country in the world," I replied, sounding like a handout from our embassy. "There are two wings of Pakistan separated by India."
>
> "Oh, India," came the relieved response. "You're next to India."

I smarted every time I heard the reference to India, with whom we had had two bitter wars. Pakistan was supposed to be one of America's strongest allies. . . .

The United States used our air bases in northern Pakistan for their U-2 reconnaissance flights including the ill-fated flight of Gary Powers in 1960. Yet Americans seemed completely unaware even of the existence of my country.[79]

Today, Benazir Bhutto takes her experiences from the land of Harvard into her everyday decisions and actions as she leads this Muslim nation.

What if Bhutto had met loving Christians while here in the United States? What if she went home not just with an education, but with Jesus? Hundreds of thousands of international students are studying in the United States right now, representing almost every part of the world. They are the best and brightest their countries have to offer. In five to twenty years, many will be the leaders of their nations. They will return home to make a difference. The question is, "Will they make a difference for Jesus Christ?"

Are you shining the light of Jesus as a natural part of your life? Are the people around you safe in loneliness and depression? If Bhutto had met you while she was studying in America, would her life have been different?

At the beginning of chapter 3, I shared the dream I had in 2016 of the points of revival light connected by an underground network of fiber-optic cables covering a football field. This grassroots revival of Jesus's light is what we are seeing across the world today—lights springing forth by the millions. Out of that dream and the prayers surrounding it have come a handful of definitions of the types of lights that are beginning to shine everywhere we look, pinpricks, pinpoints, pockets, passions, and patterns of light. Truly, "the darkness is passing away and the true light is already shining" (1 John 2:8).

Pinpricks of Light – These are small, altruistic, gracious, benevolent gestures in the name of Jesus, from one person to another, for Jesus. They may appear to be simple common courtesies, but if we had 300 million of these little pinpricks of courtesy, love, and forgiveness every day, what a changed world we would have.

Pinpoints of Light – The next size of lightbulbs holds a little more light from the source, Jesus Christ. These lights are like laser beams penetrating the darkness that go on and on through the extent of an individual's life. A pinpoint is someone who lights up the margins around them as they travel, even subtly, through life.

Pockets of Light – These are efforts, orphanages, care centers, medical centers, institutions of compassion, evangelistic outreaches, groups of individuals who light up the darkness in pockets by sharing Jesus's love. God is love. Of course, that means that all true love comes from God. Whether the group knows it or not, the origin of love is God Himself. He is the creator God. He is love, and all love comes from His source.

Passions of Light – These are unusual individuals, but can be small groups, who have such passion that they gloriously live only for one thing—exploding light, truth, love, forgiveness, and activity, even when others are not responsive to love at first. Someone once said, "God says it is so, so act like it is so, so He can make it so." God loves us. God loves everyone. God expects us to love everyone. Even the unloving, unlovable, and rejecting. Therefore, the obedience of love, the discipline of loving, says, "I follow Jesus; therefore, I love."

Patterns of Light – Patterns pray to, cry out to, live for, and act to bring God's loving Truth in our society. For example, a person or a group, like Franklin Graham and the BGEA, prior to the last presidential election, went to every state in the nation calling the nation to "Pray, Vote, and Engage," simply obeying God, believing Him for the future, and trusting Him. The concentric circles from such events, by the power of God's Spirit, overlap, and the nation begins to pray as one. John 17:21 says that God wants us as believers to have the same unity that He and the Father have, so that we can win people to Jesus Christ, and change a nation through supernatural love, forgiveness, and passion.

> *"In revival, the Church returns to the glory and power that prevailed at Pentecost." – J. Edwin Orr*

Will you be the light that Jesus is calling you to be today? We can all be pinpricks every day, and as we die to self and live for Jesus, our lives become pinpoints and passions through Christ. As Jesus joins us with other lights around us, we become a part of pockets and patterns of God's work across the earth.

Maybe you do not feel particularly shiny today. Even out of the destruction that Job experienced in his life, he could still say, "[The Lord] uncovers the deeps out of darkness and brings deep darkness to light" (Job 12:22). Pray and ask Jesus to bring the darkness to light in you. He will do it, and he will send you forth as His beacon to the world—you might not even have to go anywhere.

Revival Truths

- God is calling you to be a light of revival in your world.

- As we all shine forth Jesus, life and light begin to spread and overlap until the whole earth is a shining beacon of the glory of God.

Jesus spoke to them, saying, "I am the light of the world. Whoever follows me will not walk in darkness, but will have the light of life."

JOHN 8:12

Walking
in the Light
of God's
Word

Giving First

For whatever was written in earlier times was written for our instruction,
so that through perseverance and the encouragement of the Scriptures
we might have hope.

ROMANS 15:4 NASB

One of our critical needs is a need for encouragement. As we engage as ambassadors for Christ in our world, God meets this need for us and then calls us to encourage others. Giving encouragement involves speaking positive words to others, giving others reason to hope, and urging others to persevere in the pursuit of goals and dreams. Here are some of the ways that God wants to encourage you in your personal revival. As you read them, reflect on some of God's words that are especially meaningful to you right now in the battle of darkness versus light.

- You might say, "This is impossible."
God says, "Nothing is impossible with me" (Luke 18:27).

- When you say, "I'm too tired. I give up."
  God says, "I will give you rest" (Matthew 11:28–30).

- If you say, "I can't go on."
  God says, "My grace is enough. You can do it" (2 Corinthians 12:9).

- You might say, "I can't make it. There's no way."
  God says, "I've got what you need" (Isaiah 40:28–29).

- When you say, "I'm not able."
  God says, "I AM able. I've got this" (2 Corinthians 9:8).

- If you say, "No one gets it. No one understands."
  God says, "I have heard you, and I will be with you" (Psalm 10:17 and 91:15).

Now because God has encouraged you, consider how you might share words of encouragement with others around you that they also may "be light" in a dark world.

God, thank You for being a God who sees the times when I feel discouraged and need more of Your hope. Thank You for your encouraging words. Please help me to encourage others as together we "live light" in our world.

M6. A Spirit-empowered disciple bears witness of a confident peace and expectant hope in God's Lordship in all things.

Day 5

Impact the World for Eternity

Charlie Riggs was an oil field roustabout from New York and Pennsylvania who came to Christ in his teens. His dad left home when he was a little boy, so Charlie had to begin working at age five to help support his family. As a teenager, he worked in a bowling alley setting pins. Charlie never got to finish college because he became an officer in the military. He joined a Bible study with the Navigators ministry that began to do the follow-up for Billy Graham's crusades.

Later the Navigators opened their ministry in Seattle, and Dawson Trotman, the Navigators' founder, called Lorne Sanny, who was leading a Bible study with Charlie. Dawson asked, "How is the Bible study going?" Lorne was quiet.

"How many do you have attending?" Dawson asked.

"I just have one."

"What's his name?" Dawson asked.

"Lieutenant Charles Riggs."

"Is he faithful?"

"Oh, he's faithful."

After a pause, Trotman said, "Well, Lorne, I think you should major on Riggs."[80]

Just one! The Bible says, "A faithful man who can find?" (Proverbs 20:6). If you are faithful, then God will use you. Charlie Riggs went on to serve in the Billy Graham Evangelistic Association for forty years, doing an incredible job throughout the world. Most people are not faithful. Why is Billy Graham, the farm boy from North Carolina, "Billy Graham," the steady, consistent evangelist for five decades? It's his faithfulness.

Worship Experience
Listen to "Made a Way," by Travis M. Greene:
"We're standing here . . . because You made a way."

There are two kinds of vision: one is external and the other is internal. External vision looks at the world and follows the seemingly obvious progressive stages life offers. Many of those external stages are from true principles, such as if you work hard, you get a return. Or if you help people, they will probably help you.

A vision for the world involves internal sight and wisdom. Jesus said in Matthew 11:19, "But wisdom is justified of her children" (NKJV). Internal wisdom sees the sin and corruption of the world and weeps for the deception under which people live. Internal wisdom realizes that this world is not our home, but that eternity is. By having internal wisdom, we invest our time, talents, treasure, and testimony for Jesus's world and not our own.

Can you say, "Jesus, by faith I am going to follow your leading and Your Word today and believe that wisdom is proved by her actions? Help me to live in the real world but to also see the real, real world—that world that never dies, where the investment of my life in every way will bring the greatest return." The Bible tells us that wisdom is (1) from above, (2) peaceable, and (3) open to understanding (James 3:17). Will we let wisdom guide us as we look at our world?

We can't address the needs of the world or the workplace unless Jesus's spirit-love fills us to overflowing. Consider and pray through the apostle Paul's prayer for the Philippians. It can be our heart cry as well. "And it is my prayer that your love may abound more and more, with knowledge and all discernment, so that you may approve what is excellent, and so be pure and blameless for the day of Christ, filled with the fruit of righteousness that comes through Jesus Christ, to the glory and praise of God" (Philippians 1:9–11).

Do you have this internal sight from Jesus? Do you believe God enough to know that He made you for a purpose? If you are obedient, disciplined, and intimate with Jesus, then He will guide you into your life purpose. Use the following prayer to commit your life to God's purposes:

"Lord, help me to have internal sight. Help me not to be simply guided by what I see but what I believe. While I live in a real world, help me daily, moment by moment, to see the real, real world—that world that never deteriorates and is steadfast—Your world. Give me wisdom from above that is pure and easy to be molded to Your will. Lead me to fit into Your big picture for my life. Jesus, day by day, shape me into the person You want me to become."

Revival Truths

- Inner sight comes from God's hand.

- We can choose to live according to the world's external view or Jesus's internal view.

- We must be faithful to live from Jesus's perspective.

> Many a man proclaims his own steadfast love,
> but a faithful man who can find?
>
> PROVERBS 20:6

Walking
in the Light
of God's
Word

Any Time, Anywhere

Now hope does not disappoint, because the love of God has been poured out in
our hearts by the Holy Spirit who was given to us.

Romans 5:5 NKJV

God increased the closeness of His relationship with us by coming to earth
in the person of Jesus. Jesus lived among other men and women, talking with
them one on one, sharing meals with them, doing life together, and revealing
His feelings to them. But God's plan for increasing the closeness of His relationship with us does not end there.

When Jesus died on the cross and rose from the dead three days later,
these miraculous events restored the possibility of a close relationship with God
by dealing with our sinfulness and enabled a deeper closeness and intimacy
with God because He was able to send the Holy Spirit to dwell within us.

This means that God doesn't just relate to us as a Father who looks down
on us from heaven, nor even as a gentle friend who walks among us as Jesus
did. Rather, if we have accepted God's gift of salvation, God lives within us as
part of our very being. By the Holy Spirit, He is not only with us; He is also
in us and is thus available to love, comfort, encourage, correct, and guide us
anywhere at any time. He gives us "inner" wisdom and insight to be light in our
dark world.

Here are just some of the blessings that are available to you because of
God's Spirit. If His Spirit lives inside you, because you have received God's gift
of salvation:

- He will never leave you alone (Matthew 28:20).

- He will be your Helper and your Counselor (John 14:16; 16:7).

- He will guide you when you need to know the truth (16:13).

- He will strengthen you (Philippians 4:13).

- The Spirit will reveal the things of God to you (1 Corinthians 2:10).

- The Spirit can help you in your weaknesses (Romans 8:26).
- The Spirit intercedes for you; He prays for you (v. 26).

Stop and consider these amazing blessings that are available to you for personal revival through God's Holy Spirit. Which of these blessings gives you hope?

- As I consider the blessings that are available to me through the Holy Spirit, I am most glad to know that . . .

God, thank You for the gift of Your Son and the gift of the Holy Spirit. It's these gifts that give me hope to live a life of personal revival.

L10. A Spirit-empowered disciple practices the presence of the Lord, yielding to the Spirit's work of Christlikeness.

Looking Forward

The world is a big place, but it begins in exactly one spot—with you. Having a worldview based on Jesus's perspective is important. Sometimes we leave our country to reach the world, but we can also reach the world at home through international groups within America. In our final chapter we will put together these pieces and others in the book to see revival happen moment by moment, day by day, heart by heart.

CHAPTER 12

ONE HEART at a Time

How do you become a person who knows the Bible? You memorize one verse at a time.

How do you become a person with many friends? You build your relationships one person at a time.

How do you get to be a good husband or wife or a good son or daughter? You find the needs of another person and then try to meet those needs one at a time.

How do you live life? Whether you like it or not, it's one day at a time. One hour at a time. One moment at a time.

How do you build depth with Jesus Christ? You get to know Him by spending one minute at a time with Him.

How does revival begin? With one changed heart at a time.

A key question for each of us to ask is, "Is what I'm doing today that which will help to accomplish the results that I intend for my life?" More importantly, we should ask, "Will it accomplish Jesus's will for my life?" What results do you want in your life? Your goals? Jesus's direction?

Every day you need to ask yourself this key question. "Of all I could do, which will contribute most to that which God calls me to accomplish?"

Day 1

Daily Vision

Where are your eyes focused? Perhaps they're focused on yourself, perhaps on your job, or perhaps on your family. In spite of all the important relationships in our lives, we are called to focus our eyes on only one place: Jesus Christ. With our eyes focused on Him, we'll receive all that we require to carry out what He has placed before us. This requires a daily refocusing of our vision, a daily realignment of our spiritual eyes.

Thousands of choices face us each day. Choices about how we think, what we wear, who we talk to. Some decisions appear small and insignificant while others may be life-changing. What we often fail to realize is that every single decision builds on another. Even the smallest choices impact our lives. In the parable about the Kingdom of God in Luke 19:11–17, Jesus teaches that if we are faithful in the small things of life, we can be trusted for more important work.

In chapter 9, I mentioned the bold witness of Cassie Bernall, the Columbine High School student who died after answering yes about her relationship with Jesus Christ. She had previously rebelled against faith in her life but came to make Jesus the center of her being day by day. Her life is an example of small decisions that add up to impact a life—like being consistent in attending a church youth group. Her parents noted in an open letter to the community in the newspaper on May 1, 1999:

> Cassie's response does not surprise us. Her life was rightly centered around our Lord Jesus. It was for her strong faith in God and His promise of eternal life that she made her stand. It is clear to me that this tragic incident has been thrown back into the face of satan and his followers with an impact that is much greater than what was intended for us, God's children.
>
> To all young people who hear this, don't let my daughter's death be for nothing. Make your stand. If you're not in the local church's youth group, try it. They want you and will help support you in doing what is right. It's not easy, you'll need one another.[81]

They concluded their letter with this reminder to parents: "We are the front line in all issues regarding our children. Yes, Jesus is the author and finisher of our faith. He is the One that we give our lives to, desire to be like, want to be intimate with, and desire to make known. By following His example, we can see and should see our nation changed, one person at a time."

If Cassie had not been making daily decisions with her eyes focused on Christ, would she have been able to respond affirmatively about her relationship with Christ in the face of death? She may have been murdered regardless of her response, but what a testimony she left because of her daily faithfulness.

> *"The sense in which a Christian leaves it to God is that he puts all his trust in Christ: trust that Christ will somehow share with him the perfect human obedience which He carried out from His birth to His crucifixion."* – C. S. Lewis

We can also turn our eyes toward other people, which leads to envy. In 1 Samuel 18:6–11, Saul has been the anointed ruler of Israel, yet he hears the great acclaim being given to David. Saul begins paying attention to what David is doing rather than on the calling of God for his own life. Because Saul focuses his eyes on David, he opens the door for envy, which leads to anger and fear. Earlier, Saul had prophesied in God's strength (10:10–13); now he attempts to murder David. How does this happen? Saul's vision is clouded by not focusing on God.

One of the daily choices I face is how I see myself compared to how God sees me. The more I grow in my relationship with Christ, the more I realize how inadequate I am. Such a perspective can be healthy; however, I can focus so much on my inadequacies that I take my eyes off Jesus. An inverted pride takes over that keeps me absorbed with myself. Each day I must decide where I will focus. Will it be on Jesus, who makes me complete? Or will it be on myself? It's an important choice, one each of us must make.

If we focus on anything but Christ, we are unable to see clearly. Our vision becomes clouded with the cares of the world rather than the peace of God. There is incredible freedom in relying on Christ daily, seeking Him daily.

Revival Truths

- We need to daily focus on Christ to lead us.

- We have choices that may be small or large, but all are important.

- If we are faithful in the small things, God will honor us.

- If we focus on ourselves, we cannot see Christ.

Looking to Jesus, the founder and perfecter of our faith, who for the joy that was set before him endured the cross, despising the shame, and is seated at the right hand of the throne of God.

HEBREWS 12:2

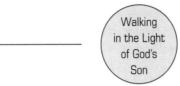

Walking
in the Light
of God's
Son

Life-changing Encounters

"Your son will live and not die." So from that day forward,
the man and all his family and servants believed.

JOHN 4:53 TPT

Just like this Samaritan father, great things happen as we encounter Jesus, walking by faith in His Word, focused on Jesus.

Reflect upon the time when you first entered into relationship with the Savior. Do you remember really desiring to please Him, to put a smile on His face, so to speak? Was a longing to please Jesus part of your "new birth" experience? When you think back on this time, did you desire to:

- Put away certain things, attitudes, or behaviors from your life?

- Avoid certain familiar patterns and places?

- Flee certain activities and acquaintances?

- Meditate upon God's Word?

- Worship with fellow Christ-followers?

- Share your experiences with Jesus with other people?

- *As I think back upon my experience of accepting Jesus as my Savior, I recall these thoughts of wanting to please Him:* _____
_____
_____
_____
_____.

Lord Jesus, I desire to please You, to walk worthy of my calling. I dread displeasing You, and I sense the Holy Spirit touching my heart, giving me a deeper motivation to re-focus on You in these ways:

1. _____

2. _____

3. _____

4. _____

5. _____

L5. A Spirit-empowered disciple lives with a passionate longing for purity and desire to please Him in all things.

SPIRIT-
EMPOWERED
Faith

Day 2

Daily Battle

Abraham Lincoln once said something to the effect that the only thing good and evil have in common is the battleground. Spiritual warfare is a daily battle. Are you willing to walk in spiritual warfare every day? Some days may be easy and some days may be hard. Are you willing to battle with Jesus? Christ has already won the victory.

Jesus guides us in knowing how to leverage His victory into every battle of spiritual warfare. Psychologist Carl Jung said that one must be "positively blind not to see the colossal role that evil plays in the world." It has required "the intervention of God Himself" through Jesus "to deliver humanity from the curse of evil; without His intervention men would have been lost."[82]

We are all on satan's hit list. From the time of Adam and Eve, when they willfully disobeyed God, the battle for our spirits has been part of life. But though the battle rages around us, the enemy is not flesh and blood: "For we do not wrestle against flesh and blood, but against the rulers, against the authorities, against the cosmic powers over this present darkness, against the spiritual forces of evil in the heavenly places" (Ephesians 6:12).

Though the battle is spiritual, our enemy doesn't usually show up wearing horns and a tail. That would be too obvious. Instead, he comes to us as he did to Eve in the garden, offering what is pleasing to our human ears and eyes. But beware, he is not our friend.

How does the enemy steal from you? Perhaps you have never considered this question, but think about it. Does he steal your time from Jesus? That can easily happen. Sometimes we may spend time watching television when Jesus has called us to another activity. That's time we allowed satan to steal.

Does the enemy steal your purity? We don't need to watch pornographic movies to lose our pure thoughts. We can read magazines that titillate us with gossip about the private lives of famous people. That contaminates a mind from being renewed in Christ. Does the enemy destroy your innocence? When we allow him to expose us to movies or books that contain material unnecessary for us to know about or to vocabulary we would never hear otherwise, our innocence can disappear. I heard a preacher once say that he was amazed at how people would pay money to have someone swear at them. It's destructive.

I'm not suggesting that we live with our heads in the sand. But if we could open ourselves to be more sensitive to the Holy Spirit and His work in our lives, we would make different choices.

Jesus has given us the tools to fight the spiritual battle:

- armor (Ephesians 6:10–20)

- every spiritual blessing in Christ (1:3)

- the authority of His name (Philippians 2:10)

- the power in His blood that gives us access to God (Hebrews 10:19–20)

- confidence in knowing that Jesus has already won the battle (Romans 8:31–39).

Worship Experience
Listen to "Raise a Hallelujah," by Bethel Music:
"I raise a hallelujah, I will watch the darkness flee"

While spiritual warfare is not the primary topic of this book, I would encourage you to read further. C. Peter Wagner has written several books on the topic of intercession and spiritual warfare (see two of them on the resource page at the back of this book). We need to keep our eyes on Christ, but let us not be ignorant of the battle at hand. Jesus told his disciples in Matthew 10:16, "Behold, I am sending you out as sheep in the midst of wolves, so be wise as serpents and innocent as doves."

Are you willing and ready to resist all the enemy offers? It takes discipline. It takes courage. But Jesus has already won the war. We just need to stay in the battle, at rest inside of Christ. Psalm 110:1 encourages us that Jesus is sitting at the right hand of the Father, having already won the victory, waiting for the day it is fully manifest: "Sit at my right hand, until I make your enemies your footstool."

Pray now and ask Jesus to give you the courage to fight, knowing He is already victorious.

Revival Truths

- Our battle is spiritual, not against flesh and blood.

- The enemy wants to steal, kill, and destroy us.

- We must daily choose to live according to Jesus and not give in to the enemy.

Submit yourselves therefore to God. Resist the devil, and he will flee from you. Draw near to God, and he will draw near to you.

JAMES 4:7–8

Walking
in the Light
of God's
Son

It's A Promise

If you love Me, you will keep My commandments.

JOHN 14:15

Why do you think God leaves us here after we've come to know Him? He could have designed things so that once we become followers of Jesus, we would automatically be lifted to heaven. Apparently, God wants us here for a reason. Matthew 28:19 reminds us of one of the main reasons that God has us here. In fact, it's a command: To help others see Jesus and follow Him . . . in spite of the enemy's attack to distort how we see God.

In this spiritual battle, some of us hear God's commands, and because we have viewed God as an inspecting god, we read John 14:15 and imagine God shaking his finger as he speaks.

Some of us may view God as disappointed in us. This kind of god might look down at you with arms crossed, shaking his head as he says, "If you really loved me, then you would be able to do these commandments. I'm not sure you really love me because you're not proving it."

And others of us may see God as a distant god. As you read the commandment above, the voice you heard may have seemed cold or disinterested. A distant god would speak the verse while seeming preoccupied with other things or more important people.

But in the face of this spiritual battle, consider this: The real God is actually quite different from anything listed above. He knows that when we come to experience His love and feel it personally, we'll want to live out His commandments. In fact, we can read John 14:15 as a promise: If you love Me, you'll keep My commandments. Hear God's heart: "I'm longing for You to love Me, knowing that, as you love Me, you'll keep My commandments."

God, as I resist the evil one's lies, help me to experience more and more of Your love for me so that I can live out more and more of Your life and love through my own personal revival. Thank You for believing in me.

M6. A Spirit-empowered disciple bears witness of a confident peace and expectant hope in God's Lordship in all things.

Day 3

Daily Victory

Earlier in this book I described having a spiritual plumb bob; I mentioned that I use Ephesians 6:10–18 daily to help keep me in alignment with Jesus. Take a moment and reread those verses on the armor of God.

> Finally, be strong in the Lord and in the strength of his might. Put on the whole armor of God, that you may be able to stand against the schemes of the devil. For we do not wrestle against flesh and blood, but against the rulers, against the authorities, against the cosmic powers over this present darkness, against the spiritual forces of evil in the heavenly places. Therefore take up the whole armor of God, that you may be able to withstand in the evil day, and having done all, to stand firm. Stand therefore, having fastened on the belt of truth, and having put on the breastplate of righteousness, and, as shoes for your feet, having put on the readiness given by the Gospel of peace. In all circumstances take up the shield of faith, with which you can extinguish all the flaming darts of the evil one; and take the helmet of salvation, and the sword of the Spirit, which is the word of God, praying at all times in the Spirit, with all prayer and supplication.

I realize that this is familiar, but I firmly believe these verses are a key to daily victory. Spiritual armor is not something extra special we utilize only when the going gets tough, but rather it is necessary clothing for our daily battle.

Imagine getting up in the morning and having a cup of coffee while you read the newspaper. It's a nice day, sunny and warm outside. You're looking forward to a day of strolling through the park with a close friend. Nothing stressful awaits you. It's a glorious and perfect morning. After your coffee you jump in the shower . . . nice and hot. You feel clean after washing off the dirt that bodies collect each day. You've covered yourself with fragrant soaps and shampoos. (Even if you're a guy, it's okay to enjoy being clean and smelling good!)

You leave the shower refreshed and revived. Then you dry off, comb your hair, maybe even dry it and style it. If you're a woman, you may add some make-up. You're all ready for a new day, right? Well, I wouldn't recommend stepping too far out of the house just yet—you're still naked.

Yet that's how we most often face the day. Naked. Unclothed in the armor that Jesus has provided. We may confess our sin and be cleansed in Christ's forgiveness. We may even put on the fragrance of God's Word. But we're still not clothed—not ready for the day. Do you want daily victory in Christ? Start by dressing for the occasion.

> *"A good solider will become well acquainted with his weapons because he needs them in battle."* – Charlie Riggs

Charlie Riggs, wrote a book entitled *Learning to Walk with God.* It's an excellent book for helping Christians see Jesus as more real in their lives. Charlie described spiritual warfare and tools for victory. It's important not only to dress properly but to carry the right weapons. Let's consider the five weapons that Charlie discussed.[83]

1. *Rely on Jesus Christ as your advocate.* Realize that God is a sovereign God, and that Jesus Christ is our advocate.

2. *Rely on the Word of God.* Riggs noted that when Jesus was tempted in Luke 4:1–13, He utilized Scripture to battle satan. We've talked about the importance of spending time in the Word, so at this point I'll say, "Just do it!"

3. *Pray . . . pray . . . pray.* I've emphasized that throughout this book.

4. *Submit to the Holy Spirit.* The Lord has created each of us to be a body that submits to a soul, a soul that submits to a spirit, and a spirit that submits to God's Spirit. Are you in alignment with God's order for submission?

5. *Have faith.* In Daniel 3:8–10, Shadrach, Meshach, and Abednego were convinced that no matter what happened to them physically, God was the spiritual victor. I am especially moved by their faith as they proclaimed in verses 17 and 18, "Our God whom we serve is able to deliver us from the burning fiery furnace, and he

will deliver us out of your hand, O king. But if not, be it known to you, O king, that we will not serve your gods or worship the golden image that you have set up." What faith!

We can be victorious daily in Christ. It is not a matter of "letting go and letting God," but of purposefully dressing for battle each day.

Revival Truths

- Jesus provides a suit of armor for daily victory in battle.

- Jesus also provides tools for our use in battle.

- Jesus has already won any battles we face throughout the day.

Little children, you are from God and have overcome them, for he who is in you is greater than he who is in the world.

1 JOHN 4:4

Walking in the Light of God's Son

Do You Wish to Get Well?

When Jesus saw him lying there, he knew that the man had been crippled for a long time. So Jesus said to him, "Do you truly long to be healed?"

JOHN 5:6 TPT

Imagine a place where grace stirred healing waters but limited the healing power to a man's ability to be first in line . . . a place where deliverance had gained a reputation but only for the fastest, not the neediest or the most downtrodden? Victory can be assured in your personal revival. That is where you find Jesus. See Him standing, observing, talking, listening. He is asking the Father, "What do you want me to do?"

There is a man lying near the pool. He is a nobody in a beautiful place, but the worst that life can offer has marred him. Jesus stands over him. "Excuse me, sir, but do you truly long to be healed?" There is no demand, only the most honest question one could ask. "Do you want the impossible . . .? Do you want the improbable . . .? Do you want what you have asked God for every day . . .? Are you ready to have your life changed?"

The man doesn't answer the question, at least not directly. In fact, his response is that healing is impossible. Not improbable or unlikely. Impossible! For some, even though they are lying every day in a beautiful place, their only identity is the sin and sickness they have come to know.

Take a moment to encounter Jesus beside your own troubled waters. Hear Him ask the question, "What do you want Me to do?" Tell Him now, and He promises to take it and place it before the Father!

Next, move towards the place you desire to be. Jesus told the man, "Get up!" Now speak up with gratitude that demonstrates faith.

Jesus, thank You that You hear me! I yield to Your grace and lean into Your mercy. I receive by faith the promise and power of Your Holy Spirit to revive me. You have met me beside these troubled waters, and now I give You praise.

L10. A Spirit-empowered disciple practices the presence of the Lord, yielding to the Spirit's work of Christlikeness.

SPIRIT-
EMPOWERED
Faith

Day 4

Daily Living

The challenge today is to live the Gospel. Those who are without Christ will look at us and ask, "Can there be a God?" Good or bad, cliché or not, we are the Bible others read. Henry Blackaby, author of *Experiencing God,* has reminded Christians of a certain expectation: Darkness will act like it's supposed to—dark. That's its nature. The problem is with the light, in that too often you can't tell the believer from the unbeliever because the fruit is the same.[84]

Of course, the question to us then is how should we live? Chuck Colson in his book *How Now Shall We Live?* maintained that in America, we are embroiled in the latest culture war, the forces of evil against the forces of good.[85]

Jesus was concerned with daily life. Read the Beatitudes, Matthew 5:1–12:

> And he opened his mouth and taught them, saying: "Blessed are the poor in spirit, for theirs is the kingdom of heaven. Blessed are those who mourn, for they shall be comforted. Blessed are the meek, for they shall inherit the earth. Blessed are those who hunger and thirst for righteousness, for they shall be satisfied. Blessed are the merciful, for they shall receive mercy. Blessed are the pure in heart, for they shall see God. Blessed are the peacemakers, for they shall be called sons of God. Blessed are those who are persecuted for righteousness' sake, for theirs is the kingdom of heaven. Blessed are you when others revile you and persecute you and utter all kinds of evil against you falsely on my account. Rejoice and be glad, for your reward is great in heaven, for so they persecuted the prophets who were before you."

In these verses, the opening of the Lord's Sermon on the Mount, Jesus wasn't speaking to a group of religious leaders. He wasn't even speaking to the "church" as we know it today. He was speaking to average people looking to live according to God's plan. I have to believe that if Jesus talked about these issues, they are important for our lives.

Jesus continues, even today, to honor the free-will choices we make. While He wants what is best for His children, He won't go further than we'll allow. Throughout this book we've discussed issues of spiritual growth that impact both personal revival and revival around the nation and the world. Brokenness. Repentance. Obedience. Prayer. Spiritual Gifts. Evangelism. In your daily life, how far do you want to go with Jesus? He is the same today as He was with the Israelites in the desert. He offered manna for that day. It is no different now. He offers us the choice each day to determine how far we'll go in trusting Him, in serving Him, in loving Him.

Ezekiel 47:3–6 presents a vivid picture of the prophet of God venturing into greater and greater depths of a river. God gives Ezekiel a vision of living water with varying depths. He leads the prophet into deeper and deeper water until is it so deep all he can do is swim. I believe that daily Jesus wants to take us to deeper and deeper waters of relationship with Him. But He doesn't push. He leads. It's up to us to follow.

Being the Mississippi farm boy that I am, I understand about roots. I understand that if a plant doesn't have good roots, firmly grounded in well-watered and fertilized soil, the plant won't make it. It can't survive any harsh changes in weather. Even if it has an uneventful growing season, it won't produce much fruit. Isn't it wonderful the tangible examples Jesus gives us to see how we should daily live? We are no different from a plant. We must have roots that grow deeply into the fertilized soil of Christ. If we don't reach down on a daily basis, we won't survive. At best, we'll be fruitless.

Jesus calls us into a deeper relationship daily—if we'll go. Where is He calling you to move deeper in relationship with Him?

Revival Truths

- As believers, the fruit of our lives should be different from that of the unbelievers around us.

- Our lives serve as an open Bible to those we encounter each day.

- Jesus calls us into a deeper relationship daily—if we'll go.

Blessed is the man who walks not in the counsel of the wicked, nor stands in the way of sinners, nor sits in the seat of scoffers; but his delight is in the law of the Lord, and on his law he meditates day and night. He is like a tree planted by streams of water that yields its fruit in its season, and its leaf does not wither. In all that he does, he prospers.

PSALM 1:1–3

Walking
in the Light
of God's
People

Seeing God

The Jews then complained about Him, because He said,
"I am the bread which came down from heaven."

JOHN 6:41 NKJV

Many today still grumble because they miss seeing Him for who He really is. Sadly, many miss Jesus because they don't encounter Him in His people. "No one has ever seen God. But if we love each other, God lives in us, and His love has been brought to full expression through us" (1 John 4:12 NLT). Pause to ask God who it is in the traffic pattern in your life who needs to experience encouragement, comfort, acceptance, or support through you.

True fellowship in which we genuinely love each other enables the full expression of God's love. This means as we experience God's love through the love of others, we see Him as He really is. As we receive acceptance from others, we'll be able to see the God of gracious acceptance (Romans 15:7). Through the comfort of a friend, we'll be able to see the One who is "the Father of compassion and the God of all comfort" (2 Corinthians 1:3 NIV).

Just as we receive this blessing of experiencing God through others, God calls us to express His presence to others, giving testimony to His glorious riches in order that they might see Him more clearly and find added hope.

Pray together with one or two others, asking for Christ to share His life through you, beginning with those close to you and with other followers of Jesus, and then extend this sharing of His love to others who need to know Him.

W2. A Spirit-empowered disciple is a "living epistle." With reverence and awe, His Word becomes real in life, vocation, and calling.

SPIRIT-
EMPOWERED
Faith

Day 5

Daily Joy

Joy is an indicator of our spiritual state. Passages in the Old Testament often connect joy with dancing, musical instruments, clapping, leaping, even foot-stamping. The New Testament associates joy with salvation, eating, drinking, or feasting. Joy is not an emotion. It's an outpouring of God's Spirit into action. It's a fruit of the Spirit, as seen in Galatians 5:22. It's impossible to experience joy without showing it. That was Jesus's intention.

Paul often contrasted the concept of joy, even from suffering, with the boasting that humans do about themselves. Our joy comes from boasting in what Christ has done rather than in anything we even think we can accomplish on our own.

Joy from the Lord not only gives us strength, it *is* our strength. Nehemiah 8 describes the events after the rebuilding of Jerusalem's walls. Ezra came before the people to read the Law of Moses. As Ezra read, the people fell to the ground to worship the Lord, weeping as they listened to the words of the Law. They recognized the meaning of the Law, and the hearts of the people had ears to hear. Nehemiah exhorted the people to stop mourning. They were to gather choice food and share it with the poor. There was no room for grieving, "for the joy of the Lord is your strength" (verse 10). After this celebration of seven days, there was a time of confession from all the Israelites and then a gathering of those chosen to live within the city walls.

The Israelites in Nehemiah 8 understood the law and repentance. This led to a great celebration of joy. Then a time of confession occurs, followed by a gathering into the city walls. This is not unlike the process of revival. God's law is made clear and people accept the atonement of Jesus with great joy. We continue on in confession and also gather others into the kingdom of God. Joy is a cornerstone in the revival process.

Just as fruit grows on a tree, we can cultivate the fruit of joy to grow in our lives. How? First, allow the Spirit of God and not the Law to lead you. Second, run from acts of your sinful nature. As soon as you recognize something as sin, repent, confess, renounce, and run from it. Third, beware of pride and envy. Fourth, recognize that God places trials in your life to cause growth. Embrace them rather than leaning away from them. Determine that you will treat them with joy rather than disgust, knowing that whatever evil is intended, Jesus will use for good. Finally, stay connected to the vine. Jesus promised that if we stay connected to Him, our joy will be complete. It will take daily discipline to grow in this area, but Jesus is faithful. Philippians 3:12 says, "Not that I have already obtained this or am already perfect, but I press on to make it my own, because Christ Jesus has made me his own." If you take the hand of Jesus and move one step along with Him, then He will take you to the perfect places prepared for you, both here on this earth and in the world to come.

> *"The highest and most desirable state of the soul is to praise God in celebration for being alive." – Luci Swindoll*

I recall an old saying in Sunday school that perhaps you have heard too: JOY equals Jesus, Others, and You. That statement brought into perspective the process for growing the fruit of joy. We focus on Jesus first; He leads us to care for others, and in the process, we also receive the care we need. We don't need to worry about ourselves when the Creator of the universe is caring for us.

Revival begins in each heart. Revival ends in each heart. Jesus has given us the joyful task of sharing the salvation of Christ with others, as we know it ourselves. That is what revival is all about. It flows from Jesus, to the individual, to the world, and back to Jesus.

Are you willing to go on this road? Are you willing to take His hand and walk with Him? Are you willing to allow Him to daily rekindle the fire He has placed within you? Be courageous. Walk in JOY.

Revival Truths

- Joy is not an emotion.

- Joy is a result of His Spirit, an outpouring of the Spirit into action.

- We can experience joy by daily focusing on Christ.

Count it all joy, my brothers, when you meet trials of various kinds.

JAMES 1:2

Walking
in the Light
of God's
People

He Delights in You

The Lord your God in your midst,
The Mighty One, will save;
He will rejoice over you with gladness,
He will quiet *you* with His love,
He will rejoice over you with singing.

ZEPHANIAH 3:17

Imagine the "facial expression" that was on the face of Jesus as you woke up this morning. In your mind's eye, picture the face of Jesus. Imagine His bearded face, eyes that are kind and gentle, a smile that is warm and tender. Imagine that as you awoke this morning, God looked down and smiled at you, His precious child.

The real God smiled, and with joy in His heart announced, "I am looking forward to sharing the day with you, into all of the places I am sending you!" This is the source of your joy-filled living as the real God, who knows you intimately and could not wait to care for you today. The Creator of the universe, who knows every hair upon your head, sees every tear that you have cried, cannot wait to show you how much He loves you. The Holy God of heaven knows your darkest secrets and deepest failures, yet because of His grace, He cannot wait to have a relationship with you.

Pause to embrace the joy of this truth. What does it do to your heart to consider a God who is acquainted with all your ways and longs to be caringly involved in your life? How does your heart respond to know that God takes great delight in you and rejoices over you?

- As I reflect upon my God who can't wait to care for me, I feel . . .

- As I consider how God rejoices over me and looks forward to spending the day with me, my heart is filled with . . .

Pause now with one or two others and say a prayer that communicates your joy, gratitude, humility, and wonder over a God who knows you and rejoices over you.

Heavenly Father, I feel . . . as I reflect upon Your heart toward me. My heart is filled with . . . as I consider how You can't wait to care for me. I feel . . . as I consider how You delight in me and rejoice over me. Thank You for being the kind of God who . . .

L4. Spirit-empowered disciples rejoice regularly in their identity as "His Beloved."

I pray that in this book Jesus is giving you a place of intimate relationship with Him to rekindle your fire, and that He is showing you the joy in sharing that fire with others. Jesus is King, and He loves us enough to ask us to participate in spreading His kingdom.

May "The Lord bless you and keep you; the Lord make his face to shine upon you and be gracious to you; the Lord lift up his countenance upon you and give you peace" (Numbers 6:24–26).

Revival will come in America, one heart at a time.

Appendices

Appendix 1

A Spirit-Empowered Faith

A Spirit-Empowered Faith

Expresses Itself in Great Commission Living
Empowered by Great Commandment Love

Spirit-empowered faith begins with the end in mind: The Great Commission calls us to make disciples.

"Go therefore and make disciples of all the nations, baptizing them in the name of the Father and the Son and the Holy Spirit teaching them to observe all things that I have commanded you: and lo, I am with you always, even to the end of the age." (Matthew 28:19–20 NASB)

The ultimate goal of our faith journey is to relate to the person of Jesus because it is our relational connection to Jesus that will produce Christlikeness and spiritual growth. This relational perspective of discipleship is required if we hope to have a faith that is marked by the Spirit's power.

Models of discipleship that are based solely upon what we know and what we do are incomplete, lacking the empowerment of a life of loving and living intimately with Jesus. *A Spirit-empowered faith is relational and impossible to realize apart from a special work of the Spirit.* For example, the Spirit-empowered outcome of "listening to and hearing God" implies relationship—it is both relational in focus and requires the Holy Spirit's power to live.

SPIRIT EMPOWERED Faith Spirit-empowered faith begins at the right place—the Great Commandment calls us to start with loving God and loving others.

"'You shall love the LORD your God with all your heart, with all your soul, and with all your mind.' This is the first and great commandment. And the second is like it: 'You shall love your neighbor as yourself.' On these two commandments hang all the Law and the Prophets" (Matthew 22:37–40 NKJV).

Relevant discipleship does not begin with doctrines or teaching, parables or stewardship but with loving the Lord with all your heart, mind, soul, and strength and then loving the people closest to you. Since Matthew 22:37–40 gives us the first and greatest commandment, a Spirit-empowered faith starts where the Great Commandment tells us to start: A disciple must first learn to deeply love the Lord and to express His love to the "nearest ones"—his or her family, church, and community (in that order).

SPIRIT EMPOWERED Faith Spirit-empowered faith embraces a relational process of Christlikeness.

"Walk while you have the light, lest darkness overtake you" (John 12:35 NKJV).

Scripture reminds us that there are three sources of light for our journey: Jesus, His Word, and His people. The process of discipleship (or becoming more like Jesus) occurs as we relate intimately with each source of light. Spirit-empowered discipleship will require a lifestyle of:

· Fresh encounters with Jesus (John 8:12).

· Frequent experiences of Scripture (Psalm 119:105).

· Faithful engagement with God's people (Matthew 5:14).

SPIRIT-EMPOWERED *Faith* Spirit-empowered faith can be defined with observable outcomes using a biblical framework.

"And He Himself gave some to be apostles, some prophets, some evangelists, and some pastors and teachers for the equipping of the saints for the work of ministry, for the edifying of the body of Christ" (Ephesians 4:11–12 NKJV).

The metrics for measuring Spirit-empowered faith or the growth of a disciple come from Scripture and are organized/framed around four distinct dimensions of a disciple who serves.

A relational framework for organizing Spirit-empowered discipleship outcomes draws from a cluster analysis of several Greek (*diakoneo, leitourgeo, douleuo*) and Hebrew words (*abad, Sharat*), which elaborate on the Ephesians 4:12 declaration that Christ's followers are to be equipped for works of ministry or service. Therefore, the "40 Spirit-empowered Faith Outcomes" have been identified and organized around:

· Serving/loving the Lord – "While they were ministering to the Lord and fasting" (Acts 13:2 NASB).[86]

· Serving/living the Word – "But we will devote ourselves to prayer and to the ministry of the word" (Acts 6:4 NASB).[87]

· Serving/loving people – "Through love serve one another" (Galatians 5:13 NASB).[88]

· Serving/living His mission – "Now all these things are from God, who reconciled us to Himself through Christ and gave us the ministry of reconciliation" (2 Corinthians 5:18 NASB).[89]

Appendix 2

A Spirit-Empowered Disciple

A Spirit-empowered disciple LOVES THE LORD through:

L1. Practicing thanksgiving in all things

"Enter his gates with thanksgiving" (Psalm 100:4 NIV). "In everything give thanks" (1 Thessalonians 5:18 NKJV). "As sorrowful, yet always rejoicing" (2 Corinthians 6:10 NKJV).

L2. Listening to and hearing God for direction and discernment

"'Speak Lord, your servant is listening'" (1 Samuel 3:8–9 NLT). "Mary, who sat at the Lord's feet and listened to his teaching" (Luke 10:38–42 ESV). "'Shall I hide from Abraham what I am about to do'" (Genesis 18:17 ESV). "His anointing teaches you all things" (1 John 2:27 EHV).

L3. Experiencing God as He really is through deepened intimacy with Him

"'Hear, O Israel: The Lord our God, the Lord is one. You shall love the Lord your God with all your heart, with all your soul, and with all your strength'" (Deuteronomy 6:4–5 NKJV). "Yet the Lord longs to be gracious to you; therefore he will rise up to show you compassion. For the Lord is a God of justice" (Isaiah 30:18 NIV). See also John 14:9.

L4. Rejoicing regularly in my identity as "His beloved"

"And his banner over me was love" (Song of Solomon 2:4 NKJV). "To the praise of the glory of His grace, which He freely bestowed on us in the Beloved" (Ephesians 1:6 NASB). "For He gives to His beloved even in his sleep" (Psalm 127:2 NASB).

L5. Living with a passionate longing for purity and to please God in all things

"Who may ascend into the hill of the Lord? And who may stand in His

holy place" (Psalm 24:3 NASB). "Beloved, let us cleanse ourselves from all filthiness of the flesh and spirit, perfecting holiness in the fear of God" (2 Corinthians 7:1 NKJV). "'I always do those things that please Him'" (John 8:29 NKJV). " 'Though He slay me, I will hope in Him'" (Job 13:15 NASB).

L6. **Consistent practice of self-denial, fasting, and solitude rest**
"He turned and said to Peter, 'Get behind me, Satan! You are an obstacle to me. You are thinking not as God does, but as human beings do'" (Matthew 16:23 NABRE). "'But when you fast'" (Matthew 6:17 NABRE). "Be still, and know that I am God" (Psalm 46:10 NIV).

L7. **Entering often into Spirit-led praise and worship**
"Bless the LORD, O my soul, and all that is within me" (Psalm 103:1 NASB). "Worship the LORD with reverence" (Psalm 2:11 NASB). "'I praise thee, O Father, Lord of heaven and earth'" (Matthew 11:25 JUB).

L8. **Disciplined, bold, and believing prayer**
"Pray in the Spirit at all times" (Ephesians 6:18 NLT). "Call unto me, and I will answer" (Jeremiah 33:3 KJV). "If we ask anything according to his will, he hears us" (1 John 5:14–15 NIV).

L9. **Yielding to the Spirit's fullness, as life in the Spirit brings supernatural intimacy with the Lord, manifestation of divine gifts, and witness of the fruit of the Spirit**
"For by one Spirit we were all baptized into one body—whether Jews or Greeks, whether slaves or free—and have all been made to drink into one Spirit" (1 Corinthians 12:13 NKJV). "'You shall receive power when the Holy Spirit has come upon you'" (Acts 1:8 NKJV). "But to each one is given the manifestation of the Spirit for the common good" (1 Corinthians 12:7 NASB). See also 1 Peter 4:10 and Romans 12:6.

L10. **Practicing the presence of the Lord, yielding to the Spirit's work of Christlikeness**
"But we all, with unveiled face beholding as in a mirror the glory of the Lord, are transformed into the same image from glory to glory, even as from the Lord the Spirit" (2 Corinthians 3:18 ASV). "As the deer pants after the water brooks, so my soul pants after You, O God" (Psalm 42:1 MEV).

A Spirit-empowered disciple LIVES HIS WORD through:

W1. **Frequently being led by the Spirit into deeper love for the One who wrote the Word**

Love the Lord thy God—love thy neighbor; upon these two commandments deepens all the law and prophets (Matthew 22:37–40, paraphrase). "I delight in Your commands because I love them." (Psalm 119:47 NIV). The ordinances of the Lord are pure—they are more precious than gold—sweeter than honey (Psalm 19:9–10, paraphrase).

W2. **Being a "living epistle" in reverence and awe as His Word becomes real in my life, vocation, and calling**

"You are our letter . . . known and read by all men" (2 Corinthians 3:2 NASB). "And the Word became flesh and dwelt among us" (John 1:14 ESV). "Husbands, love your wives . . . cleansing her by the washing with water through the word" (Ephesians 5:25-26 NIV). See also Titus 2:5. "Whatever you do, do your work heartily, as for the Lord" (Colossians 3:23 NASB).

W3. **Yielding to the Scripture's protective cautions and transforming power to bring life change in me**

"I gain understanding from your precepts; therefore I hate every wrong path" (Psalm 119:104 NIV). "Be it unto me according to thy word" (Luke 1:38 KJV). "How can a young man keep his way pure? By living according to your word" (Psalm 119:9 WEB). See also Colossians 3:16–17.

W4. **Humbly and vulnerably sharing the Spirit's transforming work through the Word**

"I will speak of your statutes before kings and will not be put to shame" (Psalm 119:46 NIV). "Preach the word; be ready in season and out of season" (2 Timothy 4:2 NASB).

W5. **Meditating consistently on more and more of the Word hidden in the heart**

"I have hidden your word in my heart, that I might not sin against you" (Psalm 119:11 WEB). "May these words of my mouth and this meditation of my heart be pleasing in your sight, Lord, my Rock and my Redeemer" (Psalm 19:14 NIV).

W6. **Encountering Jesus in the Word for deepened transformation in Christlikeness**

"All of us, gazing with unveiled face on the glory of the Lord, are being transformed into the same image from glory to glory, as from the Lord who is the Spirit" (2 Corinthians 3:18 NABRE). "'If you abide in me and my words abide in you, ask whatever you wish, and it will be done for you'" (John 15:7 ESV). See also Luke 24:32, Psalm 119:136, and 2 Corinthians 1:20.

W7. **A life explained as one of "experiencing Scripture"**

"But this is that which was spoken by the prophet Joel" (Acts 2:16 KJV). "My comfort in my suffering is this: Your promise preserves my life" (Psalm 119:50 NIV). "My soul is consumed with longing for your laws at all times" (Psalm 119:20 NIV).

W8. **Living "naturally supernatural" in all of life as His Spirit makes the written Word *(logos)* the living Word *(Rhema)***

"So faith comes from hearing, and hearing by the word (Rhema) of Christ" (Romans 10:17 NASB). "Your word is a lamp to my feet, and a light for my path" (Psalm 119:105 WEB).

W9. **Living abundantly "in the present" as His Word brings healing to hurt, anger, guilt, fear, and condemnation—which are *heart hindrances* to life abundant**

"'The thief only comes to steal, kill, and destroy'" (John 10:10 WEB). "I run in the path of your commandments, for you have set my heart free" (Psalm 119:32 WEB). "'And ye shall know the truth, and the truth shall set you free'" (John 8:32 JUB). "For freedom, Christ set us free. Stand firm then and don't submit again to a yoke of slavery" (Galatians 5:1 CSB).

W10. **Implicit, unwavering trust that His Word will never fail**

"The grass withereth, the flower fadeth; but the word of our God abideth for ever" (Isaiah 40:8 DARBY). "'So will My word be which goes forth from My mouth; It will not return to Me empty'" (Isaiah 55:11 NASB).

A Spirit-empowered disciple LOVES PEOPLE through:

P1. **Living a Spirit-led life of doing good in all of life: relationships and vocation, community and calling**

"He went about doing good" (Acts 10:38 ESV). "'Let your light shine before men in such a way that they may see your good works, and glorify your Father who is in heaven'" (Matthew 5:16 NASB). "'But love your enemies, and do good, and lend, expecting nothing in return; and your reward will be great, and you will be sons of the Most High; for He Himself is kind to ungrateful and evil men'" (Luke 6:35 NASB). See also Romans 15:2.

P2. **Startling people with loving initiatives to give *first***

"'Give, and it will be given to you. They will pour into your lap a good measure—pressed down, shaken together, and running over. For by your standard of measure it will be measured to you in return'" (Luke 6:38 NASB). "But Jesus was saying, 'Father, forgive them; for they do not know what they are doing.'" (Luke 23:34 NASB). See also Luke 23:43 and John 19:27.

P3. **Discerning the relational needs of others with a heart to give of God's love**

"Let no unwholesome word proceed from your mouth, but only such a word as is good for edification according to the need of the moment, so that it will give grace to those who hear" (Ephesians 4:29 NASB). "And my God will supply all your needs according to His riches in glory in Christ Jesus" (Philippians 4:19 NASB). See also Luke 6:30.

P4. **Seeing people as needing BOTH redemption from sin AND intimacy in relationships, addressing both human fallenness and aloneness**

"But God demonstrates His own love toward us, in that while we were yet sinners, Christ died for us" (Romans 5:8 NASB). "When Jesus came to the place, He looked up and said to him, 'Zaccheus, hurry and come down, for today I must stay at your house'" (Luke 19:5 NASB). See also Mark 8:24 and Genesis 2:18.

P5. **Ministering God's life and love to our *nearest ones* at home and with family as well as faithful engagement in His Body, the church**

"You husbands in the same way, live with your wives in an understanding way, as with someone weaker, since she is a woman; and show her honor as a fellow heir of the grace of life, so that your prayers will not be hindered" (1 Peter 3:7 NASB). See also 1 Peter 3:1 and Psalm 127:3.

P6. **Expressing the fruit of the Spirit as a lifestyle and identity**

"But the fruit of the Spirit is love, joy, peace, patience, kindness, goodness, faithfulness, gentleness, self-control" (Galatians 5:22–23 NASB). *"With the fruit of a man's mouth his stomach will be satisfied; He will be satisfied with the product of his lips"* (Proverbs 18:20 NASB).

P7. **Expecting and demonstrating the supernatural as God's spiritual gifts are made manifest and His grace is at work by His Spirit**

"In the power of signs and wonders, in the power of the Spirit; so that from Jerusalem and round about as far as Illyricum I have fully preached the Gospel of Christ" (Romans 15:19 NASB). *"'Truly, truly, I say to you, he who believes in Me, the works that I do, he will do also'"* (John 14:12 NASB). See also 1 Corinthians 14:1.

P8. **Taking courageous initiative as a peacemaker, reconciling relationships along life's journey**

"Live in peace with one another" (1 Thessalonians 5:13 NASB). *"For He Himself is our peace, who made both groups into one and broke down the barrier of the dividing wall"* (Ephesians 2:14 NASB). *"Therefore, confess your sins to one another, and pray for one another so that you may be healed"* (James 5:16 NASB). See also Ephesians 4:31–32.

P9. **Demonstrating God's love to an ever growing network of "others" as He continues to challenge us to love "beyond our comfort"**

"The one who says, 'I have come to know Him,' and does not keep His commandments, is a liar, and the truth is not in him" (1 John 2:4 NASB). *"If someone says, 'I love God,' and hates his brother, he is a liar; for the one who does not love his brother whom he has seen, cannot love God whom he has not seen"* (1 John 4:20 NASB).

P10. Humbly acknowledging to the Lord, ourselves, and others that it is Jesus in and through us who is loving others at their point of need
"Take My yoke upon you and learn from Me, for I am gentle and humble in heart, and you will find rest for your souls" (Matthew 11:29 NASB). "If I then, the Lord and the Teacher, washed your feet, you also ought to wash one another's feet" (John 13:14 NASB).

A Spirit-empowered disciple LIVES HIS MISSION through:

M1. Imparting the Gospel and one's very life in daily activities and relationships, vocation, and community
"Having so fond an affection for you, we were well-pleased to impart to you not only the Gospel of God but also our own lives, because you had become very dear to us" (1 Thessalonians 2:8–9 NASB). See also Ephesians 6:19.

M2. Expressing and extending the kingdom of God while sharing compassion, justice, love, and forgiveness
"I must preach the kingdom of God to the other cities also, for I was sent for this purpose" (Luke 4:43 NASB). "As You sent Me into the world, I also have sent them into the world" (John 17:18 NASB). "Restore to me the joy of Your salvation and sustain me with a willing spirit. Then I will teach transgressors Your ways, and sinners will be converted to You" (Psalm 51:12–13 NASB). See also Micah 6:8.

M3. Championing Jesus as the only hope of eternal life and abundant living
"There is no salvation through anyone else, nor is there any other name under heaven given to the human race by which we are to be saved" (Acts 4:12 NABRE). "A thief comes only to steal and slaughter and destroy; I came so that they might have life and have it more abundantly" (John 10:10 NABRE). See also Acts 4:12, John 10:10, and John 14:6.

M4. Yielding to the Spirit's role to convict others as He chooses, resisting expressions of condemnation
"And He, when He comes, will convict the world concerning sin and righteousness and judgment"(John 16:8 NASB). "Who is the one who

condemns? Christ Jesus is He who died, yes, rather who was raised, who is at the right hand of God, who also intercedes for us" (Romans 8:34 NASB). *See also Romans 8:1.*

M5. Ministering His life and love to the "least of these"

"Then He will answer them, 'Truly I say to you, to the extent that you did not do it to one of the least of these, you did not do it to Me'" (Matthew 25:45 NASB). *"Pure and undefiled religion in the sight of our God and Father is this: to visit orphans and widows in their distress, and to keep oneself unstained by the world"* (James 1:27 NASB).

M6. Bearing witness of a confident peace and expectant hope in God's Lordship in all things

"Now may the Lord of peace Himself continually grant you peace in every circumstance. The Lord be with you all" (2 Thessalonians 3:16 NASB). *"Let the peace of Christ rule in your hearts, to which indeed you were called in one body; and be thankful"* (Colossians 3:15 NASB). *See also Romans 8:28 and Psalm 146:5.*

M7. Faithfully sharing time, talent, gifts, and resources in furthering his mission

"Of this church I was made a minister according to the stewardship from God bestowed on me for your benefit, so that I might fully carry out the preaching of the word of God" (Colossians 1:25 NASB). *"'From everyone who has been given much, much will be required; and to whom they entrusted much, of him they will ask all the more'"* (Luke 12:48 NASB). *See also 1 Corinthians 4:1–2.*

M8. Attentive listening to another's *story*, vulnerably sharing of your story, and a sensitive witness of Jesus's story as life's ultimate hope; developing your story of prodigal, pre-occupied, and pain-filled living; listening for another's story and sharing Jesus's story

"But sanctify Christ as Lord in your hearts, always being ready to make a defense to everyone who asks you to give an account for the hope that is in you, yet with gentleness and reverence" (1 Peter 3:15 NASB). *"'For this son of mine was dead and has come to life again'"* (Luke 15:24 NASB). *(Mark 5:21–42). (John 9:1–35).*

M9. **Pouring our life into others, making disciples who in turn make disciples of others**

"'Go therefore and make disciples of all the nations, baptizing them in the name of the Father and the Son and the Holy Spirit, teaching them to observe all that I commanded you; and lo, I am with you always, even to the end of the age'" (Matthew 28:19–20 NASB). See also 2 Timothy 2:2.

M10.Living submissively within His Body, the church, as instruction and encouragement, reproof and correction are graciously received by faithful disciples

"And be subject to one another in the fear of Christ" (Ephesians 5:21 NASB). "Brethren, even if anyone is caught in any trespass, you who are spiritual, restore such a one in a spirit of gentleness; each one looking to yourself, so that you too will not be tempted" (Galatians 6:1 NASB). See also Galatians 6:2.

Appendix 3

About the Great Commandment Network

The Great Commandment Network is an international collaborative network of strategic kingdom leaders from the faith community, marketplace, education, and caregiving fields who prioritize the powerful simplicity of the words of Jesus to love God, love others, and see others become His followers (Matthew 22:37–40; 28:19–20).

The Great Commandment Network is served through the following:

Relationship Press – This team collaborates, supports, and joins together with churches, denominational partners, and professional associates to develop, print, and produce resources that facilitate ongoing Great Commandment ministry.

The Center for Relational Leadership – Their mission is to teach, train, and mentor both ministry and corporate leaders in Great Commandment principles, seeking to equip leaders with relational skills so they might lead as Jesus led.

The Galatians 6:6 Retreat Ministry – This ministry offers a unique two-day retreat for ministers and their spouses for personal renewal and for reestablishing and affirming ministry and family priorities.

The Center for Relational Care (CRC) – The CRC provides therapy and support to relationships in crisis through an accelerated process of growth and healing, including Relational Care Intensives for couples, families, and singles.

For more information on how the Great Commandment Network can serve you, your church, ministry, denomination, or movement, write or call:
Great Commandment Network
2511 South Lakeline Blvd.
Cedar Park, Texas 78613
#800-881-8008
Or visit our website: www.GreatCommandment.net

Appendix 4

Resources

Chapter 5: Prayer

P. Douglas Small, *Prayer: The Heartbeat of It All* (Charlotte, NC: Alive Publications, 2016), www.projectpray.org.

Chapter 7: Using Your Spiritual Gifts for Christ

Tim Blanchard, *A Practical Guide to Finding and Using Your Spiritual Gifts*, revised ed. (Wheaton, IL: Tyndale House, 1983).

Don and Katie Fortune, *Discover Your God-Given Gifts* (Grand Rapids, MI: Chosen Books, 2009).

Dan Reiland, *Spiritual Gifts* (Atlanta: INJOY, 1998), www.injoy.com.

C. Peter Wagner, *Your Spiritual Gifts Can Help Your Church Grow* (Bloomington, MN: Chosen Books, 2012).

Chapter 8: The Practical Results of Evangelism

Bill Bright, *A Handbook for Christian Maturity*, Ten Basic Steps toward Christian Maturity series (Orlando, FL: New Life, 1994).

Billy Graham Evangelistic Association, "Steps to Peace with God," tract (2016).

Billy Graham, *Peace with God* (Nashville: W Publishing Group, 1984; first published 1953).

Growing Strong in God's Family, revised ed., The New 2:7 Series (Colorado Springs: NavPress, 1999).

Chapter 12: Our Response—One Day at a Time

Jim Logan, *Reclaiming Surrendered Ground: Protecting Your Family from Spiritual Attacks* (Chicago: Moody, 1995).

C. Peter Wagner, *Breaking Strongholds in Your City* (Shippensburg, PA: Destiny Image Publishers, 2015).

C. Peter Wagner, *Warfare Prayer*, revised ed. (Shippensburg, PA: Destiny Image Publishers, 2009).

Appendix 5

Worship Experience Sources

Chapter 1

Day 4: "New Wine," by Brooke Ligertwood (2018).

Chapter 3

Day 4: "Out of Hiding (Father's Song)" by Amanda Cook and Steffany Gretzinger (2014).

Chapter 4

Day 2: "Into the Light," by Laura Woodley Osman (2016).
Day 3: "Trading My Sorrows," by Darrell Evans (2002).

Chapter 5

Day 2: "Clean," by Michael Fatkin, Taya Gaukrodger, and Hannah Hobbs (2019).
Day 5: "Sweet Hour of Prayer," by William Walford (1845).

Chapter 6

Day 2: "Reckless Love," by Caleb Culver, Cory Asbury, and Ran Jackson (2017).
Day 5: "Cecie's Lullaby," by Steffany Gretzinger (2014).

Chapter 7

Day 1: "I Give Myself Away," by William McDowell (2009).
Day 3: "Born for Such a Time," by Chris Burns (2013).
Day 5: "I Surrender All," by Judson Van DeVenter (1896).

Chapter 8

Day 1: "Lead Me to Some Soul Today," by Will H. Houghton (1936).

Chapter 9

Day 3: "Fall Afresh," by Kari Jobe, Sarah Reeves, and Henry Seeley (2017).

Chapter 10

Day 5: "So Will I" (100 Billion X), by Joel Houston, Benjamin Hastings, and Michael Fatkin (2017).

Chapter 11

Day 1: "For the Beauty of the Earth," by Folliott Pierpoint (1864).
Day 5: "Made a Way," by Travis M. Greene (2016).

Chapter 12

Day 2: "Raise a Hallelujah," by Jonathan David Helser, Melissa Helser, Molly Skaggs, and Jake Stevens (2018).
Day 4: "Oceans" (Where Feet May Fail), by Joel Houston, Matt Crocker, and Salomon Lighthelm (2013).

Notes

Introduction

1 Al Jazeera, "Death Toll from Devastating Cyclone Idai Rises Above 1,000," April 10, 2019, https://www.aljazeera.com/news/2019/04/death-toll-devastating-cyclone-idai-rises-1000-190410155136406.html.

2 Lori Rozsa, "Parkland Community 'Shocked' after Student's Suicide—the Second in a Week, Officials Say," *The Washington Post*, March 25, 2019, https://www.washingtonpost.com/nation/2019/03/24/parkland-student-dies-apparent-suicide-police-say/?utm_term=.f350d377f1c4.

3 CBS News, "Death Toll from Easter Sunday Terror Attacks in Sri Lanka Nears 300," April 22, 2019, https://www.cbsnews.com/live-news/sri-lanka-bombings-death-toll-easter-attack-churches-hotels-live-updates-22-04-2019/.

4 Henry T. Blackaby and Claude V. King, *Experiencing God* (Nashville: LifeWay Press, 1990), 15.

Chapter 1: A Lifestyle of Revival

5 Richard J. Foster, *Celebration of Discipline* (San Francisco: HarperCollins, 1988), 7.

6 Dietrich Bonhoeffer, *Dietrich Bonhoeffer's Prison Poems,* Edwin Robinson, ed. (Grand Rapids, MI: Zondervan, 1999), 73–74.

7 Jim Tomberline, sermon notes, Woodmen Valley Chapel Church, February 28, 1999, Colorado Springs, CO.

8 Michael Ireland, "Promise Keepers Launches New Era of Men's Ministry," Assist News Service, May 9, 2019, https://www.assistnews.net/promise-keepers-launches-new-era-of-mens-ministry/.

9 See You at The Pole, accessed April 12, 2019, http://syatp.com.

10 Trevor Freeze, "A 'Monumental' Finish to the Decision America Tour," Billy Graham Evangelistic Association, October 13, 2016, https://billygraham.org/story/a-monumental-finish-to-the-decision-america-tour/.

Chapter 2: Beginning with Brokenness

11 Joseph E. Leininger and Terry Whalin, *Lessons from the Pit* (Nashville, TN: Broadman & Holman, 1999).

12 Dan Hayes, *Fireseeds of Spiritual Awakening* (San Bernardino, CA: New Life Publishers, 1983), 51.

13   Roy Hession, *The Calvary Road* (London: Christian Literature Crusade, 1950), 28–29.

14   Adapted from the two-part article "Prodigal Nation," by Peter Marshall. See Peter Marshall, "Prodigal Nation–Part 1," *Washington Watch,* June 1998, 1, 5; and Peter Marshall, "Prodigal Nation–Part 2," *Washington Watch,* July 1998, 1.

15   Ian Murray, "Prayer and Revival," *Heart Cry! A Journal on Revival and Spiritual Awakening,* 5 (Spring 1998): 23.

16   A.T. Pierson, as quoted in "Promise Keepers" document, July 26, 1996.

Chapter 3: Joy in True Repentance

17   Mary Hutchinson, "When Mourning Turns to Joy," *Charisma,* February 2000, 49.

18   Horizon Christian Fellowship, "HCF History," https://hcf.org/history/.

19   Mike MacIntosh, *The Tender Touch of God* (Eugene, OR: Harvest House Publishers, 1996).

Chapter 4: The Foundation of Obedience

20   Mark Buntain, Sunday morning service, Life Center Church, Tacoma, Washington, winter 1988, personal notes of author.

21   Buntain, Life Center notes.

22   Wesley Dewell, *Revival Fire* (Grand Rapids, MI: Zondervan, 1995), 52, 4, 82–83.

23   Wesley, *Revival Fire*, 82–83.

24   Elisabeth Elliott, *Through Gates of Splendor* (Old Tappan, NJ: Spire, 1970), 13.

25   Elliott, *Gates of Splendor*, 26.

Chapter 5: Prayer as Relationship

26   E.M. Bounds, *Power through Prayer* (Springdale, PA: Whitaker House, 1982), 90.

27   Kenneth L. Woodward et al., "Talking to God: An Intimate Look at the Way We Pray," *Newsweek,* January 6, 1992, 39–44.

28   Pew Research Center, "Chapter 2: Religious Practices and Experiences," November 3, 2015, https://www.pewforum.org/2015/11/03/chapter-2-religious-practices-and-experiences/#private-devotions.

29   Woodward, "Talking to God," 30–44.

30   Evelyn Christenson, *A Time to Pray* (Eugene, OR: Harvest House, 1996), 181–85.

31   International Renewal Ministries, "About IRM," http://prayersummits.net/irm/about-irm/.

32   Bill Bright, *7 Basic Steps to Successful Fasting and Prayer* (Wayne, NJ: New Life Publications, 1995).

33   Wayne Jacobsen, *The Vineyard* (Eugene, OR: Harvest House,1992), 73.

34   Edward Plowman, "Citizen Jane," *World,* January 29, 2000, 21.

Chapter 6: Knowing Jesus

35   John Peters, "The History of Revivals, Part 4," *Revival World Report,* September–October 1998, 13.

36   Peters, "History of Revivals."

37   Andrew Murray, *Absolute Surrender* (Chicago: Moody, 1988), 52–53.

38   Brother Lawrence and Frank Laubach, *Practicing His Presence* (Beaumont, TX: The SeedSowers, 1973), xi–xii.

Chapter 7: Revival within Your Gifts

39   C. Peter Wagner, *Your Spiritual Gifts Can Help Your Church Grow* (Ventura, CA: Regal, 1994).

40   Sue Kline, "Sacred Work," *Discipleship Journal,* January 2000, 10.

Chapter 8: An Evangelism Explosion

41   Adapted from Mendell Taylor, *Exploring Evangelism* (Kansas City: Beacon Hill, 1964), 19.

42   Lewis Drummond, "Revival 101," class notes, Southern Baptist Theological Seminary, Louisville, fall semester 1971.

43   Charles G. Finney, *Lectures on Revivals and Religion* (New York: Revell, 1868), 15.

44   John Pollock, *Billy Graham* (New York: McGraw-Hill, 1966), 53.

45   David L. McKenna, *The Coming Great Awakening* (Downers Grove, IL: Inter-Varsity Press, 1990), 14–15, 72.

Chapter 9: A Key Time in Revival History

46   Bill Bright, keynote address, Christian Leaders Conference, November 4, 1998, Atlanta, personal notes.

47   *America's Great Revivals* (Minneapolis: Bethany House, 1970), 57.

48   *America's Great Revivals,* 169.

49   Dr. Jerry Newcombe, "Faith-based Movies Are 'Exploding' in Hollywood and

'Changing Lives,'" *Christian Headlines*, April 4, 2018, https://www.christianhead-lines.com/columnists/guest-commentary/faith-based-movies-are-exploding-in-hol-lywood-and-changing-lives.html.

50   Taylor Berglund, "59,000 Gather to Wage War against Spiritual Inaction at The Send," *CharismaNews*, February 23, 2019, https://www.charismanews.com/us/75323-90-000-gather-to-wage-war-against-spiritual-inaction-at-the-send.

51   Hazel Torres, "Holy Spirit over Iran: Revival Results in 3 Million New Believers Today from Just 100,000 in '94," *Christian Today*, July 27, 2016, https://www.chris-tiantoday.com/article/holy-spirit-over-iran-revival-results-in-3-million-new-believ-ers-today-from-just-100000-in-94/91555.htm.

52   Josie Rabbitt Bingham, "Revival Hits Army Base with 1,459 Receiving Christ," *GodReports*, August 15, 2018, http://blog.godreports.com/2018/08/revival-hits-ar-my-base-with-1459-receiving-christ/.

53   Steve Warren, "PureFlix's Pro-Life 'Unplanned' Movie Takes 4th Place in Week-end Box Office," *CBN News*, April 2, 2019, https://www1.cbn.com/cbnnews/enter-tainment/2019/march/pureflixs-faith-based-unplanned-movie-takes-5th-place-in-weekend-box-office.

54   Taylor Berglund, "Over 19,000 Saved in Manila after Billy Graham's Grandson Preaches at Historic Gathering," *Charisma*, April 11, 2019, https://www.charis-mamag.com/video/41067-over-19-000-saved-in-manila-after-billy-graham-s-grandson-preaches-at-historic-gathering.

55   Christian Ellis, "Franklin Graham's 'Festival of Hope' Reaches 94,500 Co-lombians, Venezuelan Refugees with Love of Christ," *CBN News*, April 22, 2019, https://www1.cbn.com/cbnnews/world/2019/april/franklin-grahams-festi-val-of-hope-reaches-94-500-colombians-venezuelan-refugees-with-love-of-christ.

56   Pete Williams, "Supreme Court Won't Hear Case of HS Football Coach Fired for On-field Prayer," *NBC News*, January 22, 2019, https://www.nbcnews.com/politics/supreme-court/supreme-court-won-t-hear-case-hs-football-coach-fired-n961216.

57   George Gallup, informal gathering with CEOs of Christian agencies, at Interna-tional Bible Society, Colorado Springs, 1995.

58   Alan Prendergast, "Photos: The Seven Biggest Megachurches in Colorado," *Westword*, August 22, 2013, https://www.westword.com/news/photos-the-sev-en-biggest-megachurches-in-colorado-5839869.

Chapter 10: Jesus Revived in Our Nation

59   George Barna, "The State of the Church," pastors' seminar at Compassion Inter-national, Colorado Springs, September 1998.

60 Crystal Woodall, "YouVersion Bible App Rings in the New Year with Whopping 1 Million New Subscribers," *CBN News*, https://www1.cbn.com/cbnnews/cwn/2019/january/youversion-bible-app-rings-in-the-new-year-with-whopping-1-million-new-subscribers.

61 *Time*, "Watch Billy Graham's 5 Greatest Sermons," February 21, 2018, https://time.com/18404/billy-graham-evangelism-sermons-video/.

62 James Martin, "What the Bible Says about Secrets," *New York Times*, April 10, 2019, https://www.nytimes.com/2019/04/10/opinion/sunday/privacy-religion.html?rref=collection%2Ftimestopic%2FReligion%20and%20Belief&action=click&contentCollection=timestopics&region=stream&module=stream_unit&version=latest&contentPlacement=4&pgtype=collection.

63 Sharon Begley, "Science Finds God," *Washington Post*, July 20, 1998, https://www.washingtonpost.com/wp-srv/newsweek/science_of_god/scienceofgod2.htm.

64 Bill Bright, "Ready for Revival," *Worldwide Challenge,* July/August 1995, 4.

65 Byron Paulus, "Revival in the Nation—Hope for Hopeless Times," *Spirit of Revival*, vol. 26, no. 1 (September 1996): 4.

66 Clay Renick, "Taking on the Taboo," *Today's Christian Woman*, January/February 1999, 46.

67 Bethesday Workshops, "Meet Our Team: Founder and Director Marnie C. Ferree," https://www.bethesdaworkshops.org/about-us/our-team/.

68 Email from Erin to Tom, April 24, 2019.

69 Tom Pedigo, "America—A Christian Nation?" American Family Association of Colorado newsletter 2, no. 7 (July 1997): 1.

70 Carolyn Kleiner and Mary Lord, "The Cheating Game," *U.S. News & World Report,* November 22, 1999, 55.

71 Jane E. Brody, "When a Partner Cheats," *New York Times*, January 22, 2018, https://www.nytimes.com/2018/01/22/well/marriage-cheating-infidelity.html.

72 Criminal Justice Information Services Division, "Crime in the United States," FBI: UCR, https://ucr.fbi.gov/crime-in-the-u.s/2017/crime-in-the-u.s.-2017/tables/expanded-homicide-data-table-3.xls.

73 National Day of Prayer, The 66th Annual National Observance, "For Your Great Name's Sake," May 4, 2017.

74 Karl Menninger, *Whatever Became of Sin?* (New York: Hawthorne, 1974).

75 "Publick Occurrences: The Week—The Fudge Factor," *World,* May 16, 1998, 8.

76 Allan Bloom, *The Closing of the American Mind* (New York: Simon and Schuster, 1987), 82–83, 117–18.

Chapter 11: Vision for World Awakening

77   Cal Thomas, "Cultural Danger Signs," *World,* June 6, 1998, 17.

78   Benazir Bhutto, *Daughter of Destiny* (New York: Simon & Schuster, 1990), as cited in Tom Phillips and Bob Norsworthy, *The World at Your Door* (Minneapolis: Bethany, 1997), 23.

79   Bhutto, *Daughter of Destiny.*

80   Personal conversation with Charles Riggs, spring 1975, at the Greater Mississippi Billy Graham Crusade, Jackson, Mississippi.

Chapter 12: One Heart at a Time

81   "A Letter to Our Community from the Parents of Cassie Rene Bernall," *The Gazette*, May 1 1999 (Littleton, CO), 5.

82   Carl Jung, *Aion* (1951), in *The Quotable Jung*, by C. G. Jung, ed. by Judith Harris (Princeton: Princeton University Press, 2016), 206.

83   Charlie Riggs, *Learning to Walk with God* (Minneapolis: World Wide Publications, 1986), 64–70.

84   Henry T. Blackaby, *Experiencing God: Knowing and Doing the Will of God,* revised ed. (Nashville: B&H Books, 2008).

85   Chuck Colson, *How Now Shall We Live?* (Wheaton, IL: Tyndale, 1999), 2.

Appendix 2

86   David L. Ferguson, *Great Commandment Principle* (Cedar Park, TX: Relationship Press, 2013).

87   David L. Ferguson, *Relational Foundations* (Cedar Park, TX: Relationship Press, 2004).

88   David L. Ferguson, *Relational Discipleship* (Cedar Park, TX: Relationship Press, 2005).

89   "Spirit Empowered Outcomes," www.empowered21.com, Empowered 21 Global Council, http://empowered21.com/discipleship-materials/.

Acknowledgments

Seventeenth-century French theologian and philosopher Blaise Pascal said, "Certain authors, when they speak of their work say, 'my book,' 'my commentary,' 'my history.' They would be better to say 'our book,' 'our commentary,' 'our history,' since their writings generally contain more of other people's good things than their own." Thank you to those who pray with us for revival. Thank you to those who walk with us in revival. Thank you to those who converse with us on revival. Thank you to those whose books and articles we read on revival. Each of you have contributed to this book. Through the years, ideas have come from sources long forgotten. This is our book.

The first individual who stirred the spark of and for revival that God had placed in me prior to my birth is Lewis Drummond, Billy Graham Chair of Evangelism, professor at Beeson Seminary, and previous president of Southeastern Baptist Seminary. "Dr. D," who also served as the Billy Graham Chair of Evangelism at Southern Baptist Theological Seminary in Louisville, Kentucky, literally pointed me toward my destiny. My vision for revival and for this book is largely a result of his passion.

My thanks also to Charlie Riggs, the director of counseling and follow-up for the Billy Graham Evangelistic Association for almost forty years and my spiritual mentor. He has shown me through his teachings in the preparation for Billy Graham Crusades as well as his life that there is the possibility of personal revival on a daily basis—and corporately through the church—when people are pure before the Lord through conviction, repentance, confession, and seeking Jesus Christ as one's most intimate relationship. Thank you, Dr. Riggs—and Dr. Drummond, too—for all that you have meant to the kingdom of God and to one servant boy from Mississippi.

My deepest thanks to Billy Graham with whom I had the privilege of serving many years. Though he would have called himself solely an evangelist, his heart for revival in ministry of the Word in proclamation laid the foundation in many ways for the seminal movement of the Spirit of God that we are presently seeing.

In life, there are a few times that Jesus's people are allowed into close relationships for His kingdom purposes in a way that is very, very obvious. David Ferguson has been that kind of brother for me. This is my opportunity to formally thank Dr. David Ferguson and his wonderful family and team for all they have done to promote revival, lift up vision for evangelism for the next generation, and selflessly, synergistically, and unitedly serve to further Jesus's kingdom. This is the heart of the brilliant investor in God's creation, namely Dr. David Ferguson. Thank you, David.

Thank you, also, to BroadStreet Publishing, Carlton Garborg, Tim Payne, Bill Watkins, and the many staff who helped who helped bring this book to fruition. Thank you for your wise counsel and insight along each step of the journey. Emily Adams, you brought this book into the revival era, the time of your generation's awakening to Jesus as Lord, Savior, and Merciful Friend. We never would have imagined we were praying for you when we gathered twenty-five years ago to pray and fast for revival, but you are an answer to those prayers in the unexpected form of a spiritual daughter.

Finally, the person who has inspired me most of all in the writing of this work has been my wonderful wife, Ouida, who has given us three children who love Jesus Christ—Cara, Molly, and Matt. I am grateful to them and their spouses, Matt Brown, Brian Curland, and Allison Phillips, respectively, for their endearing, prayerful support.

About the Authors

Tom Phillips

Tom Phillips is a farm boy from Mississippi whose grandfather was a circuit-riding preacher. His family's spiritual heritage originated in the great awakenings throughout the Southeast, beginning in Kentucky in the early 1800s. The Word of God as a daily guide for faith and practice bred a strong devotional life, a life of sharing God's love through Jesus, and the joy in the Lord that historically changed the southeastern portion of the United States eventually touched Tom's family.

Tom Phillips's upbringing compelled him to share his faith as a young man. Desiring to help people and share the love of Jesus through healing, he began studying medicine with the intention of becoming a surgeon. But God intervened, calling him to share not physical healing but spiritual healing with the good news of Jesus Christ, a loving and forgiving Lord and Savior. Tom's education quickly moved from medical school to seminary.

Tom yielded to God's call to a life of evangelism while in his second year of seminary. He realized the world had a desperate spiritual need, and a revived church could be the catalyst to renew society as had happened in previous revivals. God impressed upon Tom that he would share in a great revival to bring this nation back to Jesus's love and forgiveness. God's call opened a world of ministry to Tom, and he eventually had the opportunity to serve with Billy Graham. Tom has seen millions surrender to salvation through Jesus.

Emily Adams

Emily Adams grew up the middle child in a family with legacies of faith on all sides in the Four Corners of the Southwest where New Mexico, Colorado, Utah, and Arizona all meet. The Lord began tempering her at the early age of seven when she was diagnosed with a seizure-related movement disorder. Miraculously healed five years later through doctors, medicine, and diet, she now thanks Jesus for teaching her to cling to Him through the darkness of her early journey.

Emily decided to study writing in college because, as she struggled to narrow down her passions to one area of focus, Jesus showed her that with writing she could develop one passion to be able to incorporate any other. After deleting the application three times, she followed the prompting of the Holy Spirit to come as a summer writing intern to the Billy Graham Evangelistic Association in Charlotte, NC. She was privileged to begin to write the story of God's ongoing work saving and healing His children at the Billy Graham Library, where she also served the volunteer team.

A few weeks before her job at the Billy Graham Library was complete and she planned to return home to New Mexico, the Lord began to awaken Emily to experience the revival of Jesus in her life about which Tom Phillips, then Vice President of the Library, had shown her. Emily said yes to follow a new path unfolding before her as a child of revival and as Tom's assistant at the Billy Graham Evangelistic Association. Prepared for such a time as this, Emily now uses the many passions God has given her as she seeks Jesus in bringing together the generations for awakening.

To connect with the authors, share Sparks of Revival on
our podcast, and receive the latest information on the
Jesus Now Awakening Series visit us at
www.TheCenterForAwakening.com."

Also in the Jesus Now Awakening Series:…

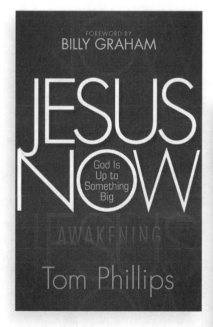

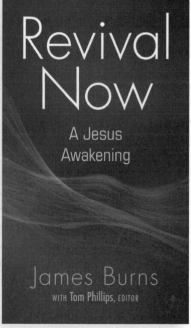